Music in New Orleans

Music in New Orleans

THE FORMATIVE YEARS
1791–1841

by

Henry A. Kmen

LOUISIANA STATE UNIVERSITY PRESS

BATON ROUGE

Library
Brevard Junior College
Cocoa, Florida

Copyright © 1966
Louisiana State University Press

Library of Congress Catalog Card Number: 66-25723

Manufactured in the United States of America by
Vail-Ballou Press, Inc. Binghamton, N.Y.
Designed by Jules B. McKee

*This book was published with the assistance of a grant
from the Ford Foundation.*

For Audrey, whose constant readiness to do battle over words, style, sense, and syntax has been indispensable. There are, I know, many men who write books without the aid of a wife, but how they do this I cannot imagine.

Preface

*T*he music of New Orleans throughout the nineteenth century deserves study on several counts. This was the only American city to maintain continuously, except for the years of the Civil War, a regular opera company. In antebellum New Orleans there were at times as many as three opera companies operating simultaneously. And there was an astonishing amount of other music, ranging from charivaris and street serenades through numerous brass bands and dance orchestras to formal concerts. The theater orchestras were always among the best in the nation and, in some years, the very best. The amount of music in the home, with its attendant activities of music trades and teaching, was enormous. Several amateur societies performed vocal and instrumental music with near-professional skill. In connection with all of this, there was a sizable amount of composing and publishing of music from songs to operas. In these respects, New Orleans was undoubtedly a cultural center—one which, in its own way, rivaled the fabled "flowering of New England" in pre-Civil War America.

Moreover, if the outstanding characteristic of America today is its successful amalgamation of many and varied nationalities and cultural traits, then New Orleans was truly, in this important respect at least, a pioneer city of modern America. Here, very early, diverse cultural groups met and slowly fused their cultures into something new, something American. New Orleans had not only the French, Spanish, Anglo-American, Irish, and German groups, but also the largest Negro population, both slave and free, of any American city. All brought with them a musical tradition or instinct or both. Add to these, West Indian music imported by refugees and visitors, the music of England and Italy heard in operas and concerts, and American folk music brought in from the hinterland by the Mississippi River sailors. These were the ingredients poured into the musical melting pot that was New Orleans.

The literary part of a national culture is a stubborn thing. It is relatively slow to influence or to be influenced by neighboring cultures. The language barrier sees to that. But music is quick to borrow and to incorporate. The ear can hear and capture new melodies and harmonies infinitely faster than it can absorb new languages. Thus music became the first meeting-ground for the many nationalities in New Orleans. Not only did they listen to one another's music, they assimilated and blended it until a new, indigenous music was born—American jazz.

The following study is concerned with the rooting and development of the major musical activities in New Orleans. The method used is that of the social historian. Which is to say, the book is not concerned with the structure and development of the music itself— that is left for the musicologist. Nor is it concerned with the anthropological approach: there is no searching for origins in the cultures of Europe or of Africa. Rather, this is a presentation and analysis of the external record of these musical *activities* as they emerged in New Orleans.

Acknowledgments

*T*wo men have helped me greatly with this book: Professor William R. Hogan of Tulane University, whose example, faith, and insistent prodding pulled and pushed me on; and Mr. René J. Le Gardeur, Jr., of New Orleans who gave graciously and without stint from his vast knowledge of early New Orleans. I am deeply grateful to both of these gentlemen. Also I wish to thank Mr. Charles L. Defour of the New Orleans *States-Item* for his enthusiasm and encouragement. Whatever errors remain in this book are mine alone.

A portion of Chapter XII has previously appeared in slightly altered form in the *Journal of American Folklore,* LXXV: 295 (January–March, 1962). My thanks to that journal for permission to use this material.

Contents

Illustrations

Music in New Orleans

" . . . they occupy much of the public mind."

Chapter One

THE BALLS

*T*he story of music in New Orleans must begin with dancing. This was the earliest sustained musical activity there; it was always the greatest—in terms of effort and quantity; and it was the source and support of opera, concerts, and various other endeavors in this music-mad city.

William C. C. Claiborne, the first American commissioner of the newly purchased Louisiana Territory, had been in New Orleans little over a month when he felt compelled to write to Secretary of State James Madison himself concerning public balls. In a letter dated January 31, 1804, Claiborne apologized for "calling your attention to the balls of New Orleans, but I do assure you, sir, they occupy much of the public mind." Indeed, he explained, the only serious disorders encountered thus far under American rule originated at these balls. Lest Madison think that Claiborne should simply stop them, he added that he had been obliged to reassure a number of anxious Frenchmen that, contrary to rumors sweeping the town, the Americans had no intention of halting the balls. To quiet this fear and to demonstrate American good will, Claiborne and his fellow commissioner, General James Wilkinson, were deliberately making a practice of attending the dances.[1]

This gesture by the new officials was good politics, for dancing was an extraordinarily serious matter in New Orleans. During the strain of adjusting to new and resented American rulers, it was characteristic that the people were most concerned about their balls. The dance came first in the hearts of fun-loving New Orleanians—so it had been and so it would be. Nearly every traveler who visited New Orleans in the early nineteenth century and who wrote about his travels, commented on the real passion this city had for dancing. Even those from France who were presumably more accustomed to a fondness for the dance and who, in some cases, had toured the French West Indies before arriving in New Orleans, were astonished at the extreme love of dancing in this remote outpost of French blood and tradition. "In the winter," said one, "they dance to keep warm, and in the summer they dance to keep cool." [2]

To a French refugee from Saint-Domingue who fled to New Orleans in 1802, it seemed that "they dance in the city, they dance in the country, they dance everywhere." The women especially would, he thought, "pass all their days and nights" at dancing if they could. An American Protestant thought that this ardor for dancing was carried to "an incredible excess. Neither the severity of the cold, nor the oppression of the heat, ever restrains them from this amusement, which usually commences early in the evening, and is seldom suspended till late the next morning." He was especially awed by their capacity to keep this up for several days in succession "without the least apparent fatigue." [3]

Another observer who called himself "a Yankee" dourly remarked that New Orleanians managed during a single winter "to execute about as much dancing, music, laughing and dissipation, as would serve any reasonably disposed, staid and sober citizens, for three or four years" even if the latter were given all year to do it in. With less disapproval a French visitor noticed young mothers at a dance nursing their babies between waltzes—a feat made easy by the cut of their gowns and made understandable by the assertion that they had dreamt of nothing but the balls since the age of seven. He could only characterize such fervor for dancing as "an inconceivable rage." Perhaps the best description though was provided by Louis Tasistro, an actor who played in New Orleans in the late 1830's. He simply called the city "one vast waltzing and gallopading Hall." [4]

Whether it was the sight of groups of people walking two miles to dance on a hot summer night in 1805, or the awesome length of a public ball scheduled to last from half past seven until daylight in 1841, there is much to show that these descriptions were not in the least exaggerated. The French Prefect, Pierre Laussat, who turned the city over to the Americans, wearily began a diary entry with "Another ball!" One of the guests at the St. Charles Hotel complained of being kept awake night after night by "fiddling and floor shaking." A certain resident solemnly warned that if "this love of the dance" gets any worse, he and his neighbors would never see bed. And no less a theatrical attraction than the famous Junius Booth found his audience depleted by the balls.[5]

Competing amusements generally had to accommodate themselves to the balls. Nearly every concert prior to 1830 was coupled with a ball, and occasionally a play or an opera was followed by a ball held right in the theater. At other times the curtain might be raised early so that the opera would be over in time for a night of dancing. Even the stellar performance of Mr. Church, who did bird imitations and sword balancing, and who capped all by playing the violin on his back on a slack wire in full swing, had to be combined with a ball! It could be hazardous to venture an entertainment too soon after a ball, as when a scheduled display of fireworks had to be canceled because, so it was said, the ladies were too fatigued from dancing to attend. Or it could simply be that a performer was unable to find a hall with an open date throughout the height of the winter season; all were solidly booked with balls.[6]

The women might be too fatigued for fireworks, but they were willing to walk barefoot through two miles of mud to get to a dance in the days before New Orleans had sidewalks. After a footbath at the door and a change into the costumes carried by their slaves, they were ready to dance for seven hours and then to brave the mud again on the journey home. At best they made the return trip in an oxcart. Later on, when it was easier to get to local dances, New Orleanians rode horseback as far as twenty miles and back to dance all night in the country.[7]

Such devotion to dancing was epidemic. Attendance records were seldom kept in the early years of the nineteenth century when people were less statistics-minded than now, yet there are indications enough of the extent of the rage to dance. Late in 1803, before the town contained many over eight thousand people, a ball in full swing was interrupted around nine o'clock by a nearby fire that was consuming the house of a free mulattress. Nearly everyone left the dance to watch the exciting fire, but when they returned they found the ballroom more crowded than when they had left.[8]

The following winter a ball was given in honor of Washington's birthday. Although the affair was intended to be rather exclusive socially, nearly four hundred people had arrived by nine o'clock. A special ball, such as the one given in 1825 to celebrate Lafayette's visit to the city, easily attracted over a thousand dancers; while an ordinary, run-of-the-mill ball drew at least five hundred.[9]

More often the papers merely spoke of a "numerous assembly." That they were reporting the truth seems clear from accounts of the exertions made by the ball promoters in coping with the crowds of people who wanted to dance. In 1809, when promoter Joseph Antoine Boniquet found that his Grand Ball Room simply couldn't accommodate all those wanting to get in, he rented an adjacent house for the overflow. More than this, he covered and illuminated the space between the two structures, thereby making room for six additional contredances. Then he raised admission prices fifty per cent. Two men, partners in the operation of a ballroom, followed Boniquet's example when they found their ballroom so jammed that there weren't seats enough for the ladies, let alone the men. And yet another manager had the happy experience of being forced to add not one, but two rooms—one at each end of the ballroom.[10]

Little wonder then that the increase in the number of public ballrooms was nothing short of phenomenal. Before the end of 1805 there were about fifteen public ballrooms. The next ten years brought close to fifteen more, and thereafter for twenty years additional ones appeared at a rate exceeding one each year. No fewer than thirty new dance locations opened for business between 1836 and 1841! Even a public bath house boasted its own ballroom.[11]

Thus by 1841 over eighty identifiable ballrooms or sites for dancing had been put into operation in New Orleans, with the majority of them still functioning. No doubt there were others of which there are no records.

In these numerous places the frequency of balls was remarkable. During a typical week at the height of the season in 1806, for example, dances were held on Wednesday, Thursday, Saturday, and Sunday in one room alone. At the close of the carnival season in 1827, the Orleans Ballroom presented a special ball for Washington's birthday on Thursday; a regular masked ball on Saturday; two successive balls on Monday (one for children and one for adults); and two simultaneous balls on Tuesday. Many of the ballrooms had a hard core of regularly scheduled balls—at least two or three a week during the winter. But in addition, there were all sorts of others: a series of subscription balls, various benefit balls, and balls on any special day or occasion. A day like Washington's birthday prompted so many Washington Balls that in 1815 one proprietor, striving to distinguish his affair in some way from all the others, called it a "Jackson Ball" instead.[12]

In a country yet very young, a certain amount of resourcefulness was required in finding commemorative events worthy of celebration with a ball. The anniversary of the transfer of Louisiana to the United States on December 20 provided one. After the battle of New Orleans in 1815, January 8 added another holiday for dancing. Indeed, this campaign offered many possibilities such as a grand ball to celebrate the very first engagement with the English on December 23; or a Jackson Ball on January 10. With Christmas and New Year's to help, that part of the year was fairly well taken care of. But in any event, a people who gathered and danced to celebrate peace with Tripoli or the anniversary of a visit from Lafayette would not permit themselves to lack for occasions.[13]

Balls attained their highest frequency during the carnival season, a stretch of from five to eight weeks between Twelfth Night and Shrove Tuesday. The idea was to get in as much fun as possible before Lent, and in New Orleans fun meant dancing. "From the very commencement of the Carnival," wrote an onlooker, "there was no thought of, no occupation, no interest in anything except dancing." This observer counted as many as eleven balls on a single evening, listened to night-long music on every street corner, and concluded that at this time of the year no man in New Orleans was "his own master; he must belong, body and soul, to the ballroom." [14]

On the last night before Lent began, the night of Mardi Gras, every ballroom in the city was open. Even the Orleans Theater, site of the French Opera, was customarily given over to a ball that night, along with its companion ballroom. The pit was floored over to join the stage as a dance floor; orchestras were provided in both the theater and the ballroom; and the two rooms were joined by a passageway erected for the occasion. This was, after all, to be the last chance to dance until after Easter.[15]

That was the theory. Practice was to taper off rather than to attempt abrupt and total abstinence. Fortunately, Washington's birthday usually fell during Lent, a fact which perhaps contributed as much to the popularity of Washington Balls as did patriotism. There were often so many that they could not all take place on the same day, but rather clustered around the birthdate. In 1837, for example, military balls honoring Washington were given on the eighteenth and twenty-fifth of February as well as on the proper day. A whole week of Lent was thus lightened. And St. Joseph's Day provided yet another traditional excuse for a spate of balls.[16]

For the rest, there were always worthy purposes to justify a Lenten ball, such as helping a widow with five children or aiding destitute orphan boys. "This," as one paper put it, "is dancing for a good purpose." Lent was also a convenient time for singers, instrumentalists, and other employees of the opera to augment their incomes by giving a ball. More often than not, however, the only excuse needed to continue ordinary balls through Lent was that the carnival season had been too short. And more often than that, the balls were simply held as usual without apology. In reality, the only abatement occurred during Holy Week, and that not too perceptibly.[17]

Nor did dancing cease during the hot, steamy summers. In 1805 John Watson recorded his astonishment at seeing groups of men and ladies "of the best families" trudge two miles and back to dance every Sunday through July and August at a new place called the Tivoli on Bayou St. John, and opportunities for summer dancing increased as the town grew. In the summer of 1838, for example, one could cross the river to the Pavillon du Chene Vert; take a steam train to the Carrollton Hotel; or ride a carriage out Shell Road to the Lake Pontchartrain Ballroom. If he preferred to remain in town, he might walk to the Arcade Ballroom or even enjoy the countryside without the trip by dropping in at the Vauxhall Gardens, which was the St. Charles Theater with the interior arranged to resemble a garden. Hardier souls could board the steamer *Mazeppa* on Saturday for a sail on the Gulf of Mexico to Bay St. Louis where "the whole place was alive with music." Here they danced for two days before sailing back to arrive on Monday morning "without losing one business hour." But as for anything else that might be lost there—in the words of one laconic observer, "That's a dangerous theme." [18]

Within the city, various "Gardens" continued to offer the opportunity of dancing a hot Sunday away. If one preferred a French atmosphere, there was Rasch's Garden on Chartres Street, Simon Laignel's Pleasure Garden in the Suburb La Course, or the Louisiana Garden on Conde Street. English tastes could be gratified at the Louisiana Vauxhall Gardens on lower Common Street, the New Vauxhall Gardens on upper Common Street, or the Vauxhall Gardens in the St. Charles Theater. The English-speaking portion of New Orleans seemed intent on having Vauxhall Gardens.[19]

But all such opportunities to dance in the summer, at least on weekends, were not enough. With the principal ballrooms such as the Orleans closed during the hot months, and with the more lavish private and public balls reserved for the winter season, the people of New Orleans grew impatient for fall. As that season approached, a reporter gauged the public mood simply but accurately: "Our ladies long for a dance—who don't?" [20]

Thus Commissioner Claiborne was not wrong when he thought dancing in New Orleans important enough to take up considerable space in his initial reports to the government in Washington. But why this should be, neither he nor any of the others who recorded the fact sought to explain. However, the conjunction of three circumstances offers a likely explanation. First is the fact that New Orleans in its first years was a lonely outpost of France, far from the mother country, and truly a city in the wilderness. France never was as able to maintain communications with her colonies as was England. Nor did Spain do any better when she ruled Louisiana. The Atlantic seaboard cities of America increasingly gained much easier access to each other and to Europe than did New Orleans to either throughout the eighteenth century. These northeastern cities, moreover, usually had hinterlands of smaller towns and villages to add support to their social endeavors. Their forms of amusement and social intercourse therefore could be a great deal more varied and more elaborate than those of New Orleans.

In that city the one form of social amusement that was most feasible and least expensive was dancing. A dance could be given almost anywhere, for a few or for many, with anything from a lone fiddle to a large orchestra providing the music. Dancing was bound to flourish among a gregarious people placed in such a situation. In addition, a considerable portion of the early population influx in New Orleans came from frontier America where for the same reasons dancing was the favorite social amusement. The frontier characteristics of New Orleans had much to do with the initial enthusiasm for dancing. And once started, a social custom has a certain impetus of its own.[21]

Second is the fact that New Orleans was America's first cultural melting pot. Of the older inhabitants, according to Governor Claiborne, not one in fifty spoke English. After the Americans came in numbers, there were at least three sizable language groups—the French, the Spanish, and the English—a condition that presented obvious impediments to many forms of amusement. But dancing easily leaps language barriers, and so its momentum increased because it could be enjoyed by all. It was the most nearly universal form of social amusement available.[22]

Finally, there is the fact that New Orleans was solidly Latin-Catholic during its first century of existence and so escaped any notions that dancing was sinful. There were no brakes to slow its enjoyment. Sunday was especially a popular day for dancing, and it was not unusual for the Louisiana French to attend worship in their ball dress and to proceed directly after to the ball. The Catholics in New Orleans assumed "that religion ought to inspire cheerfulness and that cheerfulness is associated with religion." Visiting Protestant ministers were often shocked by this attitude, and as the Protestant portion of the city increased, an occasional attempt was made either to limit the length of the season for masked balls or to prohibit Sunday dancing. But by that time the tradition was too well established.[23]

When in 1831 a number of Protestant preachers supported a move to restrict the ball season, they came in for heavy ridicule from the New Orleans *Bee*. Portraying them as men "who were ordered by God to preach to the world that the dance is a Satanic invention . . . that the Creator gave us the instinct of pleasure only so that we might procure the glory of resisting it . . . and say with a straight nose that they will roast in purgatory or even in hell, who give in habitually to the criminal penchant for dancing," the paper asked if it made good sense to insist that "from this date to that the masked balls will not be immoral . . . but after that date they will be immoral." [24]

Anyway, to be deprived of dancing was more the New Orleans idea of hell. The New Orleans *Bee* once described the city as "six months of Heaven and six months of Hell," referring to the ebb and flow of the musical season. And it was rather the Protestants who succumbed to the charms of the dance than the other way around. Even those one would think best fortified did not long resist. "The Protestant New Englander, of Puritan descent, forgetting all the maxims of his Pilgrim Fathers, as well as the practice of his youth, frequents the theatre, the balls, and the masquerade on Sundays also," wrote an observant Englishman.[25]

Perhaps this subversion of good upright people is best illustrated by the reaction of the *True American*, a newspaper whose name indicates its loyalties, to an unsuccessful attempt to restrict Sunday dancing. It labeled the instigators "Blue Skins," and avowed, "we see no reason why there should be more than one step from the Church to the Ball Room." Thus far from the paths of righteousness did "true Americans" stray in the tempting Creole city. What else could be expected when the initial steps to establish the first Protestant church were taken in a ballroom? [26]

The earliest dances, of course, must have been more or less unorganized private activities conducted on an extremely modest scale. Unfortunately, their very nature precludes the possibility of gathering much information about them. But toward the end of the eighteenth century when the first public ballroom and the first newspaper in New Orleans appeared, news and comment about dancing increased greatly. Thereafter it is possible to discern at least three sorts of private dances.

There were those given in the home, both formally and informally. Any occasion served as the excuse for a private dance: a birthday, a wedding, an anniversary, a housewarming, or quite simply the mere fact of being gathered together in a home where someone could make some kind of music. Private affairs ranged from a few dancers gathered to honor a visiting commodore of the Texas Navy with but a lone piano for music; through a modest ball in a small house with a harp, a flute, a violin, a piano, and a clarinet crowded in; to lavish affairs in pretentious homes in which three or four drawing rooms might be filled with guests who danced until breakfast at eight o'clock in the morning.[27]

One interesting variety of home dance was called a "Bal de Bouquet." This was a dance given by a bachelor, but at the house of a lady. At the outset of the carnival season, a bachelor was elected as king. He then picked a lady to be his queen and share his power which he delegated by crowning her with a wreath of flowers. At the queen's house and in her name the ball was then given. After a few quadrilles were danced, the king conducted his queen from her throne to the center of the room where she chose and crowned the next king, also a bachelor, with another wreath of flowers. He, in turn, crowned a new queen with similar ceremony and they led the next dance. The new queen gave the next ball at her house where the ritual was repeated, and so on through the carnival season. All such balls lasted until daybreak which ended the reign of the presiding king and queen.[28]

But no matter how spacious a house one owned, it couldn't always accommodate all those who should be invited in a city where dancing was so important a social function. As soon as larger halls became available then, another sort of private dance was an invitation ball given by someone in these more commodious surroundings. There was a spate of such balls during the period of transfers of Louisiana from Spain to France and from France to the United States during the months of December and January in 1803 and 1804. Because of the importance of the occasion, some record and description of these affairs have been left us; and while they were perhaps more lavish than usual, they serve to illustrate the height attained by this sort of private ball at the time that the Americans officially arrived.

On December 1, 1803, the first day after Spain formally returned Louisiana to France, the new French Prefect, Pierre Laussat, gave a ball in honor of the French flag. There was to be a dinner followed by a concert, then the dancing, and finally a late supper. Seventy-five guests attended the dinner and concert, and about three hundred more arrived for the dance. In deference to the Americans, for every two French quadrilles the orchestra played an English one. In addition, there were minuets, character dances, waltzes, boat dances, and gallopades. So infectious was the enthusiasm that elderly matrons who had long ago given up dancing again took to the floor. After supper was served at three in the morning (as it still is at the present-day carnival supper dance), dancing was resumed. Laussat wrote in his diary that at five o'clock in the morning two sets of quadrilles were still going, and at seven there remained a boat dance and a gallopade. One hopes that the musicians were well paid.[29]

Now it was the turn of the special emissary from Spain, the Marquis de Casa-Calvo, to honor the Prefect and Madame Laussat with a ball. This one, on December 8, 1803, lasted all of twelve hours, with occasional respites for the dancers (but none for the musicians who gave concerts during the rest periods). Supper was served this time at 2 A.M., possibly in hopes of an earlier termination of the affair, but none of the dancers would leave before the French guests of honor departed at 8 A.M.[30]

Of course Laussat had to return the honor, which he did a week later on December 16 with another twelve hours of boleros, gavottes, hornpipes, French and English quadrilles, and gallopades. The dance was lighted with 20 lamps and 220 candles, and relieved by 8 gaming tables, tea, chocolate, coffee, consomme, and gumbo. This affair also lasted until eight in the morning. Four days later, on December 20, the American commissioners officially took possession of Louisiana and, of course, attended a ball honoring them and the occasion.[31]

Of course, a strictly private ball on such a scale was the sort of dance least frequently given. But at those times when "everybody who was anybody" should be invited, then one was held. When the Kennedy family presented their two eldest daughters to New Orleans society in 1850, they utilized no less a place than the United States Mint Building for a fancy dress ball. "Committee rooms, offices and every apartment that could be diverted" were given over to insure a proper launching of these two girls. Costumes were rented from the French Opera Company, and the men were so enthusiastic in applying makeup that it took them a full week thereafter to remove it.[32]

In the home or out, however, there could never be enough debuts or transfers to satisfy the desire for dancing of those who chose—at least openly—to refrain from attendance at public balls requiring only the price of admittance for entry. So a third sort of private dance developed to fill the need. This was the subscription or society ball which was actually something of a compromise between the strictly private and the open-to-all public balls.

At first subscription dances were more nearly private than they became later on. Some kind of group, merchants perhaps, but more often simply "heads of families," was invited to subscribe to a series of balls in one of the public ballrooms. The subscribers held a meeting to elect a committee and to choose managers whose duties were to plan the dances, to maintain order, and to keep out undesirables. Usually six to ten dances comprised the series, at a cost of from nine to twenty dollars for each subscription. The subscribers were entitled to bring whatever ladies they "will deem convenient to introduce therein." However, convenience knows no bounds, and it soon became customary to limit the subscriber's female guests to three. Heads of families were permitted to bring their wives and daughters, but it is not clear whether these ladies were to be in place of or in addition to the ladies deemed "convenient." [33]

Keeping subscription dances fairly exclusive was the purpose and the biggest problem. For the most part these affairs were commercial ventures initiated by ballroom proprietors who were naturally reluctant to turn away any lone males wishing to pay at the door. And of course there were all those ladies inside who might be expected to welcome additional men. The subscription lists, therefore, were usually kept at the promoter's house or his office and were closed after a sufficient number had signed. Strangers were warned that they would not be admitted at the door "under any pretext," and subscribers were required to sign their names on their tickets or to be identified in some way.[34]

But there were always loopholes for determined crashers, and gradually the price of admittance became the chief measure of exclusiveness at subscription dances. By the 1830's the most select of these cost thirty dollars for a series of eight. Others, not so discriminating, offered six balls for fifteen dollars and kept no one out who would pay three dollars at the door for a single evening's admittance.[35]

In time the better subscription balls settled on procedures that afforded the maximum practical exclusiveness. The regulations for the Orleans Ballroom subscription balls in the fall of 1830 are typical: the list of subscription balls was always to be open, but late subscribers were to pay the full price of the series of eight balls—excepting those out of town or in mourning at the time of the first ball. Positively no one was to be admitted without a *personal* ticket—but strangers could obtain one from the office for three dollars. The first two ladies with the stranger cost him four dollars, but each additional lady cost him only one dollar more—a good argument for bringing three or four.[36]

On the whole, the high price seems to have accomplished its purpose. In the season of 1832–33, a severe cholera epidemic forced the abandonment of the society subscription balls at the Orleans Ballroom. But the management there proposed to give a certain number of public balls, promising to take "the most vigorous caution in the selection and decency of the company" and to provide "a vigilant police." This was in order to provide some opportunity to the "many families who delight in . . . the dance, and who would otherwise be deprived of that pleasure in consequence of the failure of the *select* parties." [37]

Subscription lists were also employed for certain single dances on holidays or to honor a famous guest. For these, the usual cost was ten dollars with dinner included. As many as could pay attended; the previously mentioned ball given for Lafayette when he visited New Orleans in 1825 was a subscription affair that drew over a thousand dancers.[38]

Even an extremely expensive subscription ball might attract more customers than were wanted. The price of the one given for Henry Clay at the St. Louis Hotel in 1843 was an incredible one hundred dollars per subscriber. Yet the list had to be arbitrarily limited to two hundred customers who, with their guests, made a crowd of about six hundred.[39]

One type of single subscription dance that was more easily restricted in size, however, was a ball that was plainly a snare for bachelors. Eight patronesses, four American and four French, were the sponsors. Each chose four more young "ladies of honor." Together these forty females were the subscribers and each was expected to bring two men. The married ladies could invite only bachelors, leaving the maidens to escort the married men. The results of this interesting arrangement are not known.[40]

Numerous as the various sorts of private and semiprivate dances were, they were far outnumbered by the public dances, the pay-as-you-enter ones that were held in the many ballrooms and cabarets dotting the city. It is difficult to pinpoint the exact time when the public ballrooms began. We do know that on February 7, 1792, Filiberto Farge presented a plan to the Spanish governor, Baron Carondelet, proposing to build a public dance hall for whites at Farge's expense. In his petition Farge said he would take for his model the hall which Governor Galvez had formerly permitted in the King's Warehouse and that had pleased the public well. Since Galvez governed from 1777 to 1782, it is apparent that there was a public dancing site in operation some time before 1782.[41]

In 1811 John Davis, who was soon to do so much to nurture opera in New Orleans, bought Tremoulet's Hotel. The former owner, Mr. B. Tremoulet, took the occasion to thank the public for its support of the past twenty-seven years. Since public dances were held in this hotel at the time and were recorded there as early as 1805, it is possible that they took place in Tremoulet's Hotel the full twenty-seven years before, in 1784 or soon thereafter. And in 1787, Governor Miro invited thirty-six Choctaw and Chickasaw Indian chiefs to New Orleans. He took them to a public ball, most likely held in the aforementioned King's Warehouse. His purpose was to make friends, and the Indians were indeed delighted, especially by the dancing ladies who seemed to these tribal chieftains to have dropped directly from heaven. This warehouse-ballroom apparently was destroyed in the great fire of 1788.[42]

But the hall proposed by Farge early in 1792 was the first intended specifically for public dancing. Farge's plan which called for the city to buy the building after four years was accepted, and construction began on the site of the former public market which had been reduced to ashes in the great fire.[43]

Such was the beginning of the famous Conde Street Ballroom, as it soon came to be known. It opened on October 4, 1792, and although Joseph de Pontalba's first impression was that "it is quite beautiful and spacious," it was not an imposing edifice. Farge's original plan was modest enough, calling for a hall one hundred feet long with boxes "such as in the theater" and a surrounding corridor for those not dancing. When built, it was somewhat smaller—a one-story wooden building, about eighty feet long by a little over thirty feet wide. To one scornful guest from Europe, New Orleans' pride was "nothing but . . . a huge barrack," having no elegant chandeliers or mirrors, dependent only on candles for miserable lighting. In fact, he declared, "The ensemble is so wretched" that any hint "of embellishment would be ridiculous." In addition, much of the time the dancers were forced to wade through mud and mire to get to the place.[44]

But they loved it. Was it not, they demanded of the newcomer or visitor, better than any in London, Venice, or even in Paris? And although this might be amusing conceit to the traveler who knew these cities, it was not so far-fetched to one familiar only with America. "I will only say," wrote William Johnson in the spring of 1801, "that the room was elegant, the ladies very beautiful, the music good, and everything that could render the evening amusing and agreeable was well adapted." [45]

One thing could not be disputed—the guests had fun there. Even those ladies who came to sit as spectators only in the boxes on either side of the hall "find their passions raised so high by the scene before them, that they cannot rest satisfied with passively looking on. Animated by the voluptuous attitudes, and significant looks of the dancers, they frequently descend into the scene of pleasure, the face, neck, and bosom suffused with crimson, and giving their hands to the first partners that offer, go down to dance with the rest, panting and palpitating." [46]

Moreover, the wish was often father to the fact, and since the structure on Conde Street was the city's principal ballroom until the rebuilt Orleans Ballroom opened in 1817, its barracks-like atmosphere was soon transformed by the ardent New Orleanians into something more nearly approximating their desires. Not only did they decorate the hall lavishly, but they changed the decorations frequently. During the single month of February in 1814, which may be taken as typical for the Conde Street Ballroom at its height, the room was first decorated "like that of the Tivoli in Paris, and hung with garlands of flowers." Seventeen chandeliers were suspended by garlands of roses, and the large mirrors were replaced with new ones. Colored glass reflected and diffused the light into every corner. To this was added a week later "a small stage lighted with colored fires, and with a decoration . . . [imitating] . . . that of Panurge in the Islands of Lanthorns." For the next week the management promised "entirely new decorations . . . the Temple of Memory and a geographical reunion of all the powers of Europe, a happy prognostick of peace and amity. The room will be surrounded with bushes, lighted with colored fires, decorated with looking glasses, and garlands of flowers with a transparent representing the successes of the American Navy." No European snob could now complain that the room lacked mirrors or was miserably lit. Rather might he wonder that it didn't burn down with all the lighting.[47]

And other ballrooms were a-building. As early as 1800 there were so many that the attorney-general, Don Pedro Barran, appealed to the governor to reduce their number in order to lessen disorder. At least one of these dance sites was elegant enough to cause the lessee of the Conde Street Ballroom, Don Francisco Larose, to appear before the city council early in 1803 with what must surely be one of the strangest requests in the history of social dancing. He had heard that some of the leading families were contemplating giving their society balls at this other place, and since he had had some business losses, he was obliged to offer his ballroom rent free for these affairs. The sponsors would have to pay only for the music, lights, and refreshments, giving Larose whatever their conscience dictated. Therefore he petitioned the city council to *order* these families to hold their society balls at his place.[48]

A few years later, in 1810, another lessee of the Conde, confronted with a similar situation, charged that a cabal was working against him in spite of the "brilliant redecorations" that had been made. He warned the wandering patrons that if they did not come back, he would turn the Conde Street Ballroom to "other uses"—a veiled threat to hold colored dances there. Thus the American way of private enterprise was beginning to replace Spanish reliance upon government interference.[49]

But it would not be long before truly splendid rooms would eclipse the Conde and gratify the dancing city. Henry Bradshaw Fearon who was traveling through America in 1817 at the behest of a group of Englishmen in order to ascertain what parts might be habitable reported: "The ballroom, at Davis's hotel, I have never seen exceeded in splendour." This was the same John Davis who later that year opened the Orleans Ballroom, one that was to become the setting for the most select affairs in New Orleans until it in turn was outshone by the St. Louis Ballroom. When Benjamin Henry Latrobe, a prominent architect, visited the Orleans Ballroom in 1819 he judged it the best to be found in America. Karl

Bernhard, the Duke of Saxe-Weimar-Eisenach, described it in 1826 as "quite long, well planned, and adorned with large mirrors." Surrounding the floor, he said, were three rows of benches arranged as an amphitheater, and behind those, several rooms for supper or other refreshments. In still other rooms, faro, roulette, and other games provided diversion for those unlucky at love. The floor itself was constructed of oak laid over a triple layer of cypress, while above and around the whole was a balcony where partners promenaded between dances.[50]

Most impressive were those gala nights when the Orleans Theater was joined to the Ballroom to make a huge, surely unequaled ball site. With the pit floored over to the level of the stage; the boxes closed with panels painted by the fine scene painters of the theater to represent a saloon, or a garden; an orchestra in both rooms allowing the dancers to drift from one to the other without pause —the grand masquerade balls at the Orleans fulfilled the boasts and fed the soul of New Orleans. It was gratifying to read on the front page of one's newspaper that "the ballroom is without a doubt the most richly decorated in the United States," or that everyone agrees these balls made the capitals of Europe envious. The Orleans Ballroom was acknowledged to be both "the ornament and pride of New Orleans."[51]

In time even this splendor was rivaled by the ballroom in the St. Charles Hotel, opened in 1837; and the latter was surpassed by the ballroom in the St. Louis Hotel after 1838. The suite of ballrooms in the St. Louis was "unequaled for size and beauty" in the opinion of James Silk Buckingham, an Englishman who published two volumes on his travels. He especially admired the painted ceiling of the largest room, and noted that the ballrooms were constantly in use. (The St. Louis Hotel burned down in 1841 but was rebuilt immediately on the same splendid scale.)[52]

In sum, it seems that the earliest halls were below European standards though impressive by American. But with the coming of ballrooms like the Orleans and like those in the St. Charles Hotel and the St. Louis Hotel, there is no doubt that New Orleans was replete with ballrooms unsurpassed in size and splendor anywhere.

But beauty and elegance were secondary. The prime reason for the existence of these halls was a functional one, and in all of them from large to small, the immense variety of dances performed demanded accomplished participants. The dancer must be ready for boleros and gavottes; for cotillions and gallops; and for waltzes, mazurkas, reels, and minuets, to say nothing of the ever-present French and English quadrilles. "The eternal quadrille" seemed to one beholder to be "given without cease," but actually there were enough other dances to make the profession of dancing master common in New Orleans.[53]

Not only were there all these steps to learn, but partners were apt to be very proficient in them. Charles A. Murray, an Englishman who had toured through most of North America, went dancing in New Orleans in 1835. "I had seen nothing so like a ball since I left Europe," he wrote. "The contre-danses were well danced, and there was waltzing without swinging, and a gallopade without a romp." Another of Murray's compatriots flatly described the Orleanians as "the best dancers in the United States." [54]

Acquiring the needed skill, therefore, was virtually a necessity. Not to dance would mean to forego too much. It was not the balls alone, numerous as they were, that would be missed, but a considerable portion of other amusements. As has already been mentioned, the great majority of concerts prior to 1830 were linked with balls, and so too were many theater offerings. In the spring of 1838, the St. Charles Theater presented an opera which was sub-titled *The Masked Ball,* and included a grand masked ball immediately after the final curtain of every performance. On eight successive nights the theater was packed for this bargain opera and masked ball.[55]

To be sure, these happened to be the eight days immediately preceding Good Friday when opportunities and excuses for masked balls may have been scarce, but New Orleans simply couldn't resist the lure of a *masked* ball at any time or for any reason. It was always fun to dance, but to hide one's identity behind a mask greatly heightened the thrill and broadened the range of permissible partners or possible adventures. A lady never refuses "any decent stranger who asks her to dance," observed one of the strangers, who

The immense variety of dances performed demanded accomplished participants; dancers had to be prepared for gavottes, cotillions, waltzes, and the French and English quadrille.

added that such dancing together "imposed no necessity for being acquainted beyond the walls of the ballroom." No necessity, perhaps, but an opportunity? Neither birth, wealth, nor color made any difference, according to Thomas Ashe who, though he was inclined to exaggerate in search of sensation, was correct enough in depicting an unusual degree of democracy.[56]

One newcomer publicly expressed his shock at seeing a sixteen-year-old apprentice boy being familiar "with a married lady whose standing in society was second to none." Most, however, were entranced with balls where the ladies had their faces covered "but every other part of their body exposed, if not to sight at least to touch," and where, as an added fillip, "they go so habited that there is no discovering whether they are black or white." No wonder that everyone who could raise the price of admission hastened to these houses of charm. The lowliest worker and the most successful men of law and business could be found here, mingling freely and happily. Did not a mask, as the New Orleans *Bee* nicely put it, "permit the proudest man to attend without scruple?" Where else in the United States was there anything like this? [57]

The excitement and the license of being masked was not the only means used to make public dances attract customers. Refreshments of one kind or another from "a cup of chocolate, or of 'beef tea,' or a glass of lemonade for six cents" to ice cream, cakes, or "excellent liquors" could usually be purchased between dances. And many of the ballrooms had somewhere on the premises a room for gambling.[58]

Proprietors vied with one another in devising schemes to make their balls in some way distinctive. One offered "Tea Parties" every Sunday evening from four to ten o'clock. Here, for only one dollar, a man and two ladies could enjoy a garden and a view of the river, as well as all the refreshments they were able to consume except liquor. That cost extra at these "Tea Parties." Another proprietor offered two hours of vaudeville on the terrace of his cafe before each Sunday ball—all for seventy-five cents a man, with ladies free. John Lege's Assembly Ballroom provided special carriages free from six o'clock on. A man could bring his ladies to those balls in style.[59]

One owner who bid fair to establish a record of some kind began his Sunday balls in the morning. For two dollars a man and one dollar a lady, breakfast was served and followed by a dress and masked ball until three in the afternoon. Then the ball was opened for additional customers who paid fifty cents a man and twenty-five cents a lady. It went on this way unto well into the night. Of course one could leave in order to attend one of the later Sunday balls.[60]

As early as 1826 the taxi dance made its appearance, the price per dance being set at six and a quarter cents. Some years later another and possibly better place charged twenty-five cents admission fee in addition to twelve and one-half cents a dance.[61]

Such competition to be different bred considerable imagination in varying the pattern of ball-giving. There were character balls to which each dancer came disguised as a certain character. The extra fun came because he intended (and was permitted) to live up to the character he had adopted. Or there was a bachelors' ball open only to bachelors and belles where the intent was that the charm of the dance would cause many to heave "the sigh of despondency at their lot of single blessedness." [62]

One promoter promised a concert of popular songs with each of his dances, the combinations to be replicas of those made popular in Paris by Philippe Musard. In 1840 another promoter appealed to the instinct for a bargain in presenting what he called a "fete champetre." The customer got fireworks, a variety show, and a "grand concert played by the large orchestra," in addition to the dance itself. More than this, those who were there at five o'clock could witness M. Lion use the new daguerreotype process to take a view of the orchestra and ballroom. Finally, during the ball the picture would be drawn for by lottery. Very little was left out of a "fete champetre." [63]

But the ballroom proprietor who perhaps showed the most ingenuity was the owner of the Jefferson Ballroom. In 1822 he turned his masked balls into gassed balls by giving "exhilarating gas" (nitrous oxide) to the dancers. At first he was very ambitious, promising to gas the "ladies and gentlemen" first, then the people of color, and finally "if practicable" some Choctaw Indians. Evidently gassing the Choctaws proved not too practicable, for by 1824 the chief occasions for gas at the Jefferson Ballroom were those nights on which "several ladies as well as gentlemen will respire it," all to the accompaniment of "good music." But with or without Indians, can television ever offer more? [64]

Children too, from the age of four, had their own balls throughout these years. One adult observer thought that these affairs were more joyous insofar as dancing was concerned than those of the adults. The children, he wrote, "leap and caper with so much more pleasure, because their amusement is their only end." (Just what other ends the adults may have had, the writer didn't say.) Another commentator three decades later was equally impressed with the way the youngsters went "bounding away to the lively music." [65]

Usually the children's balls took place in the same ballrooms as did those of their elders and frequently were followed immediately by an adults' ball. Hence the children's hours were scheduled from three or four o'clock until eight, at which time the impatient adults took over. On one occasion a children's ball ran all of seven hours —from three until ten o'clock—before the adults' ball began. If the children's balls alone were scheduled, ten o'clock at night was not an unusual closing time, and at least one ball for children, in 1811, ran from three until midnight. Thus were the children of New Orleans trained for the arduous pursuits of adult life.[66]

Training in dancing and endurance was not the only purpose served by these balls, however; here the young were taught public manners and self-possession—qualities they would use through life. Above the age of ten or eleven, they wore replicas of adult ball dress, and, garbed as elders, they learned to behave as elders were supposed to behave.[67]

One might assume that the adults had sufficient opportunities of their own to dance, but they eagerly crowded into the children's balls—so much so that these invasions became a major nuisance during the first decade or so that Americans possessed Louisiana. By the beginning of 1806 adult intrusions into the children's balls reached the point that the little ones were actually deprived of any place on the dance floor, thus causing the parents to lodge formal protests. Jean Baptiste Francisqui, the leading teacher of the day, pledged that henceforth, at his balls for children, adults would be allowed no more than two contredances at any one time—one at each end of the floor. But M. Francisqui in the same breath begged the adults to cooperate.[68]

A number of the children themselves, three years later, were moved to make a touching appeal to the public, requesting "urgently" that their elders let them enjoy their balls. They reminded the adults that they had many balls while the children had only those set aside for them; so could they not please have the free use of the hall on their own days? Apparently they couldn't, for as late as 1813, managers still announced sternly that adults were forbidden to dance at the children's balls; that they must wait until 8 P.M.; or that the room was strictly reserved for children.[69]

It was sufficient to have two fathers assist the dancing master in maintaining "order and tranquillity" at the children's balls. It sometimes took a detachment of troops to do the same for the adult public balls. Indeed, the chief detraction of the public balls was the risk of riot in one degree or another. When the Spanish attorney-general sought to decrease the number of dance halls in 1800, he argued that his purpose was to reduce disorders; and when Commissioner Claiborne called James Madison's attention to the New Orleans public balls in 1804, he did so because they were the source of the principal disturbances confronting the new American administration.[70]

The tumults that concerned Claiborne were mainly national in origin. Quarrels and jealousies among the various national groups often exploded in the ballrooms where these groups came consistently close together and in sufficient numbers to feel belligerent. This was true even before the Americans officially arrived to roil matters further.[71]

One night in 1802, for example, the eldest son of the Spanish governor persisted in asking for English dances. He, being clumsy at the French dances, disliked them. The crowd tolerated the gentleman for a while out of deference to his rank. But he abused the privilege; just as a French dance was about to begin, with seven sets on the floor, he yelled yet once more for an English quadrille. That was too much. The irate dancers began themselves shouting for the French quadrille. Friends, sycophants, and countrymen of the Spaniard joined his call for the English dance. All was din and confusion until the governor's son ordered the orchestra to stop playing altogether. Spanish soldiers stationed outside to keep order rushed in, bayonets fixed, to line up on the side of Spain. Meanwhile Frenchmen from the gambling rooms piled in to reinforce their comrades. While men cursed, drew their swords, or grabbed chairs and benches to do battle, ladies and girls cried, wrung their hands, and fainted. (Those Americans present made the most of the opportunity to carry attractive women away from the place in their arms.) A scene of carnage was prevented only by the pleas of three young Frenchmen and by the arrival of the governor himself.[72]

After the Americans officially took control of Louisiana, another source of friction at the balls was added. At one of the public dances given on January 8, 1804, to celebrate the transfer there was constant argument over whether American or French dances should be played. Matters came to a head when a square of French dancers and a square of Americans formed at the same time on the floor. Each group urged the orchestra to play its own kind of dance. One of the Americans, resorting to direct persuasion, raised his stick over a fiddler's head and tension immediately heightened (especially, one presumes, for the fiddler). Claiborne, who happened to be present, managed to calm the Americans down temporarily and the French dance was allowed to begin. But the Americans soon interrupted it, taking the floor and calling loudly for an English quadrille. Someone shouted through the uproar: "If the women have a drop of French blood in their veins, they will not give in!" The room rapidly emptied of women, ending this dance.[73]

The municipal authorities, hoping to forestall further trouble, ruled that there should be a set order of two French quadrilles, one English quadrille, and one waltz in turn. Nevertheless the argument flared up again on January 22. Women fled the hall once more as Americans and French began to collar one another and a number of soldiers entered the fray. Claiborne's fellow commissioner, General Wilkinson, ordered his military band to play "Hail Columbia" and "God Save the King" as loud as it could. Cheers followed each number. The French retorted by singing *"Enfants de la Patrie"* and *"Peuples francais: peuple de freres"* at the top of their voices, and by shouting *"Vive la Republique!"* Finally Wilkinson left, taking the music and most of the Americans with him. It was after this incident that Claiborne ordered an officer and fifteen troops to be present at every public ball to help the municipal authorities maintain order. But the attempt to force more English dances, the presence of soldiers, and the risk of repeated battles cast a pall over this first season of dancing under American rule. Expressing his hope that the next season would be better, a native reminded Americans that even the most barbarous of conquerors pay outward respect to local customs.[74]

On the whole the conquerors did in fact rapidly succumb to the charming local custom. "Already we begin to aim at select balls," observed John Watson in 1805. A young American from Kentucky whose friends back home were evidently concerned about his morals down South among the wicked French assured them they need have no fear. The only places where the races mixed, he said, were the coffee-house and the ballroom. And he added: "You may go to our English Coffee house at any or all times in the day & see five Americans or English to one Frenchman or Spaniard." As for the balls, the young Kentuckian avowed that the Americans attended only to watch the French girls dance. "Fear not for my principles," he concluded, "[since] few Americans partake of the French Cotilions [*sic*]." [75]

One may doubt whether the Americans were as immune to the spell of French dancing and French girls as this; one may be certain that such immunity could not last. With English-speaking French dancing masters eager to teach Americans, even Quakers and Presbyterians soon succumbed to the dance—and on Sunday at that.[76]

With the ballrooms being the principal place for social contact on a large scale among the nationalities, they operated as much to promote a common merging as to promote clashes. By no means did all of the early frictions over dancing end in worsening the situation. Later in the same year, 1804, in which occurred the two incidents just described, a similar situation ended differently. This time the Americans were agitating for the Virginia reel and the jig in

place of the waltz and the cotillion. To prevent just this the
Creoles, for their part, turned out in force. Both sides carried arms
to the conflict. As the noise and confusion mounted, and the ladies
as before began to leave the hall, a young girl jumped up on a
bench. Addressing the angry Americans she cried: "We have been
Spanish for thirty years and the Spaniards never forced us to dance
the fandango; neither do we want to dance the reel or the jig!"

Although the girl spoke French, her gallantry touched the astonished Americans. General Wilkinson translated her plea, ordered
the musicians to play a waltz, and then led her off to dance it while
the crowd shouted "Hurrah!" and joined the waltz enthusiastically.[77]

After the second season of dancing under American rule had
been in progress for several weeks, Claiborne wrote another letter to
Madison on the subject. Although the national groups were now
meeting frequently at the balls, Claiborne did not, as he had done
the year before, complain of disorder. Rather, he spoke of the "perfect harmony" that had come to prevail over former bitterness.[78]

In this Claiborne was a bit too sanguine. He had just been made
governor of the territory and was perhaps inclined to exaggerate
about the good feeling. The balls were indeed working for better
relations, but a miracle could not be achieved overnight. Charles
Sealsfield reported to English readers in 1826 that "Until last year
. . . the Americans and creoles stood with their ladies apart,
neither speaking nor dancing with one another. Last year both
parties seemed willing to draw nearer to each other." And the
young Joseph Holt Ingraham, who was later to gain considerable
fame as a novelist and clergyman, noticed at a children's ball in the
1830's that the French children and the American children still congregated at opposite ends of the hall, chiefly because they couldn't
speak each other's language.[79]

But increasingly the desire for a ball served to overcome the desire
for a brawl. In 1835 a rumor spread that the Americans were
conspiring to go to a St. Joseph's Day Ball at the Washington Ball
Room "armed to the teeth for the purpose of . . . driving the
French and Creoles." Consequently it was reported that the mayor
had ordered the ballroom closed for the night. This moved a group

of Americans to make a public appeal for the ball. The St. Joseph's Day Ball, they wrote, "has always been looked upon by the laborious and industrious classes in our society as peculiarly their own fete,— and hundreds who could not afford more than one ball have postponed their only holiday till St. Joseph's." The American group went on to plead, therefore, that the ban be lifted, emphatically pledging to cause no trouble. The letter was signed "Many Americans, The Friends of Peace." [80]

Thus the public balls of New Orleans played an extremely important part in overcoming national differences in America's first real melting pot. By learning to play together, the polyglot peoples of this unique American city took an early and giant stride toward necessary understanding.

By 1840 those Americans who were not yet completely "friends of peace"—insofar as dancing was concerned—were reduced to making cranky complaints about a series of "Erina Balls" at the Planters Hotel for the benefit of Catholic orphans. These balls, charged the grumblers, were but "one link in the chain of operations, by which native American children are to be brought under the influence of foreign male Jesuits, through the instrumentality of unknown foreign females." Other native-born Protestant Americans, however, at once defended the balls and denied the accusation. [81]

But if disorders engendered by nationalism gave way before the overriding desire to dance, other troubles were more persistent. When the Spanish attorney-general sought in 1800 to reduce the number of dance halls, he was concerned mainly with individual thefts, fights, killings, and similar crimes. He stated that there was not a single street in or out of the ramparts bounding the rear of the old settlement that didn't have one or more cabarets always crowded with soldiers, sailors, laborers, and slaves. These establishments were described by another as "places of riot and intoxication, crowded day and night," in which the main activities besides drinking were pilfering, gambling and dancing without end. "What can be more shameful," asked one indignant citizen in 1821, "than the scenes of prostitution and vice nightly exhibited in the Dance-houses . . . ?" [82]

What was true of these small dance halls and taverns was also true to a considerable extent of the larger public ballrooms. One of the last sessions of the city council held under Spanish rule concerned itself with the large number of indecently dressed and unclean persons who mixed at the balls with the best people of the city. The council asked the governor to exclude those not properly attired. But for the next forty years the leading ballrooms such as the Conde Street and the Orleans were forced to insist again and again that no "gentleman" be allowed to dance wearing his heavy boots, his hat, or his overcoat. Nor was the gentleman told only what not to wear. He must come "well dressed," and this was spelled out for him to mean shoes, dress coat, and a white or a black cravat.[83]

Pilfering and prostitution also were not monopolized by lower-class taverns. Thieves stole John Watson's new hat at one ball in 1805, and four days later stole his new replacement at another. Mr. Watson's frustration could have been exceeded only by that of another dancer from whom the light-fingered gentry managed to lift not only his newly foxed boots, but his stockings as well. Fancy hats, silver canes, and fine cloaks were prone to disappear or to be exchanged for inferior substitutes.[84]

A man was far more likely to be accosted at the balls, however, than to be robbed—which may have been one reason that the city fathers sought to bar children under fifteen. The English actor, Louis Tasistro, thought that most of the ballrooms were little better than haunts of assignation, "mere places of rendezvous for all the gay females of the town." [85]

Indeed, these resorts provided a rendezvous for "gay females" from many towns, if the European tourist Isadore Lowenstern may be believed. He wrote that a large part of the women at the public balls came from the North, drawn by greater and more lucrative opportunities for "pleasure" in New Orleans. In 1840 over one hundred and seventy citizens presented to the council of the Second Municipality a petition to close one of the ballrooms. The petitioners alleged that "the numerous females attending . . . are princi-pally or altogether women of the town." [86]

The biggest risk, though, was to body rather than to purse or purity. Fights and even killings consistently marred the public balls. In the words of one beholder, "scarcely a night passes without ex-hibiting some scenes of violence, frequently ending in bloodshed." Or as another lamented, "So many murders and tragical scenes have been enacted at these balls." [87]

Fights were so commonplace that they were taken for granted, seldom disturbing the course of dancing. A guest at one ball, in the short time he was present, saw two brawls "which commenced in the ball-room with blows, and terminated in the vestibule, with pocket-pistols and kicking, without any interruption from the Police." An-other reported in 1829 that battles followed each and every dance at a ball he attended. Such insouciance regarding fights so impressed the visiting actor, George Vandenhoff, that he declared that a fatal stabbing on the dance floor scarcely interrupted the music, and in-convenienced the victim's girl only for the moment it took her to find a new partner. Of course a gun fight involving several men, such as that which took place in a Milneberg dance hall in 1840, was bound to interfere more with the music. Shooting makes more noise than stabbing.[88]

Fights initiated in the better ballrooms quite often were referred to the dueling field. Here a young lad of good family and recent European education could lose his life over nothing more impor-tant than who was to have the next dance. Nor were the ladies al-ways averse to such bloodletting. Mrs. Matilda Houstoun was shocked a few days after her arrival in the city in the 1840's when an Englishman killed an American youth in a duel. "The quarrel," she wrote, "originated in the St. Louis ball-room, and was caused by the wilful and vindictive spirit of a young lady, who protested that the Englishman had insulted *her* by placing his partner above her in the dance, and that *she would have satisfaction*." One hopes she was satisfied.[89]

On the other hand, a duel had the advantage of allowing time for second thoughts to prevail. M. Letourner settled his argument with M. Garrus in 1812 by simply advertising in the newspaper that he had slapped Garrus in the ballroom. For his part, Garrus parried the thrust by advertising in the same issue that Letourner was a boasting liar. Both men lived.[90]

The incidence of fighting was always great enough to cause proprietors of all the ballrooms from the Orleans to those on the levee to take stringent precautions. Canes, swords, and any other visible weapons had to be checked at the door. This practice was generally approved. When, for example, the French consul refused to surrender his sword at a military ball, he was taken severely to task in an editorial. Pointing out that the governor of Louisiana and officers of the United States Army had surrendered their swords without a murmur, the writer suggested that the consul give a ball wherein all officers and infantrymen be required to wear or to carry their arms as they tried to dance. Checking all visible weapons proved not enough, however, and toward the end of the 1830's the custom was extended to include a thorough search of each entrant for concealed arms.[91]

Two, three, or even four managers were hired to keep order. Among other duties they were in sole charge of deciding the sorts of dances to be played. It were well that these managers be good shots; the risks were great. In 1837 one manager unluckily happened upon a certain gentleman in the street. At a ball on the previous evening the manager had questioned the propriety of this gentleman's lady. The manager missed two shots before the man closed and stabbed him to death.[92]

Much of the difficulty in keeping order was caused by the fondness for masking. A mask might give the wearer greater opportunity for stealing forbidden fruits; or for just plain stealing and other disorderly conduct. Consequently the more conscientious promoters strove persistently to exercise some control over the latitude permitted by masks.

A few examples of the rules that were made at various times give an insight into the problem. Most common was the simple demand that all masked persons be unmasked and identified before admittance. Apparently identification was not always a sufficient bar to the admission of shady ladies; therefore women might be additionally required to present a personal ticket issued directly by the management and carrying the name of each lady on it. "Not one ticket will be delivered to ladies at the door," they were warned.[93]

There were from time to time other rules requiring all maskers to leave their masks in the checkroom before entering the balls; or conversely, rules prohibiting masked dancers from leaving the ball to go into the streets with their masks on. How the whole masking business drove the managers to distraction may best be shown by a regulation made in 1834: "Ladies who may wish to go out of the ballroom, to unmask themselves, as well as such as will remain under mask, will apply for a countermask to the doorkeeper, so as to be identified by the manager, whose duty shall be to recognize masks." Clear enough for anybody.[94]

That such attempts by management failed to gain the desired result is suggested by the frequent repetition of the rules during the years under study and, more emphatically, by the efforts of the city government to control masked balls. Only two years after New Orleans passed into American hands, the new rulers were compelled to deal officially with the problem. On January 21, 1806, the city council, acknowledging that masks and disguises "were the means of grand disorders among us," proclaimed that henceforth anyone wearing a mask on the street was to be arrested, unmasked, and fined ten dollars. More than this, the council forbade all masked balls, public or private, under fine of twenty dollars against anyone giving or attending one. Finally all public balls had to be licensed. In themselves, city regulations for the balls were not new. The Spanish had had them, and one of the first acts of the new American city government was to adopt regulations for public balls. But here was an outright prohibition of masked balls.[95]

Like all legal prohibitions of something much in public favor, this one obviously failed. Toward the end of 1827 the council tried again by prohibiting all masked balls with the important exception of the period from January 1 to Shrove Tuesday. During that time licenses for single balls only could be granted (or refused) by the mayor. The cost was twenty-five dollars in addition to all previous taxes. All persons attending such a ball were compelled to unmask and to be identified by policemen stationed there. Setting time limits to the masked balls made no sense at all to the New Orleans *Bee:* " . . . they will permit masked balls after January 1. Why not after December 1, November 1, October 1!? Is there a time when we will be strong against temptation and another when we will be feeble? How ridiculous!" With florid indignation the paper asked if it weren't "time our voice was raised against so strange a tergiversation, against an abuse of power so criant, against this embargo placed on our pleasures. . . . Do we live in a civilized country or in the state of St. Peter? Is this the United States in the nineteenth century?" [96]

At the same time the paper implied its faith that this *was* the United States in the nineteenth century by reassuring readers that after a while the council would permit masked balls, or if not, the balls would simply continue under some other name.[97]

That the *Bee* was correct in its appraisal is apparent from a renewed endeavor to outlaw masked balls in 1836. Within a year this final effort at a complete ban had to be given up. Once more time limits were set, but more to save face than anything else: the time allowed for masked balls covered the important six months from November first to May first. The only other strictures imposed were to specify by name the ballrooms permitted to hold masked balls, and to make it a penal offense to admit white and colored women together.[98]

The city government had good reasons for declining to curtail the balls in any significant way. For one thing, it collected a handsome tax of from ten to twenty-five dollars or more on each of the numerous balls given. For another, the city owned, from 1796 until 1821, the ballroom on Conde Street, renting it yearly to various ball promoters. Thus a sizable direct revenue was at stake should the balls be eliminated.[99]

Indirect benefits to the city were incalculably greater. The number of ballrooms alone made them one of the major businesses of old New Orleans. And it must be remembered that most of them sold liquor and food ranging from light refreshments to a full-course dinner. When a single private ball cost as much as five thousand dollars, it is clear that the balls pumped a large amount of money into circulation each year.[100]

The supplying of costumes, moreover, was a major enterprise. Costumes could be rented directly from some of the ballrooms as well as from the Orleans Theater wardrobe. In addition, there were a number of stores devoted to this trade; at least eleven such shops existed in the period 1824–41. In them an astonishing variety of ball goods was rented or sold. Robes, garnitures, coiffures, garlands, prunelle slippers, dancing pumps for men and boys with white and colored ones for ladies, white casimer pantaloons and vests, white satin stocks, black and white silk half-hose, gowns, laces, jewelry, antique earrings, shoe and knee buckles, hairpins, wreaths, bandeaus, favors, disguises, mustaches, beards, wigs, braids, curls, and more —all expressly offered for the balls. As one shop put it, "anything from Queen Elizabeth to Potiphar's wife." Another shop claimed to have on hand over one thousand wigs alone. Then, as now, gowns and dresses just in from Paris were the ultimate.[101]

The balls were a significant aid to charity, both private and organized. A widow left with five children; a man wounded in the Battle of New Orleans; a blind man; the family of a deceased musician; or simply a poor family—these were a few of the cases helped by balls given for their benefit. Sometimes one who had merely suffered a misfortune—usually of health—sponsored a ball in his own behalf, as did Joseph Guerin. M. Guerin "flattered himself that the public, always ready to assist the unfortunate," would honor his ball in numbers. Similarly, organizations like the Society for the Relief of Destitute Orphan Boys, the Samaritan Society, or the Catholic Association for Destitute Orphans either sponsored balls or, as in the case of the last named, received a portion of the ball license fee.[102]

If to all this is added the vital support given to concerts and the opera by the balls, and if the number of music trades dependent in whole or in part on that trilogy is considered, it is fair to paraphrase a modern business leader and say "What was good for dancing was good for New Orleans."

It remains only to discuss the music played at the balls. If we assume that good music is essential for a good dance, it is surprising to find so little description of it. Travelers who were much im-

SPECTACLE.

Demain Jeudi,

LE TABLEAU PARLANT,

Opéra, muſique de *Grétry* ; précédé du

FOU RAISONNABLE,

Comédie en un aĉte de *Patrat*.

Dimanche prochain, une première repréſentation de *la-Femme juge & partie*, comédie en cinq aĉtes & en vers de *Montfleury* père & fils, ſuivie de la *Lettre ſans adreſſe*.

Mardi prochain, abonnement ſuſpendu au bénéfice de M. VALLOIS, *le Barbier de Séville*, opéra en quatre aĉtes, muſique de *Paëſiillo*.

M. VALOIS prie les perſonnes qui déſirent conſerver leurs Loges de vouloir bien l'en faire prévenir pour le plus tard, dans toute la journée de Samedi prochain.

————————

BAL DE SOCIÉTÉ

Aujourd'hui Mercredi, dans la Salle de M o'Duhigg

GRAND BAL PUBLIC

Vendredi dans la même Salle.

————

Typical 1805 advertisement for an opera, a society ball, and a public ball.

pressed by the amount and the customs of dancing in New Orleans seldom commented on the orchestras, and newspaper references to music were likewise scant.

Considering the difficulties the theaters faced in assembling just a few musicians during the first decade of the nineteenth century, it is fair to assume that the early balls had to make do with whatever could be mustered. Certainly the only man who described a dance orchestra in those years tells us that in 1802 the music for a ball that he attended was performed by five or six fiddlers whom he called "gypsies, or people of color." He conceded their enthusiasm, saying that they scraped away "with all their might," but he characterized the sound thus produced as "squeaky." On the other hand, to the presumably less sophisticated ears of an American, the music in that same ballroom sounded good.[103]

While the number of musicians multiplied during the next few years, so did the number of ballrooms—a situation that kept the managers as busy trying to find musicians as the musicians were busy playing. Often the advertisements of a ball promised that the orchestra would be a better one than last time; or boasted that "no pains or expense" had been spared in hiring the musicians; or pledged that the "greatest care" would be taken in assembling an orchestra. In spite of such pains, one of the lesser nobility of Europe, the Baron de Montlezun, who went to a ball at the Condé Street Ballroom in 1816 when that room was still the best in New Orleans, had this to say: "The music was paltry and of a pitiable effect. Six crude fiddlers were all the orchestra, ruining some melodies, cold and slow and pitiful in contrast with the fire of the dancers." The description is nearly the same as the one given fourteen years earlier.[104]

One means of enhancing ball music had been found during these years, however. In January of 1807, M. Francisqui, the dancing master, introduced a special attraction at one of his balls in the St. Peter Street Ballroom. Monsieur borrowed General Wilkinson's military band to play the waltzes. This innovation proved popular enough to be repeated a week later, and thereafter military bands frequently shared the bandstand with the more conventional string orchestras. These bands might be regular army, like the one just mentioned, or amateur, or one of the many militia bands in the city, such as the band of the Carabiniers that was popular at dances in 1814.[105]

After the Orleans Theater opened in 1819 and began importing musicians from Europe, the size and quality of dance orchestras improved. In the 1820's an enterprising ball promoter might occasionally hire the complete orchestra from that theater. But as the Orleans Theater orchestra grew in size it was seldom employed intact for a ball. Rather, the members of that orchestra, as well as those of the Camp Street Theater orchestra, and, after 1835, the St. Charles Street Theater orchestra, formed the nucleus of several of the numerous dance orchestras then needed in the city.[106]

Others were formed in various ways: the ballroom manager might advertise for individual musicians to form its orchestra; he might engage a director who would in turn hire the musicians; or he might use the services of a contractor who supplied musicians, or of a visiting band for single balls.[107]

In spite of a complaint or two that an orchestra was too small for good dance music, there was an ample supply of musicians in New Orleans after 1820. Almost every year some of those who came to the city to play in one of the theater orchestras remained to settle. As often as not they did not return to the pit in subsequent seasons, finding other musical opportunities in the city more lucrative. In this way there was a steady infusion of fresh talent from other American cities and from Europe. Likewise a number of musicians from visiting concert groups and teachers from elsewhere settled in New Orleans. It was a self-feeding process. The fact that New Orleans already had a large number of musicians made it more rather than less attractive to other musicians.[108]

Thus by 1829 even a second-rate ballroom employed an orchestra of fifteen musicians for its ordinary balls. Others used fewer or more musicians as circumstances warranted. Perhaps the best index to the range in size of the dance orchestras is found in the advertisement of a company formed in 1840 by Cobini, a local conductor, and H. E. Lehmann, the first trumpet in the Orleans Theater. They offered to furnish anything "from a pianist up to fifty instrumentalists." [109]

The company was evidently realistic enough in its appraisal of the need. In the same year a violinist, Hippolyte Dubuc, advertised his services for dancing: he alone could play the music and call the figures for up to fifty dancers, but would hire three or four other instrumentalists if needed. And Henry Didimus tells us that one of the most successful small dance halls was owned by three gentlemen who needed no other help: "One who played the fiddle, another beat the drum, and the third dealt out . . . brandy-coctail." At the other end of the scale, also in 1840, the entire Neptune Band, which claimed to have been formerly attached to the British queen, was hiring itself out for dancing.[110]

In the promotion of the balls, music got considerable attention, but not in the sense of name bands as we know them today. Occasionally the conductor's name was used, but more often the emphasis was on the musicians. Ballrooms promised their patrons an orchestra "composed in a new style"; "a complete band of musicians lately arrived from Europe"; or "great additions" to the orchestra.[111]

It was "good news for ball lovers," according to the New Orleans *Bee,* when it reported the engagement of "some reknown members" of the Orleans Theater orchestra by a ballroom. What was more, the music was to be arranged so that "each instrument will be able to display its talent." Similar good news was an occasional assurance that the same orchestra that played for the society balls would play for an ordinary public ball or for a children's ball.[112]

Of equal import to the number and quality of musicians in the orchestra was the music they would play. The incredible amount of dancing rapidly wore out the available repertoire, making it stale and boring. Accordingly the dance promoter who could promise "the newest and most fashionable" music made the most of it. He might advertise that "he has just procured a collection of handsome cotillions and waltzes," or he might pledge as a fixed policy that "every new quadrille, cotillion or waltz arriving, either from the North or from Europe, are immediately purchased and played." Just having "several new cotillions and waltzes" was worthy to be broadcast, but to be able to boast of "the newest and most current in the capital of good taste and pleasure (Paris)" was better. Best, though, in combining novelty and snob appeal was the guarantee of a new band, fresh from Europe, whose *every* tune was new, "and altogether in the French style." [113]

Otherwise the dance repertoire was freshened and enlarged, at least in the society balls, by suitable excerpts from the operas currently playing at the Orleans Theater, including the city's own opera, *Cosimo*, composed by the theater's conductor, Eugene Prevost. This, declared a pleased patron, "rendered dancing a matter of feeling." [114]

Certainly there was more praise than complaint about the ball music after 1820. Since people are generally more prone to criticize than to commend, the paucity of comment on the music itself indicates that good music was taken for granted. Those few who did mention the music found it "pretty good," "excellent," or "fine beyond compare." [115]

With plenty of good musicians then; a continual supply of the latest and best music; several splendid ballrooms; often two orchestras or an additional band; a chance for anonymity and adventure behind a mask; some possibility of a fight; abundant good food, liquors, and gambling; a variety of types of balls and of additional entertainment; those ladies and that laughing gas—it is no wonder that the harbinger of a new season in New Orleans was "Our ladies long for a dance. . . . who don't?" [116]

Who don't indeed.

"One neglects the white privets to gather black grapes."

Chapter Two

THE QUADROON BALLS

No facet of early New Orleans has intrigued writers more than the famed quadroon balls. Consequently, a few facts have been embroidered with much myth to construct a legend far removed from reality. We are usually given a highly romantic picture of beautiful and proper young quadroon girls who, except for the accident of color, might have made any man proud to win one of them for his wife. Accompanied by their mothers, they were supposed to have attended the quadroon balls for the sole purpose of meeting a white man who, although he couldn't marry a quadroon, would arrange to keep the one of his choice in a state that resembled marriage, without the ceremony. Once the choice was made, the man was expected to make arrangements with the mother to court her daughter. Or so the tale goes.[1]

Concerning the origins of these balls Herbert Asbury, one of the best-known writers on New Orleans social life, has this to say: "The origin of the Quadroon Balls, and the name of the genius who first organized them, are unknown and probably always will be." (And of other Negro dancing, except for that in Congo Square, we read very little.)[2]

Actually the quadroon balls were nothing like the popular notions about them. Negro dancing in New Orleans was at once more complex and more widespread than the legend implies. In fact, much that has been said in the first chapter about dancing generally applies with equal force to Negro dancing. It is often impossible to know when recorded observations are referring to white or to colored balls unless the writer specifically stated the fact. Since both kinds of dances were held in many of the same ballrooms, the mere name of the place an observer attended does not by itself indicate whether the patrons were white or Negro.

There are enough specific facts, however, to clear up any mystery about how the quadroon balls started; to separate these balls from their romantic aura; and to describe other, much less-written-about forms of Negro social dancing.

When the Spanish attorney-general, Pedro Barran, asked the city council in February, 1800, to reduce the number of public dance halls in order to lessen disorder, he especially singled out "the dances, given . . . with a permit from the government at the house known of as Coquet." He was referring to Bernardo Coquet, an important figure in the early history of New Orleans music, who owned a dance hall on St. Philip Street, between Royal and Bourbon streets. Barran pointed out that only free individuals, white and colored, were supposed to be admitted to Coquet's ballroom, but, he claimed, "It is the place where the majority of the slaves of this city gather." [3]

Here is a startling statement that can be understood only if one realizes that slavery in the city was quite different from the better-known pattern of plantation slavery. Many of the city slaves were skilled artisans of one kind or other who plied their trades and lived as though they were free, reporting periodically to their owners for the purpose only of making a stipulated money payment from their earnings. Harness makers, blacksmiths, farriers, hostlers, barbers, draymen, press hands, engineers, cobblers, printers, riverboat hands, midwives, bricklayers, carpenters, painters, and even druggists could be hired from the ranks of New Orleans' slaves. Others, less skilled, were hired out as laborers. Those remaining with their masters were usually trusted house servants who were given considerable latitude in their off hours. In short, New Orleans was full of slaves who, for a part or most of their time, were not too distinguishable from their legally free brethren.[4]

It was true, Barran argued, that these slaves were not supposed to be admitted to Coquet's ballroom without a written permit from their masters, but Coquet was, after all, in business, and the attorney-general politely wondered "if Coquet knows the signatures and handwriting of all the owners of slaves?"[5]

What really irked was that "These dances, by a ridiculous imitation have placed themselves to the same level of those given at Farge's house (the Conde Street Ballroom)." The luxury and ways of the white people were "impudently imitated" and those who frequented Coquet's dances were "seized by equal madness." How, Barran wanted to know, could slaves afford this? In his opinion, only by stealing from their masters.[6]

The council listened to Barran and resolved to prohibit these dances. Hereafter, colored dances would be permitted only in private homes with no whites whatsoever to be admitted—not even as spectators. No sooner was the order promulgated, however, than Coquet and his partner, Jose Boniquet, appeared before Acting Governor Vidal and confronted him with an ultimatum.[7]

During the preceding decade New Orleans' first theater had begun a struggling existence. It was highly unprofitable, losing money each season, until the shareholders could find no one to manage it. Reluctant to lose the operas, vaudevilles, and dramas staged in the little theater, several leading gentlemen of the town had gone to Governor Gayoso de Lemos for help. That was in April, 1799.

Fortunately they were able to bring the governor a proposal by Coquet and Boniquet to underwrite the theater for one year in return for *exclusive* rights to hold public dances for colored people. Aware that the losses in past years had threatened the closing of the theater, the governor had accepted this proposition because, he said, the theater would lead youth away from the vice of idleness, and anyway because he didn't want to deprive the people of their amusement.

Thus it was that Coquet and Boniquet had obtained their permit to run public dances for the colored of New Orleans with these conditions: they could hold a dance every Sunday night throughout the year, and increase this to two dances a week during the carnival season; no slaves were to be admitted unless carrying a permit from their masters; and, most important, no other colored dances were to be allowed.

Now, with the season only partly gone, the city council had prohibited these dances. So Coquet and Boniquet brought their case to Vidal who had just taken office. Already, they claimed, the theater had cost them over four thousand dollars. Since they had agreed to run the theater only in exchange for their exclusive right to hold colored dances, they informed the governor flatly that the day these dances stopped the theater would close. Faced with this appalling prospect, Vidal rescinded the prohibition. The dances could continue to the end of carnival, but Coquet must stop admitting slaves.[8]

Coquet's victory was more complete than these strictures implied. For one thing, there were other pressures for the continuance of his dances. During the following fall, in October of 1800, several officers of the Battalion of Quadroons and the Battalion of Octoroons, both of the Louisiana militia, urged on behalf of themselves and their troops that Saturday dances be held at Coquet's throughout the coming carnival weeks. The battalions had just returned from a mission to Fort Apache, during which they had undergone great sufferings and hardships. To recuperate and forget, the men needed to dance, and who would deny brave veterans small favors?[9]

For another thing, once a grievance was aired and a decision rendered, affairs had a way of resuming their usual course. Certainly a year and a half after Governor Vidal allowed the dances to continue, albeit with reservations, a new attorney-general, Pablo Lanusse, renewed the demand that Coquet's dances be prohibited, offering the same reasons as had his predecessor. The dances had continued after carnival; the luxury displayed equalled that of the white dances; and free people and slaves of both sexes attended. In fact, Lanusse added, "the numbers of slaves of both sexes attending . . . is equal to or larger than that of the free people." Soldiers out of uniform, sailors, and other such were to be found there, Lanusse protested, while decent citizens were excluded. Here, perhaps, was the real rub.[10]

One such decent citizen gave vent to his exasperation a couple of years later:

> At the corners of all the cross streets of the city . . . are to be seen nothing but taverns, which are open at all hours. There the canaille, white and black, free and slave, mingled indiscriminately. . . . [There] the father on one side, and the son on the other, go openly and without any embarrassment, as well as without shame . . . to revel and dance indiscriminately and for whole nights with a lot of men and women of saffron color, or quite black, either free or slave. Will anyone dare to deny this fact? I will only designate . . . the famous house of Coquet, located near the center of the city, where all the scum is to be seen publicly, and that for several years—to that degree that the tricolor balls . . . are not at all secret; I have several times seen the printed announcements posted at the street corners, with the express permission of . . . the civil governor.[11]

Thus it seems clear that the one place at which public dances for the colored of New Orleans were legally given was the ballroom of Bernardo Coquet on St. Philip Street, and that this house received its first official permission to hold such dances in April, 1799. More than likely, these affairs had been taking place at Coquet's before being made legal. At any rate, when the free colored militia officers asked to be allowed to hold dances there in the fall of 1800, they spoke of "the numerous dances given" previously at Coquet's house. And although Coquet was granted exclusive rights for colored dances, various smaller and less respectable taverns were doubtless not opposed to allowing a little bootleg dancing of this sort. But none could properly be called quadroon balls since neither color nor condition of servitude barred anyone from these dances. The name "tricolor balls" was as good as any.[12]

In 1805, Coquet rented his ballroom on St. Philip Street to M. Auguste Tessier, an actor and dancer in the local opera company, and moved his own mixed dances to another place he owned, the Tivoli, out on Bayou St. John. Tessier had something new in mind: he had hit on a better scheme for making money in the ballroom. In

November, 1805, he announced a plan to give two balls a week for the free women of color at which all colored men would be excluded. The events would be scheduled every Wednesday and Saturday, beginning on Saturday, November 23. Here then, in the Salle Chinoise, as Tessier shrewdly renamed the hall, were held the first true quadroon balls of which there is specific record. That is to say, balls for free colored women and white men only. Thus until a better claim is advanced Auguste Tessier must be awarded the palm for being "the genius who first organized them." For added convenience, this genius, Tessier, provided carriages at the door, and for utmost convenience, he rented rooms right on the premises.[13]

Once begun, this arrangement proved steadily popular. Within a few months, that aptly named promoter, Coquet, introduced the same restrictions on color and sex in his Tivoli Ballroom out on the bayou. Meanwhile, he waited to resume possession of his room in town where the Salle Chinoise flourished until the end of summer in 1807. That fall Coquet moved back.[14]

Unable to forget his earlier connection with the theater and the respectability it brought him, Coquet converted his ballroom into the St. Philip Street Theater. For the first seven months of 1808, theatrical offerings were the only advertised functions in Coquet's room, but it is likely that quadroon dances continued there on alternate nights. The floor remained flat and the seats were merely removable benches. At any rate, the theatrical venture was an unhappy one and as the season of 1808–1809 began, Coquet again gave his whole attention to quadroon balls. He redecorated the room rather appropriately to represent a "Temple of Love" and renamed it the Winter Tivoli. Quadroon balls were scheduled for every Wednesday and Saturday, beginning on December 10. Within two weeks Coquet was able to thank the public for his huge success.[15]

A business success in a free economy invites competition. Before a month was out, a newcomer was in the field: On December 29, 1808, the Union Ballroom on Ursulines Street offered the first of its quadroon balls. There were as yet enough nights in the week to avoid direct clashes, however; the Union's quadroon balls occupied Tuesdays and Fridays, leaving Wednesdays and Saturdays to Coquet.

Hence a man so inclined could still spend three days a week with his family.[16]

From then on, such gatherings were a permanent part of antebellum social life in New Orleans. Those on St. Philip Street continued under various names. What had been the Salle Chinoise and then the Winter Tivoli shortly became the St. Philip Street Ballroom, and years later, the Washington Ballroom. That original site and the Union Ballroom on Ursulines Street were soon joined by others: the old Conde Street Ballroom; a new ballroom on Bourbon and Orleans streets (which was not, it should be emphasized, the Orleans Ballroom, as so many have mistakenly assumed); Laignel's Pleasure Garden; the Chartres Street Ballroom (which was in the Orleans Hotel, and may also have been mistaken for the Orleans Ballroom); the infamous Globe Ballroom; and the Louisiana Ballroom. All these places gave much time to this special type of gathering in which a white man could forget the cares of home. At its height, the Washington Ballroom divided its time evenly: Mondays, Wednesdays, and Saturdays were for whites only; Tuesdays, Thursdays, and Sundays were set apart for quadroon dances. In contrast, the Chartres Street Ballroom reserved only Sundays "for white ladies." [17]

Given a choice, white men seemed to prefer quadroon dances to purely white ones which, it was said, were at all times surpassed by the former, both in the elegance of decorations and splendor of dress. But it was more than mere decoration or dress that made these dances so popular. A visitor who went to one in 1826 prompted only, he said, by a desire "to acquire a knowledge of the habits customs, opinions and prejudices" of the native population, was thoroughly delighted to find that the quadroon women "addressed me, and coquetted with me . . . in the most subtle and amusing manner." It was, he assured his readers, pure curiosity that carried him a second and a third time to these dances, even though he had to keep the matter secret from his hostesses and their friends. "If it be known that a stranger, who has pretensions to mix with good society, frequents such balls as these, he may rely upon a cold reception from the white ladies." [18]

The ladies had good reason for their coldness since the quadroon balls often drained the men away from the white balls after they had put in a perfunctory appearance, and many a lady was left sitting for want of a partner. As one male put it, "the dry stiffness of the fine ladies render(s) . . . [their balls] . . . very boring for those who do not enjoy formality. The others are marked by gaiety." Another suggested that if only the white ladies displayed more freedom at their dances, then no longer would "the company of the fair belles [be] deserted for that of the copper-colored nymphs." [19]

It wasn't, however, solely the lure of flirtation, the heightened gaiety, and the easy informality that drew men to the quadroon balls. Judging from the descriptions of wantonness and disorder that attended them, there were enough white balls replete with these qualities. It was quite simply that the quadroon affairs outdid the white ones when it came to lewdness and excitement. Alexis de Tocqueville found the laxity of morals at these balls incredible. One of New Orleans' own newspapers honestly acknowledged them to be "inter-racial orgies." A man might even find himself dancing with a girl wearing only her nightgown if he didn't watch out.[20]

In short, most of the quadroon balls, like the lower-class white balls, were fields of operations for prostitutes. Acting Mayor John Culbertson denounced them in 1835 as "sinks of the most dissolute class of women." The Globe Ballroom was variously labeled "that most villainous of all establishments"; "the saturnalia of the depraved portion of our population"; and a "moral fester on the community." The Louisiana Ballroom was called a "den of iniquity." [21]

Little wonder then that they could often deplete the more decorous balls or even the theater—especially when eager cabmen vied with one another to solicit passengers by proposing to convey them to the quadroon balls. "Every clerk and scrivener," said the observant actor, Louis Tasistro, "who can muster up a few dollars, hurries to these unhallowed sanctuaries, and launches unreservedly into every species of sensual indulgence; every flat-boatman or cattle dealer . . . finds his way to these abodes of enchantment. . . . Nor is it unusual to see members of the legislature mingle freely with these motley groups." [22]

So great an attraction could perhaps be best celebrated in poetry, and a French resident of the city was moved to try his hand:

> There vice, showing a hideous bold face
> Without dignity, unmasked, disgusts the eyes.
> There flutter the bold women
> Enticing in their walk, their favors free.
> Among these, the ebony and the dark marigolds,
> Replacing with their hue the roses and the lilies,
> More than one Helen, a little cruel,
> Sees many a Greek and many a Trojan
> Assail one another with murderous fist
> And notch each other's chins for her.[23]

But the lure of quadroon balls was not limited to excitement and the free favors of bold women. Many of the girls were beautiful and were accomplished dancers. Even a fastidious, better-class Englishman could be impressed. "I made a point of going to some of the quadroon balls," wrote Edward Sullivan, who said that he "had heard a great deal of the splendid figures and graceful dancing of the New Orleans Quadroons." After seeing these girls he reported that he "certainly was not disappointed. Their movements are the most easy and graceful that I have ever seen." He went so far as to say that he had never witnessed "more perfect dancing on any stage," and he wondered why the opera houses in Europe didn't import some of these girls for their ballets.[24]

Of course, as in the lower-class white balls, there was always danger in attending. Sullivan was not so bemused with the girls as to miss the disturbing sight of bowie knives, revolvers, and other weapons being removed at the door. In spite of this precaution, he wrote that "murders and duels are of weekly occurrence at these balls and during my stay at New Orleans there were three." Another guest likewise found his enjoyment considerably dampened by the "willing disposition for disturbance." The whole place reminded him of nothing so much as a "den of ruffians," and he prudently left after a half hour, to learn the next day that no fewer than twenty persons had been "more or less dangerously wounded" at that single dance. These diversions were not for the meek, although police were usually employed and the managers promised to maintain strict order. In the majority of quadroon balls mayhem of one kind or another was a constant risk.[25]

To be sure, not all the balls were equally disreputable. Just as the white dances ranged from brawls to the relatively select subscription balls, so too did the quadroon affairs. From the time of the first real quadroon balls in 1805, there were efforts to keep some of these dances as the private preserves of "gentlemen of distinction." Both higher prices at the door and the device of the subscription dance were employed to keep out undesirables. An admission of two dollars (the usual quadroon ball cost fifty cents) would, it was hoped, "take away all semblance of vulgarity" and admit only persons of the better class. Thus at times, observers could speak of "chaste and civil" dancing, or "the greatest decorum" at certain of the public quadroon balls, while a visitor to a subscription quadroon dance in 1842 found it to be "as orderly, decent, and well-conducted as in the salons of Paris or New York." [26]

No matter though how much more civil some of these dances were, chaste they were not. For the end sought in all the quadroon balls from the worst to the best was always the same—love without marriage. Consequently they were irresistible attractions. Contrasting a poor attendance at the luxurious Orleans Ballroom on a Saturday night in 1826 with the crowds at three or four of these balls on the same night, a citizen tersely summed up the whole matter: The men of New Orleans, he concluded, were neglecting "the white privets to gather black grapes." [27]

Confronted with a situation like that, there was only one thing the "white privets," or at least a number of them could do—plant themselves in among the grapes. During the 1830's more and more white women attended the quadroon balls, at first masked, but soon openly; so openly indeed that Acting Mayor Culbertson felt himself obliged to take official notice. In November, 1835, he asked the city council to do something about this development, saying that he knew for a fact "that at the last ball of that description there were in the rooms more white ladies than colored ones." [28]

Some of the aldermen, however, saw another reason for the presence of white women at the quadroon balls. How better than by attending them could they discover the whereabouts of their husbands? And so the council did nothing, even though the New Orleans *Bee* reported that at one dance in the Washington Ballroom two thirds of the women present were white, many of them respectable and married.[29]

Two years later the First Municipality did make it a penal offense to admit white and colored women together. But there was always recourse to the mask. As the *Picayune* frankly admitted: "They go so habited that there is no discovering whether they are black or white." [30]

Quadroon balls, of course, were only a part of Negro dancing in New Orleans. After all, the major portion of the Negro population, free or slave, was excluded from these balls. And the love of dancing that permeated all classes of whites in the city was bound to spread equally among the colored.

Balls, wherein both sexes and races mingled indiscriminately, such as those first "tricolor" balls at Coquet's house before the colored men were excluded, continued to be held. In 1855, when feeling against racial mixing was much stronger than before, the police closed the Globe Ballroom where mixed dances had until then taken place.[31]

In part, mixed dancing arose from the "crashing" of dances intended for the free colored. Sometimes in the early days, the crashers came deliberately to cause trouble—starting fights, or chewing and spitting vanilla, thereby causing an "intolerable odor." Or they might put their chewed tobacco plugs on the seats where the women sat. But whether they came for trouble or merely to dance, crashers were not welcome at the dances intended for the proud free colored people of New Orleans. In 1828 they, and others who objected to this mixing, succeeded in getting an ordinance passed forbidding any white person to enter balls catering to men and women of color under fine of from twenty-five to one hundred dollars. By this time therefore, a ballroom proprietor in the course of ordinary business might have to reserve one night a week for whites only; one for free colored women and white men; and one for free colored only.[32]

Especially annoying to the free colored was the presence of slaves at their balls. But from the time of that first complaint by the attorney-general in 1800 to the capture of New Orleans by the Union forces in 1862, the slaves managed to attend dances in spite of consistent efforts to prohibit them. As that original complaint by the attorney-general in 1800 charged, the promoter of a dance run for profit was not likely to scrutinize too carefully any colored man who had the price of admission.[33]

The law itself was soon very clear on this subject. A typical and early (1817) ordinance prescribed a fine of from ten to fifty dollars for anyone giving a ball for free colored who allowed a slave to enter on any pretext whatsoever. And for his part in the crime, the slave would get fifteen lashes. In time even the owner of a slave caught attending a ball was subject to a fine.[34]

Besides having a desire to prevent so far as possible any opportunities for slaves and free Negroes to get together where they might conceivably plan a little insurrection, many slave owners objected to such gatherings on the grounds that their pecuniary interests might be damaged. Thus in 1806 a number of owners complained to Governor Claiborne about the laxity of the police in allowing slaves to frequent taverns run by free colored men. The slaves, their owners charged, "passed most of their nights in dancing and drinking" to the point where they got too tired to give full service to their masters. And this "evil" was daily increasing.[35]

Not only might slave dancing cause a loss of return on investment, but, even worse, there was a risk of damage to the capital itself. Perhaps this is best illustrated by an indignant editorial in 1834. Two free Negroes had obtained a permit to give a dance for free colored near the levee. During the dance a fight started and a sailor was stabbed. When word of this spread through the neighboring taverns, sailors armed with axes, knives, and various makeshift weapons rushed to the ballroom, intent upon avenging their fellow seafarer.

Luckily, a gentleman who, seeking a number of his slaves, had just arrived at the scene, managed to dissuade the sailors from attacking by his promise to see that justice would be done. While the sailors surrounded the place to prevent any Negroes from leaving, the slave owner summoned policemen. They managed to arrest seventy-five male dancers, but the rest escaped. Of those arrested, two thirds turned out to be slaves. "Thus," the editor of the *Louisiana Courier* sternly warned, "but for the interference of a calm and resolute man fifty slaves might have been killed—and this for the cupidity of two free negroes." The paper demanded that these two be arrested and forbidden to give any more balls for free colored "where they may again expose our slaves to danger." Cupidity was, after all, an offense to any Christian gentleman.[36]

But in a city as generally tolerant and as ardently dance-minded as New Orleans, efforts to deter slave dancing were about as effective as King Canute's attempt to stem the tide. Taverns where the slave's money was welcome continued to multiply in spite of ordinances forbidding slaves to be in the streets after sundown. By the end of the 1830's the papers claimed that thousands of slaves nightly attended these taverns which could be found on every street. It was not unusual to arrest twenty to thirty slaves in cabarets during a single raid.[37]

So, too, the dances designed for free colored continued to admit slaves until the fact was common knowledge. A letter of complaint to the newspapers in 1839 openly referred to them as slaves' ball-rooms without arousing comment. In 1841 after a raid on one, the "Catfish Hotel," in which "banjo's were knocked in—and ivories were knocked out," the *Picayune* frankly acknowledged that "Catfish Hotel was heretofore considered impregnable." [38]

The papers themselves used the conversations among slaves about their balls for humorous sketches as when Sam Johnsing and Pete Gombo discuss a forthcoming ball at Dinah Jone's [*sic*]. Sam chided Pete: "Guess your massa not at home, an you ain't got no pass, and can't get one, no how you fixes it . . . Dat's a stumper I know." But Pete replied with warmth: "I doesn't car 'bout that; I goes to that ball, dat's cartain; pass or no pass—I'll take de sponsibility." [39]

That's the way it went—pass or no pass, the slaves of New Orleans had their balls. It is true that they might be apprehended and whipped and their owners fined, but as often as not their masters, too, were willing to "take de sponsibility." On the eve of the Civil War a slave owner wrote in her diary: "There is a ball to-night in aristocratic colored society. This is Chloe's first introduction to New Orleans circles, and Henry Judson, Phoebe's husband, gave five dollars for a ticket for her. Chloe is a recent purchase from Georgia. We superintend their very stylish toilets. . . ." Henry was free, but Phoebe and Chloe were slaves. The occasion celebrated by this particular ball was the secession of Louisiana from a union that was proving harmful to slavery.[40]

"The playhouse in St. Peter Street, condemned as unfit repeatedly."

Chapter Three

THE OPERA: BIRTH

Opera was New Orleans' cultural glory throughout the nineteenth century. This city had its own self-supporting, resident company which, for much of the century, offered the best opera to be found in America. Its superiority was especially marked before the Civil War when the presentation of opera in other American cities was sporadic and transient. At its prewar height, opera in New Orleans represented a cultural flowering in the old South that differed only in kind, not in degree, from the vaunted flowering of New England. Its presence in New Orleans was decisive in encouraging and setting the tone of numerous other musical activities. Without it the city would not have been able to boast as it did in 1837 that "the little musical enthusiasm prevailing in the United States is nearly entirely concentrated in New Orleans." [1]

The story, therefore, of how America's first permanent opera company—and for a long time its only one—came into being and survived is worth reconstructing in detail, in so far as possible. For in large part the story of antebellum opera in New Orleans is the story of early opera in America.

Tradition has it that New Orleans' theater was started in the fall of 1791 by some actors and musicians from Cap Francais in Saint-Domingue, refugees from the Negro uprisings in that West Indian island. Directed and managed by Louis Tabary, they are said to have given performances in homes and tents, or even in the open, until a structure on St. Peter Street was either built or converted to house them.[2]

This account of the beginning of New Orleans' opera appears to be one of those legends that gain credence through repetition rather than evidence. The story reached full absurdity only recently when Tabary and his fellows were solemnly cited in a study of minstrelsy as being "a Negro troupe of comedians and entertainers" performing in New Orleans in 1791. So grows a tale.[3]

To be sure Louis Tabary, as we shall see, did more than any other man prior to John Davis to promote and maintain the early theater. It is also true that Tabary was a refugee (a white one) from Saint-Domingue. But since he was fifty-eight years old when he died in 1831, Tabary would have been barely eighteen in 1791, hardly old enough to be an experienced actor, managing and directing a troupe. The truth is that Louis Tabary, born in Provence, had emigrated to Saint-Domingue early in 1803 and remained there until the summer of 1804. Sometime between then and the following summer he moved to New Orleans where he followed the career of actor and director in the theater for a quarter of a century, during which time he saw the infant opera that he had nurtured grow to maturity.[4]

In similar fashion, the origin of the early performers has been oversimplified. Some had been in Saint-Domingue, but even they did not all come directly from there to New Orleans. A few sojourned first in New York or Charleston. Others of the group came directly from France. Nor did they come in a troupe in 1791. Rather they filtered in over a period of years.[5]

As for the theater itself, notarial records show that one Louis Alexandre Henry purchased a site on St. Peter Street on June 4, 1791, and proceeded to build a theater. On October 1, 1792, the government issued a set of regulations for the theater which was due to open three days later. Designed to insure order, the regulations set the time for the opening of the ticket office, and the curtain time. They forbade interruptions and hissing, as well as smoking, the latter prohibition being especially motivated by a fear of fire. Since all ages, sexes, and classes were expected to be present, the use of improper language would be punished—even by prison if necessary.[6]

On October 4, 1792, the theater on St. Peter Street opened its doors for the first time. According to Pontalba who attended the opening performance, only two of the actors were even tolerable, while the actresses were "fit only to be run off with a broom to their backs." But bad theater is better than no theater, and in any case the twelve loges had been rented in advance for two hundred and fifty to three hundred dollars each. So the theater continued giving performances. After one season, however, Henry was replaced as manager, and after one more season, as owner. On March 15, 1794, the theater was incorporated with forty (or forty-two) shares at two hundred dollars each. Under the new regime the theater managed to keep operating and to acquire some better performers. But what kind of music, if any, accompanied this early activity is almost entirely a matter of speculation.[7]

The first definite reference to opera in New Orleans appears in the year 1796. On February 24, the wife and young son of Pontalba left New Orleans for France where she soon received some letters from her husband who had stayed behind. On March 4, 1796, he mentioned the theater and on March 19 he referred to a meeting of the shareholders of the theater and to his rental of a box accommodating four persons. He saw a play on Sunday, May 8; and two weeks later, on Sunday, May 22, 1796, he attended a performance of the opera, *Sylvain* by Andre Gretry, who has been rated "one of the best musicians of that epoch." Here then is the very first opera in New Orleans of which there is record.[8]

This is not to say that the May 22 playing of *Sylvain* was the first performance of opera in the city. In fact Pontalba's letters make it clear that *Sylvain* had been done previously. Pontalba's son, Celestin, who was four and a half years old, had heard *Sylvain* enough times before he left for France in February to be familiar with some of the verses. Nor does it mean that *Sylvain* was the only opera played. While Pontalba did not specifically name any other, he did mention a subsequent performance on July 17, which apparently was the opera *Blaise et Babet* by N. Dezedes. Undoubtedly other operas were given at the time Pontalba wrote—and before.[9]

By now the theater was in considerable financial trouble. Pontalba complained to his wife that "the management is going very badly, it is being robbed, the actors make the rules, and not one of those employed does his duty. If this continues we will be forced to give up the theatre." He had been visited on July 21 by a number of the shareholders who appealed to him to straighten out the finances and "begged me to take direction. I could not refuse, and I am going to be the *bete noire* of the actors for I found myself forced at once to lay down some rules against which they immediately protested." [10]

But Pontalba's efforts and new rules apparently failed to relieve the situation, for we recall from our discussion of quadroon balls that, when Messieurs Coquet and Boniquet offered in 1799 to underwrite the theater in return for exclusive rights to operate balls for the colored population, they reminded the governor that the theater had been losing money for the past few years. We saw also that these gentlemen were granted the permission sought, and how in this way the popularity of these dances helped finance the theater for the rest of that season.[11]

In the same year (1799) that Bernardo Coquet took over the management of the theater we find the next specific mention of an opera performance. On September 3, 1799, a playbill advertised the premiere performance of *Renaud d'Ast* by Nicolas Dalayrac, one of the most popular composers of his time. From then until November 10, 1805, there is no extant record of performances. Several facts, however, indicate that the theater was closed during much of that interval. Pierre Berquin-Duvallon, who lived in New Orleans from the latter part of 1799 to May of 1802, reported seeing comic pieces shortly after his arrival. But he added that the theater closed soon thereafter because of a misunderstanding between the civil and military authorities (probably over seating), and had remained closed for about two years. Then some efforts were made to reopen it, and Duvallon mentions one semiamateur performance. But even this

slight attempt to restore the theater caused the dispute over seating
to flare anew, and it seems to have been closed again early in 1802.
It was still not open when Dr. Sibley visited New Orleans in September of that year except for an occasional Sunday show by rope
dancers or the like. Early in that same month, the newspaper *Le
Moniteur de la Louisiane* carried a proposal for a new theater in
which the shareholders of the "former theatre" were invited to exchange their shares for ones in the new venture.[12]

A new theater was too much to hope for yet at a time when the
existing house could not make a go of it. For about one week in
November, 1803, "the physician Meyere" put on a "scientific show"
in which he apparently made a woman disappear in a magic box.
Outside of this, there seems to have been no theatrical activity, and
even Meyere chose to perform his act in a private house, perhaps
because the theater was so badly run down. As Dr. Sibley said,
". . . the whole House is Roughly Built and now Looks Shabby,
the Paper that once covered the Rough work is peel'd off in spots
and very much defac'd." The theater was ordered closed by the city
council on December 12, 1803, when that body received a report
that the building was about to collapse. For a while thereafter the
building was mentioned in the papers only as a landmark to locate
other houses. After an inadequate gestation, New Orleans' infant
opera was almost stillborn.[13]

A spark of life remained, however, soon to be nourished into vigorous growth. Shortly after the condemnation of the theater building, a newly arrived actor named Jean Baptiste Fournier undertook
to repair the existing structure. Toward the end of September, 1804,
Fournier wrote to the council requesting a new inspection and on
November 28 the council approved the re-opening of the theater. At
the same time the council ordered a number of police regulations
posted that indicate some of the difficulties which had beset the theater in the past.[14]

Article I forbade anyone to appear without a ticket. It especially
threatened punishment for those who gained admission "by cun-
ning or violence." Article II prohibited making "fanciful demands"
on the orchestra to play "this or that tune." The management

pledged itself to play the various national airs—but any person who disturbed the orchestra in this regard ran the risk of being hailed before a magistrate.

One way of "disturbing" the orchestra was revealed by Article V which began by stating, "No one will be allowed to throw oranges or anything else . . ." Article IV forbade constant clapping or hissing. It was desired, the council said, that the pieces played would contribute to harmony, good will, and good manners, for alone on these rests the permanence and success of the institution."

Undoubtedly the theater, like the balls, had been the scene of national frictions revolving about the music to be played. Evidently the various national groups demanded their own patriotic airs, applauded these and hissed others, and threatened the orchestra if it did not satisfy the conflicting demands. Now, with the theater about to be re-opened, the council was taking steps to ward off any recurrence of such actions. It was a wise precaution in a city where the jolt of merging cultures and new allegiances was sharp.

Whether owing to the regulations or to a desire not to lose the theater again, the re-opening was all that the council had hoped it would be. On December 20, 1804, the first anniversary of the transfer of Louisiana was commemorated with a show during which the audience behaved in a manner that the *Louisiana Gazette* approved and wished to see continued. At the close of that month, Governor Claiborne wrote to James Madison that "the two descriptions" of citizens had been meeting frequently at the theater for several weeks "in perfect harmony." The only sour note was sounded by the governor himself when on two occasions shortly thereafter he failed to take off his hat in the theater—a boorish oversight which insulted his audience and caused the *Louisiana Gazette* to ask him whether he thought he was among "Indians or Yahoos"? In case he had any lingering doubts, the paper acidly informed him that he was now among "a polite and polished people." [15]

It is clear then that the theater got started again late in 1804, but was opera in the repertoire? A complaint of another sort throws some light on this. Early in June of the following year the Superior of the Ursuline nuns wrote to the governor to protest a "late performance at the theatre" which ridiculed their order. The objectionable show was scheduled to be repeated the following Tuesday which would have been June 11, 1805. Claiborne dutifully passed the complaint on to Mayor James Pitot, but it is doubtful that the latter took any action.[16]

The piece which hurt the feelings of the good sisters must have been the opera, *Les Visitandines* by François Devienne, for one year later the abbess renewed her protest, and Claiborne again wrote to the major saying that this was the same piece that had given offense the year before and specifying Sunday, June 22, 1806, as the date of this most recent affront to the nuns. Since we know that *Les Visitandines* played on this date, it must also have been the object of complaint during the previous June.[17]

It was shortly after the nuns sent their initial protest to Claiborne that the name of Louis Tabary first appeared. In July, 1805, he sent a letter proposing a new theater to the city council. He was then thirty-two years old, a man of great energy and persistence if not always of good business sense, who would give the rest of his life to the New Orleans theater, undismayed by obstacles and failures. With the advent of Tabary, the story of opera in New Orleans may be said to have begun in earnest. The infant would yet undergo many crises, but it would survive.[18]

That the rejuvenated theater had better prospects than before is indicated by signs of competition and inner strife that cropped up almost at once. We recall that Jean Fournier had made the repairs and had been named the director of the theater in 1804. Tabary's above mentioned proposal to the city council that he build a new theater was signed by him as the director. Perhaps at that time he meant director of the proposed theater, but in March of 1806, Tabary let it be known that he was "taking possession" of the direction of the theater as of March first, and that henceforth all communications concerning the theater were to be addressed to him. There can be no doubt here: Tabary had replaced Fournier as director of the St. Peter Street Theater.[19]

Already, under Fournier's direction, the little house had done much. From June, 1805, to the end of February, 1806, at least twenty-three opera performances were staged, twenty-one of them in the four months of November through February. No doubt there were more. Those we know about included sixteen different operas by nine composers, among them Pierre Monsigny, Dalayrac, Gretry, François Boieldieu, and Étienne Mehul, all stalwarts of the opera in Paris—at that time the opera center of the world. On December 10, 1805, the St. Peter Street Theater presented Giovanni Paisiello's *Il Barbiere di Siviglia* (a "rowdy comic version of the famed tonsorial tale" that still played in the summer of 1960 to standing room only in Stockholm's famed Drottningholm Court Theater). It was a first for New Orleans, possibly for America, and it played again on January 5. *Le Calife de Bagdad* by Boieldieu (December 25, 1805), *La Fausse Magie* by Gretry (January 9, 1806), *Euphrosine* by Mehul (February 15, 1806), were also listed as premieres. Most likely the other operas had played before. Among the latter was Gretry's *Richard, Coeur de Lion* which was to become John Quincy Adams' favorite opera and which is sung today in Paris. Gretry was the most popular composer in New Orleans at this time, judging by the number of performances, and in popularity Gretry was closely followed by Dalayrac.[20]

Here surely is an amazing record for a town which as yet boasted only twelve thousand people—over one-third of whom were Negroes. But Tabary had even more ambitious plans for the theater. Within a month after he took over the direction of the St. Peter Street Theater on March 1, 1806, he issued a call for the shareholders to assemble at the theater. They met early in April to grant Tabary direction of the company for the next three years. Thus armed, the following month Tabary used three full pages of the *Moniteur* to publish the proposal for a new theater that he had sent earlier to the city council with the aim of soliciting popular support for the project. He had already purchased a 70 by 153-foot lot on Orleans Street, between Bourbon and Royal streets, and had hired the architect, M. Hyacinthe Laclotte. Laclotte was renowned, so Tabary said, for the theater he had built in Bordeaux. Tabary promised to yield nothing to the theaters of Europe and to import actors from France.[21]

To help achieve his vision Tabary sought thirty shareholders. No share was to be under a thousand dollars—five hundred down and the balance in six months. A share would draw 8 per cent interest paid quarterly, and grant to the holder a free pass to all of the regular performances, which was to say that the pass was not valid for benefits and special occasions. Since he intended to be the sole owner eventually, Tabary optimistically reserved the right to buy all shares within six years after the theater opened, but the shareholders would retain their free passes for four years further. Meanwhile Tabary alone was to administer and direct the playhouse.[22]

Tabary claimed to have the endorsement of the governor, the mayor, the city aldermen, and the territorial legislators; and before long he made public a letter of approval by Governor Claiborne. Early in June he announced that he was hiring workers and was taking bids on materials. On October 6, 1806, with the governor, the mayor, the aldermen, and the shareholders looking on, Tabary himself laid the first brick. Thus began the famed Orleans Street Theater.[23]

Thus began also Tabary's troubles. Five months after he had confidently wielded the trowel, he was forced to suspend building operations. The shareholders were slow in paying, and Tabary owed M. Boutmy $1,710 for bricks. That gentleman, being more concerned for his business than for the future theatrical glory of New Orleans, had obtained a judgment and was threatening to seize the works. As if this were not enough, voices arose in question of Tabary's trustworthiness. He in turn swore that he had always given a full accounting of the money thus far raised; had even advanced all the money he could from his own pocket to keep construction going; and he now called for a meeting of the shareholders to convince them of his honesty and to ask their help in finding a way to satisfy the brick contractor.[24]

In the midst of this crisis a new complication arose. Bernardo Coquet, who had underwritten the theater eight years earlier with his "tricolor" balls, was bitten by the theatrical bug again. The city was informed that the Salle Chinoise, his house on St. Philip Street where these racially mixed dances took place, would open as a theater early in April, to be known as Les Varietes Amusantes. On April 18, 1807, Tabary's new rival entered the arena with some comedies and vaudeville. There was a gallery for persons of color, as in the older theater, and shows were promised every Wednesday and Saturday "without interruption." Nothing had been spared, the backers said, to make the new theater "agreeable." Above all, they would be "zealous" to procure a good orchestra—a zeal which before long enabled them to boast an orchestra containing all of four musicians.[25]

For Tabary, April was simply a bad month. It brought him not only competition, but financial problems as well. Before the month ended a sheriff's sale of the ground and the partially completed masonry of Tabary's hopeful venture on Orleans Street was posted for May 20. But May brought a ray of sunshine when, four days before Tabary's partially constructed theater was scheduled to be sold to the highest bidder, the rival theater on St. Philip Street was forced to offer its colored shades and wooden benches to anyone wishing to buy.[26]

Apparently a group of dissident actors led by Fournier had simply installed benches in Coquet's ballroom to make a theater. In any case, the notice signaling the end of this first competitive effort was signed by none other than M. Fournier, the man who had repaired the St. Peter Street Theater and had been director there until Tabary displaced him in 1805. With the benches removed the Salle Chinoise returned to its tested money-maker—the balls for free colored women and white men. The news of all this must have sweetened Tabary's bitter dose a trifle.[27]

Encouraged perhaps by the failure of his rivals or simply buoyed by his ever-lively hopes, Tabary pleaded again in June for public support so that he could resume the halted construction on Orleans Street. That he could at this time argue for a theater which would seat 1,448 persons evinces the man's remarkable faith. In the first place, it was not easy to keep the small existing theater filled. Among other things, the management had to resort to the eternal gambling instinct to sell tickets by proffering a lottery of passes good for six months. One hundred tickets were put up—half to win and half to lose. It cost eight dollars to draw a ticket, but then another eight dollars had to be paid if the ticket was a lucky one. In this way the theater collected twenty-four dollars for a six-month pass which cost the winner sixteen dollars. At the same time the management moved against unfair competition by warning that the practice of selling personal passes or subscriptions at the door was forbidden and must cease, "or proper steps would be taken." [28]

In the second place, Tabary's troubles were mounting. His old rival, Fournier, somehow turned the tables after failing on St. Philip Street; he replaced Tabary as director of the St. Peter Street Theater. Then, early in October of 1807, Tabary's creditors obtained a court order against him, and the harassed actor was forced to plead for a limited extension of time to pay his debts. A few days later he played five different roles in a comedy. Possibly he was trying to earn money faster.[29]

But Tabary and his clique could not long remain content under Fournier's direction, especially when there was an alternative. Bernardo Coquet still had his ballroom on St. Philip Street as well as his urge to participate in theater life, if only as angel. Soon Tabary and another actor from the St. Peter Street troupe, Louis Douvillier, were deep in plans to try a theater once again in Coquet's place.[30]

In the meantime, discord among the actors grew sharp enough to cause some patrons to complain that it was hurting the shows. How deep the bad feeling went is well illustrated by Mlle. Laurette Fleury, the elder of two sisters who were extremely popular singers. When that lady heard a mere rumor that she intended leaving the St. Peter for the new theater, she grew so indignant that she published a strong denial in both the *Moniteur* and the *Courier,* the two leading New Orleans newspapers of the day. She vowed that she would "continue to play in the theater of M. Fournier as soon as her health would permit, and if, by some unforeseen event, this director should be forced to close his theater, she would then retire completely from the stage." Better retirement than dishonor.[31]

Midway through January, 1808, the public was officially told that a new theater would soon open. A larger stage was promised, one which would "permit operas of the first composers," and better ballets. Also, the managers said that they expected some new performers. Here, for the first time, the theater was called Theatre de la

Rue St. Philippe. But it was the same building owned by Coquet
that had been the Salle Chinoise, and for a brief interlude, Les
Varietes Amusantes—27 St. Philip Street. On January 30, 1808, the
new theater opened its doors with the opera *Une Folie* by Mehul
which had last played at the St. Peter Street Theater the previous
summer.[32]

The advent of a second theater playing opera did not stop the St.
Peter. The new theater opened on a Saturday; on Sunday, the day
following, the St. Peter played a three-act opera, *Felix,* by Monsigny. The next Wednesday saw Gretry's famous *Richard, Coeur de
Lion* at the St. Philip, followed on Thursday by Nicolo Isouard's *La
Ruse Inutile* at the St. Peter. So at the beginning of 1808, New Orleans, though still a small town of around fifteen thousand, found
itself with not one, but two opera houses, which, according to one
impressed visitor, were generally both crowded.[33]

Such attendance might have been possible for a while at the
height of the carnival season since the two theaters ran on alternate
nights, allowing the same patrons to attend both. The St. Philip was
open on Wednesdays and Saturdays with an occasional Monday,
while the St. Peter took Thursdays and Sundays with an occasional
Tuesday. Four operas were played during the first week of competition and again during the week of February 20–26. Mostly though
there were three operas a week. However, when one adds ballets, it
is possible to find weeks such as the one of March 20–26 when four
operas and a ballet made a total of five such offerings.[34]

For a time it seemed the town could absorb such a cultural dose
and that the new theater would succeed. In March a printed cast
shows that Tabary and Douvillier had been joined at the St. Philip
by the dancers M. Francisqui and M. Tessier as well as by Miss
Eugenie Fleury, the younger of the singing sisters. And in April,
Miss Laurette Fleury, she who swore to retire rather than leave
Fournier at the St. Peter, graciously joined the new company.[35]

Now as long as these rival theaters agreed to split the week so to
speak, they could continue to function at least, even though they
may have been taking the pitcher to the well dangerously often.
Such cooperation could not be expected to last long, however, in
the face of past jealousies and present human nature. Then too,

there was the temptation to offer Sunday showings when attendance would be best. A direct clash was inevitable. It came on the Sunday of April 24, 1808, when for the first time both theaters scheduled performances—Della Maria's very popular *L'Opera Comique* at the St. Peter, and *Captain Cook,* a three-act pantomime-ballet, at the St. Philip.[36]

Angry questions were raised at once: "A subscriber to both theaters, stranger to their quarrel, demands to know where he should go when they both play on the same day? If he goes to the one does he thereby lose his ticket to the other? A shareholder in the two theatres asks the same question." Most revealing was the query of a musician. He had been playing in both theaters, and now he pointed out that if subscribers were willing to "sacrifice" their money, the musician, "who receives it, owes two engagements. Which of the two will he fill?" [37]

There was the bind. The theaters might be able to split the audience to the disgust of shareholders and the financial harm of all, but they could not very well divide the limited number of musicians without courting musical disaster. So the Sunday quarrel was patched or at least shelved, and the theaters resumed their split week arrangement.[38]

But not for long; the battle was joined afresh on Sunday, May 8, when both theaters posted three-act operas: Monsigny's *Le Deserteur* at the St. Philip and Dalayrac's *Azemia* at the St. Peter. The following Sunday both houses opened again although the St. Philip put on a drama—perhaps indicating that the musicians stayed at the St. Peter where two operas were staged. But the next Sunday they both played operas again, and on the last Sunday in May it was the St. Peter that retreated to a drama, leaving the opera for the rival theater.[39]

Throughout June the Sunday strain on musicians was eased by this alternate switching from opera to drama or vaudeville, which required less in the way of an orchestra. The St. Philip had operas on the first and fourth Sundays; the St. Peter on the second. On the third Sunday of the month they both played dramas. Then on the first Sunday in July, both theaters not only scheduled operas, but the same opera at that—*L'Opera Comique.* It was a one-act opera, however, and was preceded by a four-act comedy at the St. Peter, while at the St. Philip *L'Opera Comique* came first, followed by the two-act opera *Une Folie*. One cannot help imagining at least some of the musicians playing their three acts of opera at the one theater while the four acts of comedy played at the other, then dashing four blocks between the theaters to be in time for the closing opera at the St. Peter.[40]

In any case, the situation was intolerable. Both theaters again scheduled operas for the Sunday of July 17, but on the Friday before, Tabary and his partners, Coquet and Douvillier, made a truce offer. Addressing all the shareholders of either theater, they submitted a plan to reunite the theaters. It gives us a good picture of the problems of opera in New Orleans in 1808. The peace-seekers reminded their readers that the theater on St. Philip Street had given only a few presentations before "the public was convinced of the inconvenience of two theaters in this town," and they stated flatly that there were "at this time" neither enough actors for two satisfactory troupes, nor "enough population to sustain them." Therefore, they argued, a reunion was necessary for the "pleasure of the public, the profit of the entrepreneurs, and the fortune of the permanent players."

They then frankly assessed both theaters. The St. Peter was in a state of decay so bad as to cause "sound fear" of actual risk to the spectators unless the shareholders underwrote burdensome repairs. Even if repaired to the point of safety, the house was still too small for the grander operas and shows; and, worst of all, it had no easy exits in case of dreaded fire "which one is unable to prevent no matter how much care is taken."

The St. Philip they considered large and more commodious, with a stage as big "as one could wish for all sorts of dramatic enterprises." Its main deficiency was that the floor lacked "elevation below the loges." (One is reminded that this building was originally a ballroom.) Now it would be easy, they said, to slope the floor; moreover, this could be done in such manner as to provide exits enough to remove any danger from fire in the neighborhood.

Tabary, Coquet, and Douvillier therefore proposed that the two troupes unite and use the old St. Peter for the present. At the St. Philip, besides elevating the floor, they would build "around the sides, and the facade, a wall of bricks, high enough to support a second tier of loges, and a new tile roof. And above the entrance and the stairs, a foyer for the convenience of the audience between acts." When the work was completed, sometime in the fall, the company was to move permanently to the St. Philip.

To finance the merger and renovations, the shareholders of the St. Peter would advance one hundred dollars per share to pay for half the estimated cost of eight thousand dollars. Coquet would pay the other half personally as well as any amount over the estimate, and at the end of six years he would reimburse the shareholders. After the troupe moved to the virtually new theater, the shareholders of the St. Peter would sell that building entirely for their own benefit, reserving only for the St. Philip "the decorations, theatrical utensils, illumination, orchestra, and all others that aid theatrical presentation." But they must promise not to dispose of the St. Peter "in any way advantageous to another theatrical troupe." Finally, the shareholders of both theaters would have passes good for six years from the date of accord and "their customary preference in location of loges on the non-subscription days."

Tabary and his friends urged all concerned to accept as soon as possible, promising to begin work at once so that "the public will enjoy next winter the advantages this reunion is able to achieve." [41]

A sensible proposition it would seem; but the rift between the two groups was too deep to be bridged that simply at this time. During the rest of July and August, 1808, the theatrical advertisements made it clear that the St. Philip, its hopeful proposal having been spurned, was in trouble. Operas were staged exclusively at the St. Peter while only an occasional vaudeville could be seen at the other theater. By August 17 both Fleury sisters had returned to the St. Peter, and in another week so had Tabary. In fact, he was back as boss, once again ousting Fournier as director.[42]

After so recently detailing the physical deficiencies of the St. Peter Street Theater, Tabary now needed to reassure the public. Performances ceased after August 21, and a few days later, Tabary announced that a repaired theater would open on September 1 with new decorations, new repertoire, and new novelties, all designed to "render the Spectacle agreeable for next season." He suggested that people should hurry to subscribe. In the upper loges they could reserve a seat through eight shows for the price of six dollars and in the lower loges for five dollars. Or they could buy eight individual tickets for five dollars, or for only four dollars if they were people of color. The subscribers could use, loan, or sell their tickets any way they chose, except to sell them at the theater door at show time in direct competition with the box office. Tabary's liberality could extend only so far.[43]

Whether many actual repairs were made is doubtful. A patriotic play with military band and dancers occupied the theater on August 28 and an opera was played on August 30. The formal opening of the "new theater" was set back from the first of September to the fourth, but the opera announced for the first took place as scheduled. Thus the theater was really closed for six days only.[44]

At any rate the old St. Peter had won the field, while Coquet approached the finish of his most recent attempt to establish a theater. On August 27 his dwindling group played what they called the first and last performance of a "heroic-tragic-comedy in prose verse and songs" entitled *La Mort de St. Philippe tue par St. Pierre.* St. Philip didn't die at once, however, for the show was repeated on September 3; and even that was not quite the end. Coquet was stubborn, and if he had lost Tabary he had gained Fournier once more. Within a week after the second "Death of St. Philip" Coquet announced that the Theatre de la Gaite, formerly the St. Philip, would soon open.[45]

This last gasp was drawn on September 17 when a couple of little plays were staged. A week later the Gaite presented yet again *The Death of St. Philip, Killed by St. Peter,* and this time it was final. Shortly thereafter a number of theatrical costumes, scripts, scores, and other properties were offered for sale. They had belonged to Fournier who had abandoned them to his creditors. Art is long but funds run short. The building, after having been offered for rental and for auction, was re-baptized, and under the name of the Winter Tivoli it returned to its safe and sure function of housing the racially mixed balls. One thing remained of its former theatrical glory—the scenery was used to decorate the hall, appropriately enough, as "the Temple of Love." [46]

With the return of the St. Philip to its older profession as a temple of love, the St. Peter had the season of 1808–1809 all to itself. But the deficiencies in the structure were still there, and not all the performers had returned. The ascendancy of the St. Peter lasted only through the winter. On May 31, 1809, the St. Philip was again used as a theater when the "reunited actors" gave a show there for the benefit of a poor family. And in June, Philip Laroque, a musician and orchestra leader, began selling new subscriptions for the St. Philip. The "actors reunited in the society of the theatre de la rue St. Philippe" gave their first regular performance on Sunday, June 11, with a piece aptly titled *Le Resurrection de St. Philippe, ou le Petit Bonhomme Vit Encore,* followed by an opera. The good little man indeed lived again, for after this, performances during the summer were given exclusively at the resurrected theater. The whole crew seems to have moved over to St. Philip Street.[47]

Toward the end of August, Coquet, ever-hopeful, proposed a new plan. "For a long time," he said, "the public of this city wished to have a vast, commodious play house." Certainly Coquet wanted one whether the public did or not. So he was ready to try again. Reminding everyone that "the playhouse in St. Peter Street [had been] condemned as unfit repeatedly," he assessed the situation there as impossible. At his own place he acknowledged two main deficiencies: the flat floor, mentioned before, and the lack of "upper boxes for women of color." He would remedy these nicely and would as well enlarge the theater and add a hall—in fact the plans were already drawn and could be examined in the coffeehouse—if he could but borrow twelve thousand dollars for five years. To this end he hoped to sell shares for three hundred dollars each and mortgage all his property as security. In place of interest on the loan, the shareholder would be admitted free to all the ordinary performances during the five year period.[48]

This proposal fared better than the one of a year before. There was a brief flurry of dissension on September 20, 1809, when the St. Peter played an opera and again a few days later, when both the-

aters advertised *L'Opera Comique*. However, the St. Philip canceled
its performance, and the actors proclaimed that they were reunited
(again) and had agreed on a procedure. They would play one week
at each theater in turn for a total of eight regular shows a month;
and the shareholders of either theater would be entitled to use their
passes at both. Thus was removed one of the chief barriers to unity.
Both theaters were to be repaired, although subsequent events show
that the repairs on the St. Peter were to be slight, only enough to
permit its use while the St. Philip underwent a major overhaul.
During October and November, 1809, the theaters alternated more
or less as promised; but in December and throughout most of 1810,
only the St. Peter was open. It was during this time that the St.
Philip was virtually rebuilt.[49]

The new playhouse was scheduled to open on December 7, 1810;
and, in anticipation, the stockholders of the older house made plans
to sell the entire establishment including the grounds. On December 1 the scenery, costumes, decorations, curtain, machinery, scores,
and scripts were auctioned off. Two of the troupe had benefit shows
coming to them, however, and they were allowed to use the props
for these on December 2 and 9. Both these performances were
operas.[50]

Thus the performance on Sunday, December 9, 1810, marked the
end of New Orleans' first theater. It also serves to demonstrate what
the modest but important theater on St. Peter Street had accomplished for the community in little more than ten actual seasons of
operation. For this final offering was a three-act opera, *Pauvre
Jacques,* composed and conducted by Philip Laroque, a local musician long associated with the theater. Laroque had already seen two
of his operas, *La Jeune Mere* and *Nicodeme dans la Lune,*
produced—the first one three times. Better encouragement for local
musical development is hard to imagine. The scenery was painted
by Hyacinthe Laclotte, who also lived in New Orleans and worked
as an architect, engineer, and drawing instructor, as well as a set designer. He and others like him brought skills to the area that enriched it greatly and that would not have been available in such
quantity had it not been for the theater.[51]

Most impressive though was the sheer wealth of musical entertainment made available to the people of New Orleans. From the time when Tabary first became director on March 1, 1806, to its closing, the St. Peter Street Theater, with a small assist from the one on St. Philip Street, gave at least three hundred fifty-one performances of seventy-six different operas. The works of thirty-two composers, the best in Europe, had been brought across the Atlantic and the Gulf. No other city in America and not too many in Europe could match this outpouring of opera.

Dalayrac was by far the most popular composer in this interval, having sixteen of his works performed eighty-seven times; and Gretry came next in popularity, with sixty-one performances of twelve operas. The favorite single works, however, were Mehul's *Une Folie* which was given fifteen times, followed by Della Maria's *L'Opera Comique* with fourteen playings. Dalayrac's best-liked opera, *Adolphe et Clara,* played eleven times, a record matched by Gretry's *Sylvain.*[52]

The grounds and buildings of the St. Peter Street Theater were put up for sale on December 28, 1810, and a little more than a year later, they were once more offered at a sheriff's sale. But never again did the place function as a theater. After being sold in 1821, it was destroyed to make way for a new building.[53]

"Long voyages have been undertaken."

Chapter Four

THE OPERA: INFANCY

$\mathcal{D}$espite the success of Coquet's plan to rebuild his theater on St. Philip Street, thus providing New Orleans with a better playhouse, a few stubborn men continued the struggle to complete the theater started earlier by Louis Tabary on Orleans Street. Early in December, 1809, the same month that the extensive repair on the St. Philip Theater was begun, a small group of trustees met to consider abandoning further efforts to construct the Orleans Theater. They needed more money if they were to continue. The money pledged to this venture through shares of five hundred dollars each would have been sufficient; but the money was to be paid in installments of one hundred dollars every two months, and the shareholders were behind in their payments.

The trustees warned that if the arrears were not paid by the time of the scheduled meeting, the enterprise would have to be given up and the grounds and preliminary works sold. Showing a fine disregard for Coquet's intention to make over his St. Philip Street house, the trustees of the Orleans admonished their shareholders that failure to pay up on their shares would mean the end of theater in New

Orleans, since it would remove the only place proper for it. Whether this brought more funds or merely more promises, the trustees' meeting resulted in inviting masons, carpenters, and others to study the plans and to submit bids by December 15.[1]

A year later, when the St. Peter Street Theater closed for good and the new St. Philip Street Theater took its place, a part of the Orleans Theater, which had now been under construction on and off for over four years, was completed. The stores in the building and an apartment fronting on St. Ann Street were ready for occupancy on January 1, 1811. But the Orleans Theater itself was still a long way from opening. Coquet's new St. Philip Street Theater remained unchallenged, and for the next few years this former ballroom for the colored was the seat of New Orleans' opera. One might say that the first decade of the nineteenth century belonged to the theater on St. Peter Street; the second—more or less—to the one on St. Philip Street. Of course balls continued at the St. Philip Street location, but if any colored or mixed balls were held there during its time of dignity as the center of opera, they were not advertised. And the ballroom now adjoined the theater instead of occupying the same room.[2]

Humid weather prevented the paint in the new St. Philip from drying in time for its scheduled opening. But at last, on December 20, 1810, the new theater opened with a double bill of opera: those two proven favorites of the city, Gretry's *Sylvain* and Dalayrac's *Adolphe et Clara*. A full house, for the opening at least, was certain.[3]

Besides providing the growing city with a much better playhouse for French operas and dramas, as well as with more elegant surroundings for the balls and concerts that New Orleans was so fond of, the St. Philip served the city in another way during its first season. Late in April, 1811, one William Duff made arrangements with Coquet to rent the theater once or twice a week, as convenient, for the rest of the season. Duff had gathered a small group of actors together, and on April 26 "the American Company" gave two comedies, *The Doctor's Courtship* and *The Unfortunate Gentleman*. This was the first time that an organized troupe performed English drama in New Orleans.[4]

Meanwhile, the Orleans Theater slowly progressed. The committee in charge offered three repossessed shares for sale in May, 1811, with the inducement that "the magnificent building" was nearing completion. By July, the shareholders were able to hold their meetings in the foyer of the theater itself, as well as in the coffee room. And late in August the brick and joiner work was put up for bids. For the moment the sun seemed to be shining on the theatrical fortunes of New Orleans.[5]

It proved to be only a summer sun, unfortunately, whose warmth soon gave way to the colder winds of fall. As October approached, the committee for the Orleans confessed its inability to pay the workmen. It had already failed twice to obtain necessary help from the shareholders; the committee now threatened that if no funds were forthcoming, it would turn over all accounts, wash its hands of the whole business, and consider itself exonerated.[6]

Before the year was over, the St. Philip too was in trouble. Coquet bowed out as manager, leaving the theater to the actors who took charge on a cooperative basis. That Coquet was abandoning an unprofitable situation is intimated by a pledge from the actors to reduce the price of subscriptions because money was "very scarce." They also promised to raise the curtain at a fixed time so that those who lived far from the playhouse could reach home at a reasonable hour. M. Laroque, musician and composer, was named cashier, and the actors' society was headed by A. Daudet and Fournier, whose persistence if not his success must be admired. An immediate falling off in the frequency of shows gives further hint of financial troubles.[7]

Two months later, the stockholders of the eternally building Orleans Theater were in worse trouble. A suit against each of them individually had been filed in Superior Court. On top of this, in May, the plans for the theater, containing all elevations, profiles of the walls, and so forth were somehow lost or mislaid, and a reward had to be offered for their recovery. It had now been almost six years since Tabary proudly laid the first brick; and it seems that all this was more than he could bear, for one week after the loss of the plans was admitted, he requested work as a private tutor, claiming that he wished to be done with the stage. But either no one hired him or he had a renewal of heart, for he continued in the theater.[8]

The year of 1812 was a low point in the fortunes of New Orleans opera. In the third week of June, the actors at the St. Philip complained that they had run at a considerable loss for the past two months and were tired of seeing the theater deserted, either because of bad weather or what they sarcastically called the "pursuit of more important objects" by Orleanians. For the rest of the summer they proposed to give benefits only. What they were really up against was the fact that heat, disease, and reduced population made it extremely difficult to sustain the theater through a New Orleans summer. Even so, the benefits were fairly frequent during the remainder of that summer, and three new operas were produced. Attendance at these operas suggested that more frequent new productions might help.[9]

In August, the suit against the stockholders of the Orleans came to a head when the property, described as seventy feet on Orleans Street, around sixty feet on St. Ann, with one hundred and fifty-five feet between streets, was ordered to be sold along with the building at a sheriff's sale the following month. And there were even further complications. One William Brand said that he had observed with interest the announcement of the pending sale. He warned that he held a privileged claim of four thousand dollars and fifty-seven cents and would seize the theater from whoever bought it.[10]

As if this were not enough, the ill wind currently buffeting New Orleans' theaters blew the top right off the St. Philip on August 19, when a severe hurricane struck the city. The roof ended in the hands of an enterprising tin-smith who bought it to make "tin spouts, cannisters, lanterns," or anything else in the tinnery line. It was the end of November before the shorn theater could operate again.[11]

The house re-opened with a benefit to help Coquet ease his losses from the hurricane, then ran as before. And as before, there was trouble over the entries, especially when the proceeds were designated for the benefit of some one performer. On those occasions, the recipient tried to insist that all admissions be paid ones, a desire that irked the shareholders, one of whom bought space in the newspaper to air his annoyance. Addressing himself to one of the actors, Louis Douvillier, who had advertised that anyone wishing to attend his benefit must buy the ticket directly from him, "Roger, Share-holder" charitably said that no doubt Douvillier was simply misin-formed. Roger then served notice: "Let M. Douvillier, or any other person who might publish such advs. be appraised that when Mr. Coquet built his theater, he created ten shares, and that the share-holders . . . were allowed their entry twice a week, until they should be reimbursed of the $300 advanced by them, without being held to apply to anybody." [12]

Roger had a case, but so had the actors. They were operating on a cooperative basis and Coquet was no longer directly involved. They had been deprived of any place to perform while the theater was roofless. In the summer of 1813, after seven months of renewed operations, they repeated the plea for better support than they had had the summer before. They had received no salary for a long time, they said, and had even suffered a loss. However, they pledged to redouble "their careful work" and dared to hope for a better re-sponse.[13]

Somehow, in spite of the heat, the war, and "diverse sentiments," this determined group of actors kept the theater alive. With Tabary again their manager, in January, 1814, they put the shareholders on notice that January 31 would mark exactly six years since the St. Philip began. After that date, the free passes so long enjoyed by the shareholders would expire. To get that burden off their backs must have been a great relief to the actors.[14]

Somehow too there was still life in the battered committee of ad-ministration for the Orleans Theater. One tenth of the property was offered for sale in the summer of 1813, and two years later the committee requested all who had claims to present them. More than this, a dividend was promised, probably earned from the store rents and similar sources.[15]

At long last, on Thursday, October 19, 1815, the opera *Un Quart Heure de Silence* by Pierre Gaveaux was presented in the Orleans Theater, the city's third and newest playhouse. A few days later, M. J. Turpin announced that he had rented the theater twice a

week on nights when no play was scheduled to give grand balls beginning November 4. The floor of the pit would be raised to the
height of the stage, making, he said, a "most beautiful dancing
room." [16]

The theater was new but the personnel was the same. Operas at
the St. Philip ceased as the actors simply moved to the Orleans.
Other than location, the only discernible change was in managers,
as A. Daudet replaced Tabary. But that was nothing new for the
New Orleans troupe. The older theater filled in with regular balls
every Tuesday and Saturday, thus joining its still older sister, the
St. Peter, which was doing the same every Wednesday and Saturday.[17]

One might have thought that the luck of the Orleans was due to
turn for the better, now that the theater had opened at last. But the
misfortunes that seemed to be its destiny continued. The place
couldn't be heated properly: early in January, 1816, in response to
many complaints, Turpin decided to move his balls back to his
Navy Hotel in order to spare the ladies from the cold in the theater.
At the same time the theater was seized again in a creditor's suit
and offered for sale at Maspero's Coffee House. And before that
month was over, M. Coeur de Roy, a principal musician and prime
mover in the company, fell out of the first balcony, severely injuring
himself. His fellows hastened to arrange a concert to help his "truly
disastrous situation," but because of rain, the performance had to
be postponed to "the first fair day." [18]

The courage of this band of actors, singers, and musicians in the
face of repeated adversity was admirable. Daudet, the manager,
optimistically announced three days before the scheduled sale of the
theater that he had just obtained three hundred and twenty new
plays and operas from France—nearly all of which had played in
Paris within the last two years—and he promised to present the best
of them soon. In spite of temperature, seizures, or accidents, the
company seemed determined to stand by its new playhouse.[19]

They struggled on through February and March of 1816, giving
ten operas in each of these months, but the effort was proving too
great. April found them ready to concede defeat, and they rather
fittingly chose the thirteenth day to admit that "after having done

all they could to sustain their enterprise, (they) are obliged to renounce an enterprise that has become too burdensome." For the remaining two months of their engagement with the shareholders, they would give only benefits, "a sacred obligation of the management." They thanked the subscribers who had encouraged and sustained them to the present and "regretted infinitely" that the zeal and care of the troupe had been in vain. With a last streak of stubbornness they pledged always to seize any occasion to prove a friend to the arts.[20]

During the remainder of that gloomy month they gave three operas for the promised benefits and one more on May 2. Then, on May 5, as if they had not had enough harassment, a major flood forced them to suspend even the benefits for a month. On June 6, they gave their last opera, *Ninon chez Madame de Sevigne* by Henri Berton, and closed their unhappy season, perhaps hoping for better times next year. But Lady Luck, who had never smiled too sweetly on the first Orleans Theater, deserted it completely that summer when a fire utterly destroyed the place and wrote *finis* to as dismal a saga of misfortune as ever the Greeks had imagined. This was just about ten years after Tabary had laid the first brick.[21]

The performers thus deprived of their new theater were substantially the same ones who had started in the old St. Peter. There had been additions of course, and a few had retired or left, but many, like Tabary, had been with the group for ten years or more. Although they had come from elsewhere, they were now permanent residents of New Orleans, a truly local company. Continually faced with discouraging obstacles, they had nevertheless given operas to the city regularly and frequently—a remarkable achievement.

In the 5½-year interval between the final performance in the St. Peter Street Theater and the fiery end of the first Orleans Street Theater, no fewer than three hundred and fifty-five opera performances were presented, representing one hundred and two different works by twenty-five composers. Dalayrac was still the favorite composer: nineteen of his operas were performed a total of seventy-six times. His *Maison a Vendre* was one of the two most popular single operas. It played fourteen times—a record matched only by Luigi

Cherubini's *Les Deux Journees*. The other leaders in popularity were Gretry, with twenty-seven performances of twelve operas; Berton, with thirty-five performances of nine operas; Mehul, with thirty-eight performances of eight operas; Isouard with thirty performances of ten operas; and Gaveaux with thirty-one performances of nine operas.[22]

The most striking display of the spirit and enterprise of the company was the introduction of forty-three new operas, an average of eight a year. Considering the rehearsing, scenery, and costumes required for each new production, one can only marvel at this rate. Probably most, if not all, of the new works were premieres for America, as well as for New Orleans. Notable among them was Mehul's *Joseph*, first played in France on February 17, 1807, and introduced to New Orleans on April 21, 1812. Henry Krehbiel has written that the music in *Joseph* "is marked by grandeur, simplicity, lofty sentiment and consistent severity of manner." *Joseph* "will always command the admiration of impartial musicians," said Gustave Choquet; and Hanslick compared it with one of Mozart's operas. It became and remained one of Carl Maria von Weber's favorite works. One of the earliest operas to be based on a Biblical story, *Joseph* called for a completely womanless cast and was possibly the first all male opera. This fact alone, to say nothing of the more difficult music, shows in some measure the audacity of the New Orleans troupe. After its introduction in 1812, *Joseph* was performed eight more times before the Orleans Theater burned down.[23]

A company of men and women with such spirit could not long remain discouraged by the loss of their theater. As fall came on that year and the snap of a new theatrical season could be felt in the air, they made ready to try again. Reminding the people that "misfortunes too well known" had deprived the actors of the opportunity to offer their plays for several months, they said they were "newly reunited" and would open soon on the familiar boards of the St. Philip Street Theater which they had deserted last year for the ill-fated Orleans. To help defray "the extraordinary expenses occasioned by the improvements made in the Theatre, which has been disposed on an entirely new plan, and decorated by M. Pilie," the actors requested that the public pay, on opening night only, prices augmented to one dollar and a half for box seats and to one dollar for the pit and gallery seats. Children's admission would remain at fifty cents. Thereafter prices would revert to the usual one dollar, seventy-five cents, and fifty cents respectively.[24]

These high hopes were soon dashed. The opening date had to be set back from October 31 to November 3, with the promise that prices would not be raised and that slaves would be admitted to the amphitheater for fifty cents. They opened with Berton's *Ninon,* the same opera that had proved to be their last at the Orleans. The company proposed to run twice a week, but by the second week in November, they were forced to reduce their operas to one a week for the rest of the year.[25]

There is no telling what the future of opera in New Orleans might have been had John Davis not now entered the scene. However good Tabary may have been as an actor and director, he had repeatedly proved a poor business manager, as had Fournier and Daudet and the others who tried. Coquet had lost money as a backer, and the actors' cooperatives were equally unsuccessful. Davis himself constantly lost money on the theater, but he always had other successful ventures going which made up his losses. Why he continued his one losing enterprise for almost eighteen years can only be guessed. It may have been the gambler's hope of eventual success; or, more likely, his love of the theater and of his role in it. At any rate, John Davis was one nineteenth-century American business man who did much for the arts. Ultimately he too withdrew, but when he did, he left New Orleans' opera with the status, maturity, and tradition to continue for almost a century more.

John Davis was born in Paris in 1773. Like many other young Frenchmen in that day, he emigrated to Saint-Domingue only to be forced out of that island by the revolution. He came to New Orleans from Cuba in 1809, when he was thirty-six years old, to engage in various entrepreneurial activities. Within two years of his arrival, he entered the hotel business by purchasing Tremoulet's Hotel on the levee, usually known as the Marine or Navy Hotel because of its proximity to the United States Navy Yard. This hotel, which Davis promptly renamed the United States Hotel, was equipped for recreation as well as for lodgings. Besides the usual rooms, it offered food, baths, billiards, coffee, and the like.[26]

Davis bought Tremoulet's Hotel in the spring of 1811. That summer, in partnership with another man, he built a tavern on Bayou St. John where he rented out flatboats and other craft and began the construction of another hotel. Soon thereafter he broadened his interests to include the manufacture of Spanish cigars and "good tobacco," the sale of furniture and "other goods," and the importation of lime, tar, and kindred products from across Lake Pontchartrain. Later on he ran a gambling room in his Orleans Theater and elsewhere.[27]

Altogether, these activities enabled him to leave a large fortune when he died in 1839. But the honors accorded him then came not because he was a successful business man, nor because he was a veteran of the Battle of New Orleans, but because it was really John Davis "who gave Louisiana a French Theatre." [28]

Just as Bernardo Coquet had earlier interested himself in the theater through his success at running dances, so too did John Davis. The hotel he bought from Tremoulet in 1811 contained a ballroom where dances had taken place for many years. Always ready to expand any profitable activity and undismayed by the possibility of British attacks on the city, Davis leased the old Conde Street Ballroom late in 1814 and installed Messrs. Bertus and Sel, two dancing teachers, to direct the balls there. He was operating this ballroom in 1816, the year in which the Orleans Theater building burned down, and apparently he was contemplating leasing the ballroom attached to the theater when it should be completed. He had, perhaps, taken some steps in that direction when the fire put an end to his plans. At any rate, Davis stated on October 5 that he had given much thought to establishing a new ballroom until the fire "destroyed in a few minutes this fine building." Therefore he promised to "display new pains" in embellishing the old Conde Street room where Bertus and Sel would again direct the balls. His "sweetest reward" would come from the "felicitations of a sex true appreciators of the zeal and pains of those who made it their study to please them." Obviously Davis considered himself an expert in this pleasant study.[29]

Whether spurred by the hope of further sweet rewards or by crasser concerns, Davis continued to give thought to the burned ballroom and theater. Before much over another month passed, he bought the ruins and the grounds. He promised to rebuild the structure in the shortest time possible, but more elegantly than before, and to import a number of artists from Europe. This would of course be expensive, he said, but he relied on the "liberal ideas of an enlightened public," one eager to see rebuilt an edifice which would do honor "to most towns in Europe." [30]

To attain this goal, Davis proposed to employ a means of financing "until now unusual in this city"—namely a tontine. There would be enough shares at one hundred and fifty dollars each to form capital of seventy thousand and fifty dollars. With this he would build the structure—he hoped within one year after the subscription was filled. The completed building would be Davis' to use as his own for five years. Then he would turn it over to the shareholders to manage themselves or to rent as they saw fit. If they chose to rent it, Davis was to have first preference. So far this was like any other stock venture, but now the tontine came in: as each shareholder died, his share was to go to the remaining shareholders, with income always equally divided among them, until they were reduced to ten. Then the building would belong to the ten survivors in full property.[31]

With Davis thus proposing a new theater and offering prospective shareholders a chance to bet their lives, another showman joined the game. Cayetano Mariotini had been bringing his circus from Havana to New Orleans for a number of years. In 1816, Cayetano's Circus opened on Saturday, April 6, and ran through the summer into September, featuring equestrian dances by Cayetano and his wife and, of course, two horses. Thus he was in New Orleans when the Orleans Theater burned, an event which evidently gave him ideas, as it had John Davis.[32]

Accordingly, as the height of the winter theatrical season approached, Cayetano proposed adding a "vast and commodious" theater to his circus, the whole to be called the Olympic Circus. Here he would give comedies and operas, as well as grand pantomimes such as those staged in Franconi's Theater in Paris. Cayetano therefore offered six-month subscriptions for fifty dollars each, and promised to construct some well-lighted bridges to ease the passage from the city to his Olympic Circus which was located in Circus Square —alternately known as Congo Square—in the rear of the city. Thus New Orleans had once again two new theaters in the offing, while the one theater operating, the St. Philip, was failing to maintain its goal of two shows a week.[33]

Cayetano moved with dispatch, and on Washington's birthday, 1817, in spite of severe competition from the balls that that day always called forth, he opened his Olympic Theater with a reliable ballet, *La Mort du Capitaine Cook.* He also had a reliable cast, for it was the same that had held forth in the earlier theaters. One thing was different—the show opened with a display of horsemanship.[34]

New Orleans' latest impresario claimed that he had spared no expense and had reunited (once again) the artists of the city. He promised to run every Thursday and Saturday and never to permit a postponement for any pretext whatever. Alas for good intentions, the very next performance was postponed because "of the great labor involved." This was Rodolphe Kreutzer's opera, *Paul and Virginia,* the first opera scheduled for the new theater; its final scene depicts a great wreck when the ship *St. Geran* is struck by lightning and sinks with Virginia on board. To bring this off, Cayetano hired M. Leriche, a former machinist at the Theater Feydeau in Paris.[35]

With the opening of the Olympic, opera moved again out of the St. Philip Street Theater, leaving that house only some amateur benefits and occasional traveling performers. In the light of events to come, however, the St. Philip was well enough off. After a total of five operas were staged at the new location, M. Leriche, the late Parisian theater machinist, was seeking any sort of carpenter or machinist work. Cayetano had been unable to employ him since April 6. And after one more opera given on April 20, Cayetano himself was in Parish Court with a petition of bankruptcy. He died a short time later.[36]

This season was one of the worst the actors had known since the theater started. Following Cayetano's bankruptcy, two more operas were produced at the Olympic in May; three in June; and two in July—most of them coupled with a horse show. Here ended the first season of the Olympic Theater. An opera was scheduled there for August 31, but was evidently cancelled, and no further entertainment took place in the vicinity for a time save in a nearby pit where bulls, bears, tigers, and dogs were pitted against one another. Lest this be not revolting or gory enough, a bull was saddled with fireworks.[37]

As always when in trouble, the actors cast eyes on M. Coquet and his enduring refuge on St. Philip Street. On July 26 they were back in Coquet's theater with an opera. Exactly one month later they staged another, and one more in the next month. But they were getting ready to have another real try at it. In October they increased the pace from one to two operas a month and promised to use a better oil in the lamps—a kind that would neither smoke nor stink.[38]

As November, 1817, began, this indomitable crew prepared to embark on another season. Calling themselves the Actors Company of the St. Philip Street Theater, they thanked the public for the encouragement received and pledged a new effort to produce good shows that winter. Especially would they endeavor to present new operas lately in from France. All this at the rate of only four dollars for eight shows in the pit and second loges, or five dollars in the boxes. Coquet's St. Philip Street Theater was in business again, marking around twenty years since that gentleman's first association with the theater.[39]

From November 9 to December 12 they managed to give nine operas at the St. Philip before the availability of another usable theater tempted some of the group to split off again. These latter reopened the Olympic on December 14 with Gaveaux' opera, *La Jambe de Bois,* and the customary horse show. The dissidents at the Olympic were able to give just nine operas in over three months, however, and are of interest only in that their attempt illustrated the drain caused by internal division—and in that they premiered and repeated *La Servante Maitresse* by Giovanni Pergolesi. This was the opera better known as *La Serva Padrona,* introduced at Naples in 1733, which "has served as a model of comic operas since." It had two characters only, accompanied by a string quartet and occasional horns, being thus more within the limited capabilities of the small company at the Olympic.[40]

The majority of the performers in New Orleans remained at the St. Philip, giving operas steadily through 1818, summers included.

Income for the theater, if not for the French performers, was increased by the arrival in New Orleans of the first thoroughly professional English company to visit the city. It was managed by Noah Ludlow, who rented the St. Philip for an average of two nights a week from January 13 to May 1. And after March, performances at the Olympic ceased. In September its elimination as a competitor was signally completed when Coquet himself offered for sale, "together or separately," the framework and covering of the rival theater, thus indicating that the structure was never really more than a glorified tent.[41]

In the meantime, John Davis had completed part of his project in Orleans Street—the more profitable part. Regular public balls for adults and children, plus sixteen subscription balls were planned for the new Orleans ballroom, which opened on Thursday, November 20, 1817. At the same time, Davis announced that the tontine to raise funds for the theater was half filled, and he hoped it would be completed before the end of the year. If it was, he promised, the theater would open before January, 1819.[42]

A short while later, he claimed to have the major part of the shares sold, a statement which would have sounded more convincing had he not simultaneously offered shares to contractors in return for work or materials.[43]

This hint that all was not well with Davis' tontine was confirmed the following summer when he admitted that the tontine had failed to reach its goal, whether by sales or barter. Another discouraging sign was that the St. Philip had to threaten its subscribers to pay up or face the law. But John Davis was resourceful and determined to see his theater built. He decided to continue on his own, with whatever help he could get from friends and with the aid of his other businesses. That fall he served three-dollar dinners in the Orleans ballroom on Sundays and had the coffee room in operation. He had the building far enough constructed to mortgage it for a loan of fifteen thousand dollars from the city.[44]

But for the season of 1818–19, the St. Philip had the stage to itself as the only theater in New Orleans. Davis originally hoped to have the Orleans Theater ready early in 1819, but the failure of the tontine delayed his plans. It is a tribute to his industry and to the success of his other ventures, especially the balls, that he managed to make his target year, even if late in that year. Time was running out for the St. Philip.

On November 11, 1819, "Feuilleton," a column of general comment in the *Louisiana Gazette,* reported that two agents who had been sent to France by Davis had returned. With them they brought two actors, one each for comedy and opera; two actresses, one of them a cantatrice; a conductor; and a few musicians. Even better news was that more additions were yet to come. Four days after the first report, "Feuilleton" declared that every friend of the arts impatiently awaited the arrival of the ship, *Union,* bringing more performers from France. According to the column, everyone hoped for the success of "so great an enterprise." The theater, "Feuilleton" declared, offered a means of existence to many who, in turn, spent their money in the town. Therefore all were urged to cooperate. The combination of the former players with the new would permit a greater variety of roles, more new operas, and better casting. Indeed, the column promised, there would be a multitude of charming operas as yet known of in New Orleans only by the success they had obtained in France.[45]

On November 19, prices for the new theater were posted. Seats in the first and second rows of boxes, the gallery, and the parquet were all one dollar and fifty cents each. The pit seats were one dollar, as were the third-row box seats which were reserved for the colored. Subscriptions for the dollar and a half seats were offered at one hundred dollars a year. These entitled the holder to two shows a week, on Thursdays and Sundays; hence the subscriber got one hundred and four shows for one hundred dollars. For the dollar seats, subscriptions cost seventy dollars a year.[46]

Descriptions of the Orleans Theater are meager. It formed part of a complex of buildings which included Davis' Hotel and the Orleans Ballroom. Together they made a "considerable pile of brick buildings . . . with a very handsome front and interior," according to a contemporary directory of the city. But the theater itself was neither large nor pretentious, never seating many over thirteen hundred persons. The lower front was Roman Doric with a second story of Corinthian Composite. One interesting feature inside was a section of latticed boxes for persons in mourning who didn't wish to be seen enjoying the opera. Later on it was admitted that the loges were not well placed; that there were locations where one could neither see nor hear well; and that sound from the corridors intruded at times. But for the time and the place, it was a splendid achievement. Quite fittingly, the opening performance was dedicated to John Davis who deserved it, the announcement implied, for nothing had been spared, enormous sacrifices had been made, and "long voyages have been undertaken." It was all true.[47]

The new theater, conceived by Louis Tabary almost fourteen years before, opened on Saturday, November 27, 1819, with familiar fare. "Washington's March," played as an overture by the orchestra, had been used so often to kill time before a late curtain at the previous theater as to be a bore. It did give the audience a chance to settle down and appraise the new edifice and improved orchestra. The two operas chosen for the opening—Boieldieu's *Jean de Paris* and Berton's *Les Maris Garcons*—had also been played many times before at the older theater, and thus made good vehicles for assessing the new company.[48]

In fact, the next fifteen operas at the new theater were likewise old friends to the New Orleans audience. The promised new selections could wait until some of the other newness had worn off. This was, to be sure, good box office procedure as well. It was not until January 19, 1820, that the first new opera *Le Rendezvous Bourgeois* by Isouard, had its American premiere in Davis' new theater.[49]

Another link with the familiar was of course the presence in the new company and new orchestra of many of the artists and musicians from the old—presumably the better ones. It is indeed hard to

ORLEANS THEATRE.

(FOR THE OPENING.)

On Saturday the 27 of November 1819,

(For the benefit of Mr J. Davis,)

(SUBSCRIPTION SUSPENDED)

A Representation of

JEAN DE PARIS,

An opera in two acts, the music by the celebrated Boyeldieu.

TO BE FOLLOWED BY

The Married Batchelors

An opera in one act, music by Berton

The whole to begin with a Compliment for the opening of the Theatre

Before the curtain is raised the music will execute the March of General Washington

The manager of the Orleans Theatre has thought that that beautiful piece of music executed with the utmost precision, could not fail to please every good American. In consecrating a new Temple to the arts, it was natural that the first idea should be directed towards the hero of liberty, for liberty is the mother of arts, towards the soldier-citizen, whose illustrious labours and proof and wisdom, did so powerfully contribute in founding the happy government under which we live.

For the letting of those boxes which subscriber will not keep, apply on Thursday to Mr. John Davis.

The curtain shall rise at 1-2 past 6 precisely.

Advertisement announcing the opening of the Orleans Theater. The program was designed to appeal to both French and American patrons.

say whether the Orleans Theater opened with a new imported troupe and orchestra augmented by selected members of the earlier company; or with essentially the same old outfit enlarged and strengthened by imports. In either case it was a dream come true.

The retention of Louis Tabary as manager of the new company lends strength to the latter interpretation (as well as to our sense of justice). On the other hand, most of the leads in the operas, the first chairs in the orchestra, and the conductor's podium were given to the new arrivals. Moreover, the arrival of fresh talent from France did not cease with the docking of the ship, *Union*. A month after the theater opened, for example, M. and Mme. Cheret joined the company. He was a violinist, dancer, singer, and composer, while madame both sang and danced. An opera composed by Cheret himself was soon on the boards at the Orleans.[50]

Thus was the Orleans Theater, the famous home of French Opera in antebellum New Orleans, built and launched. It resembled its two predecessors in owing its birth to the efforts of ballroom promoters, and its nourishment, at least in part, to the money provided directly and indirectly by New Orleans' passion for dancing.

After fire destroyed the first Orleans Theater in 1816, John Davis spent a little over three years getting the rubble cleared and the second theater built. For the actors they were years of despair, quarrels, and hope. But whatever mood predominated, work continued. One hundred and forty-five performances were staged, encompassing seventy-nine operas by twenty-five composers. The only sign of wavering faith was a sharp reduction in the number of premiere performances of which there were only five. Dalayrac continued to be the favorite composer; thirteen of his operas were played thirty times, over one fifth of the total number of performances. The most popular single work was *La Jambe de Bois* by Gaveaux, given eight times. Berton, Boieldieu, and Gaveaux each had over fifteen performances, while Gretry's showings declined to eight. It was still an impressive feat, averaging close to fifty operas a season. More struggles and more despair were yet to come; but from the opening of the second Orleans Theater, the general course of opera in New Orleans would be upward.[51]

"Let us end this cruel uncertainty."

Chapter Five

THE OPERA: YOUTH

Not all of the instrumentalists who had spent many years playing for operas in New Orleans were invited to join the new orchestra at the Orleans Theater. Those passed over were not without work, however, for they were undoubtedly employed by the Virginia Company, a group of American performers who arrived in the growing city at the beginning of 1820 and rented the St. Philip Theater. The Americans were managed by James H. Caldwell, a man whose arrival in New Orleans was to have important musical consequences—one being that he later brought Italian opera to the city.[1]

Caldwell's company at the St. Philip Theater opened early in January and played the operetta *Rosina* on January 8. But apparently too few musicians remained at the St. Philip to provide an adequate orchestra, for the Virginia Company had been in the city only a few days when it issued an urgent appeal for good musicians. Especially needed were players of "flutes and clarionets, horns and violins," who were promised liberal terms on "immediate application." Whether or not many musicians answered its call, the Ameri-

93

can company gave five operas while in the St. Philip Theater. Among them were two drawn from the novels of Sir Walter Scott: *Guy Mannering,* scored by Henry Bishop, and *The Lady of the Lake,* with at least some of the music by Rossini. Both of these were later to become very popular in New Orleans.[2]

But the St. Philip Theater was by this time—at least in Caldwell's eyes—"an old and dilapidated" playhouse, and so in February the Virginia Company moved to the Orleans Theater, which they rented on Mondays, Wednesdays, Fridays, and Saturdays, when the French company was off, for one hundred dollars a night. Whether Caldwell employed the Orleans orchestra or brought with him the one he had assembled at the St. Philip is not clear. A profusion of concerts on the nights in question, in which many of the Orleans musicians participated suggests that Caldwell retained his own orchestra, at least in part, and perhaps added some of the Orleans players. At any rate, the Orleans Theater, in its first year of operation, had the sound of English musicals as well as French operas within its walls.[3]

The Virginia Company left New Orleans toward the end of March, but before leaving, it played one more English opera at the St. Philip. This was on a Tuesday night, March 7, when the French opera occupied the Orleans Theater. The primary reason for using the St. Philip again was that this opera, *Love in a Village,* was given to raise money for the free colored victims of a recent fire in Savannah, Georgia. The benefit, arranged by a number of free Negroes, was given before an audience consisting entirely of free persons of color.[4]

Caldwell probably made money on his first season in New Orleans, although he claimed not. One thing was certain—he would return. He had engaged to share the Orleans Theater with Davis' French company for the next three seasons, a privilege for which he was willing to pay ten thousand dollars a year.[5]

French operas continued at the Orleans throughout the summer of 1820. Davis and Tabary had not yet learned what to do about the season of heat and disease. As one devoted patron put it late in July: "We remark with satisfaction that in spite of the extreme heat which keeps so many from going to the theatre, the administration of the Orleans Theatre, far from being discouraged, continues to show new works and with as much care as in France." Then disease succeeded where heat had failed: a severe epidemic moved the city council to order the theater closed for the month of September. This of course meant that Davis owed subscribers the canceled performances; he was forced to work in six extra shows when the theater resumed, in order to satisfy the arrears. If he was not yet discouraged with the summer theater, he soon would be. John Davis was too good a businessman to continue a hopeless game.[6]

Nor was business quick to pick up in the fall. December was close at hand when a subscriber observed that a recent audience was "not overflowing." Even so, he wished ardently that other nights were equally well attended for the sake of Davis who had done so much and who "deserved more recognition and reward." Thus from the start, opera at the Orleans Theater found the going hard. Fortunately it did not have to stand alone. Both the singers and musicians could give frequent balls, preceded by a concert, to help them earn a living.[7]

As he began his third year of operation in December, 1821, Davis showed that he had learned one lesson. Subscriptions for whites were reduced to eighty dollars for reserved chairs in the first loges and parquet; and sixty dollars for unreserved chairs in those locations. Free people of color could buy a pass to their section for fifty dollars. This modest sum still entitled the subscriber to two shows each week, every Thursday and Sunday the year round. Moreover, Davis promised to increase the repertoire with new selections and to enlarge the company with performers "hourly expected from France." [8]

Davis' intention naturally was to strengthen his box office receipts with fresh talent, and no doubt the appeal of his theater was enhanced by the new arrivals. But this policy also worked against him in a predictable way. As more imports from France arrived, some of the regular performers at the Orleans were displaced. Together with those who had been left out of the Orleans company in the first place, plus one or two independent immigrants from France and a few imported by Davis who had either quit or been fired, there were

Within one week in 1820, the Orleans Theater offered an opera, two grand balls, both preceded by children's balls, and a combined concert and ball.

enough performers outside of the Orleans Theater to form a rival troupe. And of course the St. Philip Street Theater was just waiting to be used.[9]

So New Orleans, with a white population of slightly over twenty thousand, was again surfeited with two French opera companies, to say nothing of Caldwell's company at the Orleans. This time there was an ample supply of actors and musicians for both theaters— only the customers were spread thin.[10]

From February 9, 1822, through April, the St. Philip ran in opposition to the Orleans. At times each gave the same opera in a single week, or ran rival operas on the same night, usually on Sundays. Moreover, there are hints that several of Davis' company were not above helping their rivals in the St. Philip on those nights that Caldwell's Americans occupied the Orleans. Such three-way competition caused Davis to try combining balls with his shows. At first only the patrons in the first row of boxes were entitled to remain for the ball, but soon all customers were invited, those in the pit being required to pay an extra half dollar if they wished to dance. The best answer to competition though is to offer more for the money, and Davis came to think that he should undertake the recruitment of a really good troupe himself. In May, 1822, he sailed for France.[11]

When Davis returned that fall after six months abroad, he brought with him twenty-two fresh actors and musicians, and more were to follow. Among them was a *corps de ballet* capable of dancing both serious and comic ballets. It was, in fact, the first real ballet group to appear in New Orleans. Davis had also acquired welcome additions to the repertoire, including Rossini's new version of *The Barber of Seville*. This famed opera, in its entirety, was first presented to New Orleans on March 4, 1823, just seven years after its introduction in Italy, and almost three years before its first performance in New York. Thus, beginning with the season of 1822–23, opera at the Orleans Theater was played by a company almost wholly imported, one of substantial size and artistry, and possessed of a proper ballet. The only question was whether a small, provincial, and isolated community, part slave and part free, could support such an ambitious undertaking.[12]

By the end of May, 1823, it was clear that receipts were falling behind expenses. Davis turned over the management to two of the actors, Auguste Douce and A. B. St. Esteve—a move that was promptly praised in the French newspaper, *L'Ami des Lois,* as a step toward better times. But the newspaper also implored the public to give better support to an institution whose fall "these two artists have arrested." The men were not miracle workers, however, and the paper feared that they could not long operate the theater without help. Therefore *L'Ami* called for voluntary subscriptions, insisting that "we must maintain the French theatre." [13]

Before long the new managers made an appeal that rang all the changes. They had consented to take direction of the theater, they said, only because of their wish to please the public, their love of the arts, and "the attachment that all good Frenchmen carry in their hearts for the mother country." They asked if this beautiful establishment, which owed its existence to the patriotism of John Davis, would be allowed to fail for the lack of some slight succor which "no Frenchman would hesitate to give if he consulted his heart." Closing the theater would be a real loss to the town, they argued, in customs and mores, in law and order, as well as in recreation.

And the public must not fool itself that the theater, if once closed, would ever open again. "The artists . . . worthy of the public would not be able to exist, would be forced to return to France. Would they ever come again when, in the most fortunate times the place could offer, it permits itself to be deprived of a pleasure that is nearly a necessity?"

Faced with so glum a prospect, the managers appealed to all "who know well how useful an establishment like this is to civilization, . . . to the brave and likeable youths of this town . . . who should vividly desire the prosperity of an establishment created for them, [and] to the commercial interests favored by the theatre." In fact, now was the time for "all enlightened persons" to come to the aid of the theater.

As a practical step toward the desired end, the managers swore, for the duration of the crisis, to have but one goal—to pay the artists enough to exist. They themselves would gladly work without pay until more fortunate times. And the subscribers, for their part, could yield their Sunday passes and be content with Tuesdays and Thursdays or Fridays, when the new shows would always be repeated. "If we can achieve this the theatre will be sustained. In the contrary case we regret that our efforts and the noble and generous conduct of John Davis towards us, will have been in vain and we will be forced to dispose of a burden we cannot carry without the help of the public." [14]

Of all the reasons advanced for supporting the theater, the one which probably struck home the most was the call to patriotism. It was an argument that would be used frequently as long as the French opera existed. Already the island of French culture in New Orleans was threatened with inundation by the increasing tide of Americans rolling into the city. The French theater and opera became the best rallying point for a cultural rear guard action by a national group anxious to preserve its identity. At any rate, the subscribers were quick to respond, yielding their Sunday passes unanimously, emboldening the managers to hope that this action would permit them to carry on until December. One immediate result was that the orchestra, which had left, returned to the theater.[15]

The summer emergency was weathered, but another was in the making. One way to reduce expenses was to cut salaries. As the winter of 1823–24 approached, it became apparent that the performers would not receive the pay scale of the previous season. A large number of them suspected, however, that their pay cut was merely exploitation on the part of management; and with the St. Philip Theater ever handy, these distrusting ones prepared to play there again. John Davis reacted quickly. Resuming personal direction of his theater, he put his case before the populace. "A few artists unwilling to conceive that the embarrassed state of business does not permit offering them the same advantages as formerly, have abandoned this theater to go to that of St. Philip street. I am afraid they will be disappointed in their expectations, and that their fate at that Theatre will not be so favorable as that which I offered to them." Then Davis prepared to do battle. Until the others returned, "the artists who have remained faithful to me, are going to prove to you by their zeal, how desirous they are of deserving your approbations." [16]

The unfortunate split left thirteen performers at the Orleans Theater, while nine went over to the St. Philip—among them Louis Tabary. In the total troupe were four married couples who divided evenly—two couples at each theater. At least domestic harmony was preserved. The rebels named their group the Theatre des Varietes and opened at the St. Philip on Sunday, October 12, 1823. Bernardo Coquet, that on-again, off-again impresario who owned the house, was in the theatrical business once more.[17]

Thus a dismayed observer sighed, "the troupe of the Orleans is again divided . . . either because of the caprice of the actors, or the abandon in which the public has left the theatre." He thought the latter motive the more likely, since "poor receipts on the one hand and heavy expenses on the other does not fill the cash box, and an actor never learns so well his role as when he is well paid." The writer claimed to take no sides in the dispute: this was, after all, a free country where an actor had a perfect right to leave a disagreeable situation. However, everyone "should groan sincerely over the wavering of an establishment which would honor this town if it were directed with more firmness, if it were a little more encouraged by a population rich and enlightened." He went on to analyze the prospects: for a time "curiosity and caprice" should draw patrons to the St. Philip, but ultimately the larger number of subscribers and the more beautiful room would bring them back to the Orleans. In the meantime, the lack of a sufficient company at either theater would prohibit performing many of the better selections for months or even longer.[18]

Another, who agreed that two theaters could not possibly exist where one had scarcely made expenses, resorted to the appeal that was rapidly proving its effectiveness: the call on patriotism. He urged the performers to consider well that a prolonged division meant an irreparable loss to the French. In the end it was a concerned Creole who brought the two factions together after six months of separation. "All honor to him who has done this service to the old Louisiana population," expressed the sentiment of most French Orleanians.[19]

Before returning to the Orleans company, the actors at the St.

Philip insisted that they must give the owner, M. Coquet, proof of their gratitude by helping him to defray the expense of fitting up his theater once again for their use. Accordingly, they played a benefit for him on Saturday, November 29, 1823. It was the final French performance at the St. Philip and marked the end of Coquet's quarter-century of association with French opera in New Orleans. Coquet wasn't entirely finished with opera, however: a Spanish troupe from Havana gave Ferdinando Paer's *Le Maitre de Chapelle* and a few other shows at the St. Philip during the following January.[20]

The French company was reunited just in time, for in another month it was faced with vigorous competition from the first American theater to be built in New Orleans. James Caldwell, who had been renting the Orleans Theater on the nights not used by the French, had begun constructing a theater of his own on Camp Street, in the American section of town, in 1822. Caldwell's new theater, modeled somewhat after the Chestnut Street Theater in Philadelphia, neared completion late in 1823, and on New Year's Day, 1824, it opened for business.[21]

In one way it was probably a relief to Davis to get the Americans out of his theater. Their presence there had caused a good deal of friction, climaxed when the French doorman of the Orleans Theater was killed by one of the Americans. On the other hand, the erection of an American theater meant that American offerings would no longer be confined to the less desirable nights, when the French performers rested. Henceforth, the Americans and their orchestra, which Caldwell claimed was made up of the best musicians in the city, and which the *Louisiana Advertiser* called distinguished, would compete directly for a share of the public on the more popular nights.[22]

This new competition, plus the inherent difficulties of trying to maintain opera where the population had not yet reached thirty thousand free inhabitants, caused the financial crisis of the Orleans Theater to worsen. By March, 1824, when the new American theater had been operating only three months, the French company made a pressing request for thirty thousand dollars which it needed at once. The people of New Orleans were urged to remember that the theater provided a setting for balls which "would make many capitals of Europe envious," and from which all classes profited directly or indirectly. Moreover, the theater had put around three hundred thousand dollars in circulation, had boosted commerce, and was a good influence on public manners. Yet the artists could scarcely pay for their return passage to France.[23]

To remedy this situation, citizens were asked to buy one thousand new subscriptions for the ordinary shows at thirty dollars each; to cease neglecting the theater for the balls; and to attend the theater more often than merely on the opening nights of new productions. (In regard to the latter request, the company pointed out that a piece, to be good, had to be repeated frequently.) Finally, employment would have to be found for the performers who remained during the summer.[24]

As the crisis in the theater deepened, so did the anxiety of the New Orleans French to preserve their culture. "It boosts our native tongue," explained *L'Ami des Lois* in urging support for the theater. Citizens "who loved their country," should gather as soon as possible "to conserve an establishment truly national," pleaded a letter writer. One who called himself *Un Viel Amateur* spoke of the absolute necessity to conserve the "tongue and customs of our ancestors" through the theater. And one of the new subscribers who had answered the call hoped everyone shared with him "the urgency of succoring an establishment . . . from which we should for a long time draw an advantage in maintaining our tongue and ways." Frenchmen who assembled to ponder ways and means of helping the theater were described as men "who love well their country." [25]

Those who weren't so concerned with preserving the French tongue and ways were asked to reflect on the general advantages the Orleans Theater provided for Louisiana. Where else could one find "an amusement more useful and less dispensable." Young men especially could here learn good taste and manners; they would—or so it was claimed—cease frequenting "the houses of chance and debauchery." And the price was within reach of all: only thirty dollars to "buy some refreshing days from dangerous society." [26]

Nevertheless, as April reached its end, too few Orleanians had availed themselves of the chance to escape dangerous society, and the problem was still acute. Not enough had been done, according to one ardent advocate, and ruin faced the theater. The spirit was there, he said, but direction was lacking. June first, when contracts must be renewed, would soon arrive, and it was time to conclude negotiations. "Let us end this cruel uncertainty," he pleaded.[27]

The cruel uncertainty was in fact rapidly being resolved. On June 6, 1824, the company gave its last opera at the Orleans Theater—Boieldieu's *Le Petit Chaperon Rouge,* and left New Orleans for Havana on its way home to France. Davis closed his theater for the first time since it had opened four and one-half years before, and New Orleans was deprived of opera during a substantial number of months for the first time since John Davis had made opera his concern.[28]

Already the Orleans Theater had done much to further the cause and to establish the tradition of opera in New Orleans. By importing artists from France it had improved the quality of performances, while at the same time enlarging the troupe and orchestra. It had introduced thoroughly professional ballet to the city, as well as the latest compositions from the world of opera. Above all, it had strengthened the cultural ties of the New Orleans French with the homeland; had made these New World residents more aware of their French heritage and more determined to preserve it—a determination that would play an ever increasing role in making opera a part of New Orleans.

In its four and a half years of existence thus far, the Orleans Theater, together with the brief revivals at the St. Philip Theater, had given the city four hundred and sixty-four performances of one hundred and forty operas by fifty composers—an average of about two operas a week. Boieldieu became the favorite composer during this period: eleven of his operas were performed seventy-seven times. In second place was Isouard with sixty-nine performances of thirteen operas. The former favorite, Dalayrac, had dropped to third place with sixty-three playings of his operas. He still had the greatest number of operas produced, however—nineteen in all. The most popular single opera was Boieldieu's *Jean de Paris,* which played seventeen times, followed by Isouard's *Joconde,* given fifteen times.

No fewer than fifty-two new operas were introduced in these four and a half years. Nineteen of these were played once only, while another ten received only one additional playing, a fact which illustrates one of the major difficulties confronting the New Orleans troupe. Amateurs can afford to produce an opera for one or two showings; professionals cannot. There is, however, no way even the best professionals can tell in advance which productions will prove popular. Several of these costly failures were by lesser known composers, but such tested composers as Mehul, Kreutzer, Herold, Gretry, Gaveaux, Isouard, and even Dalayrac, contributed their share of unpopular operas. Every new production was a gamble.[29]

In part, this first closing of the Orleans Theater resulted from the natural slack in theater-going in a New Orleans summer, and in part from the difficulty of supporting a pretentious company of mainly imported talent. When the opera company was composed of artists who were year-round residents of the city, most of whom had supplementary sources of income and who operated on a more or less cooperative basis, it could afford to produce shows that yielded little or no profit; and it had little to lose by playing a few operas throughout the summer. Even so, the company had fared none too well. But John Davis, who was confronted with the problem of paying salaried artists the year round, could not operate this way. For him the summer receipts were simply insufficient.

Davis seemed slow to learn this lesson, for understandable reasons. He was really caught in a dilemma. If he hired French artists for one winter season only, he had to provide two-way passage each year, to say nothing of paying annual recruiting expenses. On the other hand, if he desired to keep a given troupe in New Orleans for a longer period, he faced the summer problem.

With his usual optimism, Davis remained undaunted. He sent to France again to recruit another troupe; and more than this, he took advantage of the closing of his theater to remodel the interior. Among other things, he added "arabesque ornaments relieved in gold and . . . a collection of the most magnificent birds, that gracefully interrupt the . . . regularity in the construction, and in the connexion of the arabesques." When he had finished, one newspaper proudly boasted that the "Orleans Theatre, that might before have vied with the handsomest theatres of Europe, will now be unrivaled either for richness or the fine tastes of the Decorations." Gradually Davis was finding a new ally for French patriotism as a support for his theater—civic pride.[30]

Toward the end of 1824, the Orleans Theater prepared to open again. But first a substantial number of subscriptions were sought, since experience had proved that the theater simply could not rely so much on the proceeds from non-subscribing patrons. To this end, prices were reduced to sixty dollars a year for the best seats, and forty dollars a year for the others, for two shows weekly. Both the interior and the company were new, said the management, and so too was ticket policy: henceforth no one would get a ticket until he had paid for it. Credit transactions had hurt the theater too much in the past. With one thing or another, it wasn't until January 13, 1825, that the Orleans was opened again, after being closed for over seven months.[31]

The same old trouble was quick to reassert itself; the very first heat of summer knocked the props from under this renewed attempt. Before the year was out, Davis was being sued by the city council for arrears on money advanced him by that body. He was also behind in paying his performers, causing some of them to straggle home to France. Consequently it had become more and more difficult to mount operas. In the entire last half of 1825, only twelve were performed.[32]

Ever hopeful, Davis asked that enough subscriptions be bought in advance to guarantee the first six months of operation in 1826, but he was soon forced to admit failure. The result was that after two operas in January, no more were performed at the Orleans, except for one benefit show on June 1, until the theater closed on July 9. It was proving impossible to mount operas with a troupe so depleted in numbers and in spirit.[33]

The financial plight of the Orleans Theater was again the subject of much comment but of little action. Speaking of an opera singer who was departing because Davis was unable to pay him, the editor of the *Argus* bewailed the loss of a musician "superior to all those we have heard before him . . . and probably to all those we will hear after him." This editor went on to criticize the public for "the indifference and coldness with which the last propositions of Davis were received." Has it already been decided, he asked, "that our French Theatre will collapse, that we will coldly let it fall in ruins, without the least effort to prevent it?" [34]

Another, calling himself "Johannes," even suggested that the only way to save the theater was to drop opera altogether because it was too expensive. This writer argued that a good drama troupe of around sixteen members would not cost over twenty-six thousand dollars a year, whereas a comparable operatic troupe would cost at least fifty thousand. Furthermore it was easier to obtain first-rank actors than first-rank singers. Johannes reminded his readers that opera had never been self-sustaining, that even in the great cities of Europe it existed only with government aid. How then, he asked, could anyone hope that New Orleans could support opera? Therefore, to try to remount opera in New Orleans would inevitably mean the end of the theater, since it was evident that receipts sufficient to keep a dramatic troupe solvent fell far short of the enormous expenses of opera. Johannes urged people to consider the poor receipts for some time past, although he admitted that these were due in part to a drop in cotton prices and to an exceptionally cold winter that froze the river and prevented the usual number of winter visitors from traveling. Johannes closed his assessment of the situation by requesting all good men to consider ways and means to relieve Davis from "the embarassment [sic] he has been in since the last theatrical year." [35]

Still another writer slyly added to the appeal of French patriotism and civic pride an appeal to the ego. The inhabitants of New Orleans must come to the aid of the theater, his argument ran, to "justify the general opinion of their good taste and wisdom." [36]

Not patriotism, nor civic pride, nor "good taste" sufficed to save the situation for Davis this cold year. Frenchmen flocked to Caldwell's American theater on Camp Street where the orchestra was highly praised in the local press and where on Saturday, March 18,

1826, Caldwell introduced Karl Maria von Weber's opera, *Der Freischutz*, to New Orleans.[37]

Although derided by Europeans—one of whom commented acidly that "the late Carl von Weber would not have been delighted at witnessing the performance of his *Der Freischutz*, here metamorphosed into the Wild Horsemen of Bohemia"—Caldwell's presentation was well received. "The Kentuckians expressed their satisfaction in a hurrah which made the very walls tremble," said an observer. In the next month *Der Freischutz* was repeated four times.[38]

In contrast, when the Orleans Theater presented a benefit opera on June 1, after five months of no operas, it had to borrow musicians from the Camp Street orchestra and from the Philharmonic Society, a mixed group of amateurs and professionals. And for this performance, perhaps in desperation, the Orleans employed a sales trick of mailing quantities of tickets, and then announcing in the press on May 31 that all those not returned by 10 A.M. the next day would be considered bought, with payment expected. This was hardly a way to win friends or to increase attendance.[39]

Davis tried one last device to bolster his theater's finances that year. He brought in a well-known female star named Gireaudeau whose "face, bust, and figure," rather than other less exciting assets, did draw well. But when Miss Gireaudeau took sincere praise of her more obvious talents as an insult and refused to appear further, John Davis surrendered. "I am accustomed to experience losses, and it is not with receipts like the last two that I can repair them. Had Miss Gireaudeau played on Sunday last, instead of making $180 I would have received 7 or 800. Had she played the day before yesterday the house would have been full, but as it was there was nobody. . . . [Why] . . . this enormous difference I do not know;—all I know is that I am the victim of it." One suspects sarcasm when Davis said he failed to understand "this enormous difference." He had eyes and should have been able to see why Miss Gireaudeau's presence made that difference.[40]

One thing Davis did know: Miss Gireaudeau's defection had cost him money. His own estimate was fifteen hundred dollars, which he said would have compensated for only part of his losses during the past year. On this gloomy note Davis closed his theater, but not before suffering a final blow when his leading actress and her husband refused to play in the closing performance on July 9. Their contracts had terminated the day before.[41]

With the imported troupe gone home to France, the local performers took over the Orleans Theater to give a few Sunday operas. But they too soon abandoned the effort, finding the crowds so poor as to make it not worth their while.[42]

In view of his unhappy experience, one might have expected John Davis to cry "enough" and turn his energies to other less taxing pursuits. On the contrary, he was ready the following fall to try again with a new imported troupe. Somehow his own stubbornness; the pull of the theater; the fact that the balls at the Orleans were generally profitable; and the opportunities for musicians, dancers and singers to augment their incomes by teaching and by playing for the dances, combined to give New Orleans another chance to embrace opera. On November 29, 1826, the ship *Nestor* disembarked a fully prepared opera company. Four days later they reopened the Orleans Theater for a new season with *The Barber of Seville*. They had everything but a sufficient audience.[43]

Within a week the editor of the *Argus* voiced a novel and lofty appeal for customers. Pointing out that the productions of this new company were good, the editor asked why the attendance was so poor. "All know," he wrote, "that it is neither charitable nor Christian to ruin afresh a poor director of the theatre." But the absent patrons seemed to be disposed to be neither charitable nor Christian in this regard, and in another month the ultimate call on French patriotism was sounded once more: "Oh men ungrateful! In vain does the director take pains to cross the ocean for talent . . . disappointed, benumbed, . . . his room and his cash box empty . . . ; in vain does he implore the public in the name of the beautiful French tongue, spoken of old, that we speak yet, and that soon we will not speak if we show the same apathy to all that which conserves our idiom." [44]

Patriotism, being presumably stronger than feelings of charity or religion, could perhaps bring the French to the opera, but in the end it was quality that kept them there. The troupe assembled by Davis for the season of 1826–27 was better than ever before, and it was good by any standard. Among the married couples in the Orleans Theater this year was Mlle. Alexandre and her husband. A slight and graceful lady, Mlle. Alexandre danced as well as she sang. She soon became the darling of New Orleans and remained so as long as she was in America. She usually drew a good house, giving performances that set a standard by which her successor would be measured. Mlle. Alexandre was outstanding, but the rest of the company did not disgrace her, and the audience grew steadily larger.[45]

Not only did the level of performance reach a new high, but an opera was introduced this season which captured the musical hearts of New Orleans much more than anything offered previously. On Tuesday, February 6, 1827, Boieldieu's masterpiece, *La Dame Blanche,* received its American premiere, only one year after its introduction in Paris. It proved an immediate hit and was repeated on Wednesday and Thursday, the first opera in New Orleans to play three nights in a row. What a relief it must have been to all concerned to read, for a change, that "at an early hour the theatre was filled almost to overflowing." "The beautiful overture answered the most sanguine hopes," reported the *Argus.* And as for the performance, this newspaper said it had seldom seen so satisfactory an ensemble. All in all, it was "far superior in every respect to anything of the kind ever before offered in this city." [46]

Within a week, *La Dame Blanche* played for a fourth and fifth time. Before the season ended on June 12, Boieldieu's opera was given six more times, the last four each advertised as "positively the last time" and repeated only because of overwhelming requests. Indeed *La Dame Blanche* was chosen for the closing night of the season when it was hoped that enough money would be taken at the door to repair the front of the theater.[47]

Although it was Boieldieu's music that won New Orleans, with the overture and various airs from his opera dominating concert programs this season, the fact that *La Dame Blanche* was based on two Scott novels, *The Monastery* and *Guy Mannering,* undoubtedly helped in a city devoted to Scott. And who could resist a cast performing entirely in Scottish costumes? [48]

Another new opera which achieved almost as much success was *Der Freischutz* by Weber. To be sure, a version of this stirring opera had played in New Orleans the year before, at Caldwell's theater on Camp Street, but that truncated performance could hardly be compared with the production at the Orleans Theater. Entitled *Robin des Bois* by the French, this German opera was introduced in May, and after a short time while its new and different sounds were being absorbed, it became a favorite. *Der Freischutz* has been freshly recorded in 1960 and hailed as "one of the most melody-laden, professionally adroit compositions ever created for the stage." [49]

Despite the financial doldrums that beset the French theater until the company and productions of the 1826–27 season began to take hold, the followers of French opera fared well enough. In the two and one-half years from January, 1825, to June, 1827, they were treated to no fewer than one hundred and thirty-eight performances of sixty different operas. They could also, if they wished, hear a considerable number of English operas at the American Theater, including English versions of two French operas by Kreutzer— *Lodoiska* and *Paul and Virginia.* Among the twenty-seven composers whose operas were played at the Orleans Theater, Boieldieu, aided by the introduction of his highly successful masterpiece, *La Dame Blanche,* now ranked first. Nine of his operas were given thirty-five playings. After him, in the order of their popularity, came Dalayrac, Isouard, and Auber. Eleven new operas had made their appearance, among them *Der Freischutz* and the aforementioned *La Dame Blanche.*[50]

John Davis now had opera performers and repertoire at his Orleans Theater that could draw crowds, at least during the winter. But as summer approached, past experience and present indications demanded that something be done to hold this fine troupe together. Merely trying to sit through another summer of heat and sparse attendance at the Orleans would be to court a repetition of the dismal story of past years. He had too good a company now to sit supinely by and risk another dissolution of his troupe.

Davis as we have seen was a bold and energetic man. He came to grips with his problem in characteristic fashion. Sometime before the end of May, 1827, he determined upon his solution: Two days after his theater closed on June 12 with *La Dame Blanche,* Davis and his company set sail for New York. He would assault the great Northeast itself with his French opera.[51]

Chapter Six

THE OPERA: LEAVING HOME

On Friday, July 13, 1827, the company from New Orleans opened at New York's famous old Park Theater with a double bill of French operas—*Cendrillon* by Isouard and *Maison a Vendre* by Dalayrac. By the time it left the Park on September 22, Davis' group had played operas forty times in a little over two months. They went next to Philadelphia's Chestnut Street Theater; in three weeks, from September 28 to October 20, they gave sixteen opera performances and then returned to New York to give four more. These two cities were treated to ample variety since the total of sixty performances encompassed thirty-two operas and fourteen composers. Boieldieu's *La Dame Blanche* led the list with six playings in New York and two in Philadelphia; *Robin des Bois (Der Freischutz)* by Weber appeared four times in New York and twice in Philadelphia. *La Dame Blanche* was introduced in New York on August 24, two years after its world premiere in Dresden (1825) and a little under seven months after its American premiere in New Orleans on February 6, 1827. *Der Freischutz* had played unsuccessfully in an English version in Philadelphia three years before. Of the thirty other French operas that made their debuts in the North, six were by Boieldieu, five by Isouard, five by Dalayrac, three by Berton, and two by Auber.[1]

This first venture of the New Orleans Opera outside its home precinct gives us a good index to the quality of America's own opera company. Northern audiences and critics had no considerations of Creole patriotism nor civic pride to color their judgment. And this was the same company that had played in New Orleans during the preceding winter. There was but one addition for the trip. The first violinist of the Havana Opera visited New Orleans in May, and Davis persuaded him to come along. Sometime during the tour a few new importations were expected to join the company, but that would be later.[2]

Moreover, the first visit of the company in New York occurred when that city was still savoring its first prolonged taste of grand opera. Manuel Garcia had brought "the first Italian opera troupe to visit the New World" to New York for a "very successful" season in 1825–26. Besides being eminent in his own right as a tenor, teacher, manager, conductor, and composer, Garcia had sired an imposing trio of singers, among them a daughter soon to become the world renowned Madame Malibran. With his family and others, Garcia presented Italian operas in New York, including that city's premiere of *The Barber of Seville*. (That this is often considered America's introduction to Rossini's masterpiece—and that an authority on the 1830's could write in 1949 that "American opera really began with the Manuel Garcia Company"—only illustrates how unaccountably little is known about the New Orleans opera.) [3]

The 1827 tour of the North was an unqualified critical success. Davis' company was especially praised for its balance in quality. "It is not often the same troupe has five good singers," said the New York *American*. "This company is as good as those heard in the provinces of France and superior to those heard in the Capitals of Europe outside France." The orchestra was hailed as the largest and best ever heard in the North, even before the addition of more musicians just arrived from Germany. In Philadelphia the orchestra's impact was heightened by the fact that this was the first time that city had heard the horn properly played. Paradol, the conductor, aroused uniform enthusiasm, especially for his style on the podium. Above all, the entire group was lauded for its attention to detail, exactness of production, and ensemble. This was a company —not just a star or two surrounded by hack singers and slipshod production.[4]

Davis and his "joyful company" left New York aboard the ship *Margaret* on November 2, and arrived "all in fine order" at New Orleans by the end of the month. On December 2, 1827, they reopened the Orleans Theater with Boieldieu's *Jean de Paris*. After their glowing success in New York and Philadelphia, they might have expected a fine reception at home, but once again the season commenced with indifferent crowds. As before, the combination of Sunday night and a popular opera like *Robin des Bois* usually brought in enough money to repair the losses of Tuesdays and Thursdays. Or a new opera would draw well for a while. But Sundays come only once a week, and new productions are new only for a short time. Attendance was still a matter for concern late in March.[5]

A lesser man might well have given up the whole effort, but John Davis instead prepared to try the North again and to expand the 1828 itinerary to include Boston. And this despite the fact that a good part of the musically successful 1826–28 company had returned to France. Davis simply proposed to meet in Boston a number of new personnel recently engaged in France by his son. This untried troupe would actually make its debut in Boston.[6]

The reinforcements did not arrive in Boston until August 21, after a crossing that took seven weeks. Davis, who had been waiting in Boston trying to feed and pay the rest of his organization since July 25, couldn't afford extensive rehearsals. He immediately gave an orchestra concert which included a Haydn symphony; and on Monday, barely four days after that long sea voyage, the new company opened with Boieldieu's *La Dame Blanche*. Five more operas were performed in Boston before the company moved to New York —this time to the Chatham Theater. After four operas in New York, they journeyed to the Chestnut Street Theater in Philadelphia where they played from September 16 to October 18, 1828.

They returned to New York for four days and then back to Philadelphia to remain from October 28 to November 5. In all, these three cities heard forty-four opera performances and two concerts. Among the eight operas presented for the first time in the North were Spontini's greatest opera, *La Vestale,* given on October 30 in Philadelphia; Auber's *Fiorella* played on November 3, in Philadelphia, only two years after its premiere in Europe; and Mehul's *Joseph,* introduced in Philadelphia on October 15. (*Joseph* and *La Vestale* are considered important operas today.) Finally the French version of Rossini's *Le Barbier de Seville* was played for the first time in all three cities visited.[7]

Davis' second invasion of the North received even warmer acclaim than the first. The orchestra was judged to be better, if possible, than the previous fine aggregation. Several more instrumentalists were imported from Germany, and Davis brought with him from New Orleans an excellent flutist, M. Jandot, who had been playing in the orchestra of Caldwell's American theater on Camp Street. Jandot and his father had emigrated a few months before from France where the father was the first clarinetist in the Bordeaux Theater. "Not a single fault was committed by the instrumental performers," according to one Philadelphian, "and this in itself furnished a great treat to those who, like us, have generally been obliged to make great allowances, even for the best orchestra we could assemble."[8]

The vocalists, too, were again praised for their evenness of quality. In New York they were said to be "in sharp contrast to the American theatre which has a star, but then has buffoons in the secondary roles." In Davis' company, according to this comment, none was mediocre.[9]

The opening night in Boston was marred by one outburst of rowdyism, the reason for which was reflected in the only adversely critical article to appear. A writer in *The Bachelor's Journal* of Boston called the French language a gabble and complained that "it was perfect nonsense to the spectators." He advised the troupe never again to leave New Orleans. Although he admitted the music was excellent, he said it was too "Frenchified."[10]

When the news of this incident and barb reached New Orleans, it drew a fierce retort. The New Orleans *Courier* offered the item for the "laughter and pity" of New Orleanians. It had thought that Boston was the center of intelligence in the United States, the *Courier* said, but now it realized that Bostonians were too ignorant to appreciate the New Orleans opera. "A cock fight . . . would be more to the taste of Bostonians than the French opera. . . . But we know that in New York, Philadelphia, Baltimore, Charleston . . . they love this Frenchified music, altho' it would be unable to produce such powerful effects on the nerves of Yankees, as the mighty Orchestra of Fiddlers who play their reels." [11]

Actually Boston didn't deserve such sarcasm. The mayor of that city and several leading citizens apologized for this one display of bad manners, and when the Boston engagement ended, Bostonians acknowledged that "we have never before heard so good theatrical music." [12]

Nor, for that matter, had New Orleans. Davis' company was back home again on December 7, 1828, with a new opera and the improvement was quickly noticed. When *The Barber of Seville* was played on Sunday, December 21, the consensus was that it had never been done so well before. Perhaps because of this high quality, or perhaps because the Boston incident still rankled, there were no complaints about attendance this season. Late in July, 1829, the troupe departed again for the North, but this trip would omit Boston.[13]

Davis' third summer tour was marred by the deaths of two of the company during the voyage and by the departure for France of his star soprano, Mme. Alexandre, at the close of the tour. On the brighter side, Davis engaged in New York a corps of ballet dancers which was better than anything yet seen in New Orleans. The leader was Benoni, who had been first dancer of the Theatre de la Monnaie in Bruxelles, and his wife, Mlle. Feltmann, the premier danseuse at the same theater. Mlle. Feltmann's father, a fine comedy dancer, and her five year old daughter, already an accomplished dancer, were included, while another mother and daughter, Adele and Esther Ravenot, made up the rest of the corps.[14]

The 1829 tour, in which Baltimore replaced Boston, marks another step in the artistic growth of the New Orleans company. Most of the previous repertoire required relatively light voices, but now the operas of composers like Auber and Herold, and the addition of more of Rossini's operas, made greater demands upon the performers. Opera was steadily developing, becoming more complex and difficult musically. If at first Davis' lead singers were not all up to these increased requirements, this was again more than compensated for by the excellence of the whole. And the orchestra needed no compensations. Augmented once more by additions in New York and Philadelphia, it was capable of playing the more advanced compositions without trouble. Among these were Rossini's *La Pie Voleuse* (*La Gazza Ladra*) and his *Dame du Lac,* as well as Herold's most recent opera, *Marie,* all given for the first time in the North.[15]

On Sunday, November 22, 1829, the troupe was home again to open the season with *Marie.* New Orleans was now increasingly aware of the treasure it possessed in its resident opera company. Although the deserted house was not yet a thing of the past, and severe monetary crises were yet to come, the constant improvement in quality, the repeated acclaim in the North, and the steady growth of the city were combining to ease for a time the financial doldrums which had so often discouraged the company. New Orleanians were especially delighted with the new corps de ballet. It was proudly held that the theater in Bruxelles had been unable to replace Benoni and that Estelle Feltmann's debut at the Grand Opera in Paris had been brilliant. The success that these dancers enjoyed in the North before coming to New Orleans enhanced their appeal. One new ballet, introduced on a Sunday, drew more patrons than the Orleans Theater could hold. For the first time a fairly regular column of opera news, comment, and criticism appeared.[16]

It was therefore, a serious blow to Davis when in February, 1830, John Caldwell enticed these dancers away from the French theater to present them in his rival American theater on Camp Street. However, two could play that game. The Camp Street Theater had engaged a renowned singer, Madame Feron, now in the United States after years of success in San Carlo, La Scala, the Paris opera, and in London. Caldwell introduced her on March 3, in *The Bar-*

ber of Seville. Although the supporting cast was miserable, the orchestra poorly directed, and Madame herself was required to insert such songs as "The Arab Steed" and "An Old Man Would Be Wooing," she presented a definite challenge to the Orleans Theater. But soon a rumor spread that Madame would shortly appear at the Orleans, where she would have support worthy of her talent. At least twice the Camp Street managers vigorously denied this rumor in the press and advised the public to hear Madame Feron now, at the Camp Street Theater, while there was still a chance. April 3 was to be her "positively last appearance" in New Orleans, yet ten days later she opened at the Orleans Theater in Rossini's *Barber of Seville,* with the kind of support that only the French company could give. She sang four more operas there before the end of April. Davis had repaired, at least in part, the damage caused by the loss of his ballet troupe.[17]

The fourth northern journey (1830) to New York, Philadelphia, and Baltimore saw a further reorganization of the company. One of the newcomers was Gregorio Curto, a bass singer from the Paris Opera. (Curto would settle in New Orleans to become an influential teacher, conductor and composer, numbering among his vocal students, years later, Minnie Hauk. Indeed, she attributed her great career in no small part to the solid foundation given her by Curto.)[18]

Another newcomer was Mme. St. Clair, who had the difficult task of replacing Mme. Alexandre, a favorite wherever she sang. But St. Clair, although not pretty, was young and possessed a pure, fresh voice. Her performance in *The Barber of Seville* stood the comparison admirably, not only with her predecessor, Mme. Alexandre, but with Malibran as well. In fact, the 1830 company was held to be, on the whole, superior to that of 1829.[19]

Davis had intended to return to Boston to commence the fourth tour, but the ship carrying indispensable replacements from France was late and the dates for the Park Theater in New York were set, so the company had to skip Boston. Charles-Simon Catel's *L'Auberge de Bagnieres,* Jean François Le Sueur's *La Caverne,* and Gretry's *Zemire et Azor* were the only new presentations, while the favorite was Rossini's *La Gazza Ladra,* which played five times.[20]

During this summer, M. Develle, Davis' chief set designer and scene painter, occupied his time by entirely redecorating and repainting the Orleans Theater. Hence the new company found a fresh house awaiting it when it disembarked from the ship "Ann-Mary-Ann" on November 10 after a seventeen-day voyage from Baltimore.[21]

Lest there be too much of the new, an old favorite, *La Dame Blanche,* was chosen to open the season of 1830–31 on November 14. "Thanks to Davis, all is of the best, nothing is neglected," exulted one enthusiastic viewer. Everyone was urged to attend. For if Rossini, plus St. Clair, Letellier, and Curto couldn't fill the house, warned the *Courier* it would "bespeak a want of taste in our public" that all should be very unwilling to admit. Mme. St. Clair especially was hailed as the best singer ever heard in New Orleans. (In December, when the rival American theater on Camp Street brought Mrs. Pearman to the city, she was described as the only singer in America who might compare with St. Clair, thus claiming for New Orleans the two best sopranos in America.)[22]

Nevertheless, it seemed prudent to invoke French patriotism and civic pride again. The *Courier* urged New Orleanians to remember that their opera was unique in the United States. Just as the Greeks had their Parthenon and the Romans their Pantheon, so New Orleans had its French opera, this journal observed. "It is the pride and hope of the generation raised on the ruin of the old French regime."[23]

One reason such pleadings continued to be necessary for the support of this better-than-ever opera company was the lure of the "tricolor" balls, those same mixed gatherings that had helped finance the opera in its beginnings. "Public taste is vitiated and led out of its legitimate channels by those abominable places" as one moralist put it. But also there were many who tired of what seemed to them the endless singing and recitative of French opera. Highly trained, serious singers in legitimate opera, then as now, were not always attractive to the average man. When the Camp Street Theater offered *The Marriage of Figaro* with Mr. and Mrs. Cramer Plumer, few came, in spite of the argument that "one good opera . . . [is] worth a hundred mediocre tragedies." A singer of light popular songs, Clara Fisher, followed the Plumers in the same theater and drew well. Her style, according to the *Courier,* "tho' not so scientific as that of the Plumers, has infinitely more of nature and sentiment, which is ever sure to please the many, while but few are capable of enjoying an artificial display of music." [24]

Of course this view was strongly disputed by opera supporters, one of whom described Miss Fisher as merely "the favorite puppet of the 'Punch and Judy' portion of the theatrical world." But the newspaper had the last word, pointing out the inescapable fact that "the Plumers have sung to comparatively empty benches . . . [while] Miss Fisher has constantly attracted good houses." And why? Because "the highest attainments of art . . . please only those who have made it their passion or their study." [25]

On the other hand, there were those who argued that what the theater needed was more rather than less demanding music. "It is now evident," said one, "that if Mr. Caldwell wishes to unite and attract the immense and opulent audience of this city, he must strengthen his orchestra, provide operatic talent and cultivate the opera." Nor could Caldwell claim that he had tried better music and found it wanting in attraction for the customers since his theater had "never been provided with superior music." [26]

Such advice was worth a try. It so happened that two married couples of outstanding singers were in New Orleans at this time— Mr. and Mrs. Plumer and Mr. and Mrs. Pearman. Caldwell strengthened his orchestra with teachers and amateurs to accompany all four singers in a performance of Boieldieu's *Jean de Paris.* "As strong a cast as it has ever been produced with in the United States," said one of the American newspapers in the city, thus getting in a sly dig at the French company which had performed *Jean de Paris* many times.[27]

Thus the season of 1830–31 saw more and better operas in New Orleans than ever before. Besides the regular offerings at the Orleans Theater by the steadily improving and enlarging French company, there were more than a few major operas at the American theater on Camp Street where Madame Fearon, the Plumers and the Pearmans had been introduced to New Orleans.

For the fifth consecutive summer, Davis took his company, now over fifty strong, to New York and Philadelphia in 1831. The musical event of this trip was *La Muette de Portici*, Auber's greatest opera, which was introduced in New York on August 15. *La Muette* played four times in New York and three in Philadelphia. (Its American premiere had been on April 29, 1831, in New Orleans.) Auber, Rossini, and Boieldieu were the most frequently played composers this summer. Besides *La Muette de Portici*, other Northern premieres were Rossini's *Le Comte Ory*, Louis Herold's *La Clochette*, and Auber's *Fra Diavolo*, all of which had played previously in New Orleans. In general, Davis' company was as well liked in the North as before.[28]

Unfortunately, the company was marred by dissension that arose among Davis and some of his players. Two of them departed for France, while the conductor and his wife took their time returning to New Orleans. In consequence, although Davis was expected to come back to New Orleans with a group considerably strengthened by the addition of some highly paid singers, the truth was that the company was unable to present anything more than vaudeville for a week after beginning the home season in late November.[29]

When Rossini's *La Gazza Ladra* opened the opera season on December 4, the home fans were quick to criticize. "An immense crowd filled our beautiful theatre early last Sunday night," wrote one, "and everyone waited impatiently the roll of the drum, the signal for the commencement of the overture. . . . A profound silence reigned—finally the drum rolled, and, thrilling with pleasure, I awaited the trill on the fourth beat of the measure. But what extreme surprise, not an instrument blew together!" And when the clarinet finally came in, it was a half tone flat, a fault which annoyed all through the opera since the clarinet has a major part in *La Gazza Ladra*. Even so, this listener insisted that the orchestra was the best in the land, needing only a better first clarinet.[30]

Undoubtedly the rest of the season's performances improved over this unpromising start, but the absence of much newspaper comment, as well as a noticeable lack of benefits for the stars, suggests that the company was indeed somewhat under par. This alone might well have discouraged Davis from attempting a sixth summer tour in 1832. If he was undecided, the widespread prevalence of cholera in the North that summer made a tour unadvisable in any case. Apparently the players were simply left to get through the summer as best they could. In late May, a number of them appearing in an orphans' benefit were advertised as "attached to the late company of Mr. Davis." [31]

On October 25, the cholera hit New Orleans, to spread devastation such as none this city of epidemics had yet known. In the space of ten days one of every six inhabitants died. The dead could not be collected fast enough, and coffins were soon unobtainable. Many of the dead were simply weighted and dropped into the Mississippi; others were gathered in a heap and burned. Many unembalmed and largely unidentified bodies were simply buried in hastily dug, large common graves. [32]

Although the cholera epidemic had run its short but dreadful course by the time the Orleans Theater commenced the new season with *La Dame Blanche* on Sunday, November 25, 1832, the effects of the plague could be seen in the attendance. Women especially stayed away, either in mourning or from fear of venturing out. And the company itself had at least eight newcomers to replace those who had returned to France. [33]

The result was, according to the *Courier,* that *La Dame Blanche* was not as well performed as in the past. The company as yet lacked ensemble, the choruses were weak, and the orchestra suffered from reduced numbers. However, the new conductor, Andre Huny, formerly director of the orchestra at the Theatre Feydeau in France, provided gratification and hope. "What could he do . . . with a complete orchestra and the necessary chorus?" asked one, while lavishing praise for what he had done "with the few elements he had." And although smaller than desired, the orchestra was still "strong and brilliant in the distinguished artists that compose it." But no matter how accomplished the conductor and individual musicians might be, the essential lacks remained. "In spite of all the zeal of the orchestra leader and his talent, one cannot hide that . . . [the opera] needs an orchestra more full and rich, and more sonorous

than the orchestra and chorus we have now," said Guillaume Montmain, who was probably the city's first regular critic.[34]

This general tone of disappointment continued throughout the
season of 1832–33. The lead tenor had too light a voice for grand
opera; likewise the soprano; the bass sang well enough but couldn't
act; a corps de ballet was sadly missed; the new operas presented
had bad lyrics and plots—"all cliches of the theater"; the duets
lacked color; too many of the premieres were already years old in
Paris; and similar complaints.[35]

Little wonder then that Davis tried startling devices to improve
attendance. No less an opera than *The Barber of Seville* was coupled with a duel on the stage. A troupe of ten acrobats, the Ravel
family, was brought in at the beginning of April to remain for over
a month, appearing along with various operas.[36]

In a way these acrobats did enhance the appreciation of opera in
New Orleans. On a Sunday, May 19, the Orleans gave Michele
Enrico Carafa's little opera, *Jenny*. This was the first time since
April 2 that an opera did not share the stage with the Ravel acrobats. "The opera Jenny has completely reconciled the true lovers of
the French theatre of this city," sighed Guillaume Montmain. "Not
that the opera Jenny is a masterpiece, almost to the contrary, but
because it has succeeded in putting an end to these interminable
representations of tight rope, tours de force and pantomimes, very
extraordinary no doubt, but little appropriate to the only . . .
palladium of the tongues of our fathers in New Orleans." [37]

When the news got about that Davis intended to try the North
again with this company, Montmain could only remark, "I wish it
pleasure, but I doubt that with the elements composing it it will
have a huge success—but God's will be done." Yet this tour, the
sixth and final one for John Davis, turned out much better than
Montmain expected. For three months, from July 19 to October 16,
1833, the company of fifty strong played in all four northern cities
of Boston, New York, Philadelphia, and Baltimore with great success.[38]

Bostonians were all appreciation this time, proclaiming the orchestra one of the best they had ever heard, even though their own Handel and Haydn Society orchestra had then been in existence eighteen years. The music alone was said to be worth the price of entry. But again it was the ensemble that drew the highest praise. Gottlieb Graupner, Boston's best known musician, who had played in Haydn's orchestra in London and was one of the three founders of the Boston Handel and Haydn Society, added his double bass to the French orchestra during its stay in Boston.[39]

New York was equally pleased, noting that "the French opera has perfectly succeeded. The house was full at each performance." Here, too, the ensemble was singled out: "Our English opera has some better singers, but for the . . . whole, the French have it over the others." Four more operas were introduced in the North: *Zampa* and *Le Pre aux Clercs* by Herold; *Le Philtre* by Auber; and *Le Dilettante d'Avignon* by Jacques Halevy. *Zampa* played eight times and in all four cities before the tour ended.[40]

In some other respects, however, the company did not fare so well. A citizen of Boston publicly denounced the personal conduct of these strangers in that proper community. And dissension, a perennial hazard for any large troupe on the road, took a severe toll. No fewer than five of the leads departed to Havana. The remainder of the company arrived finally in New Orleans in November "sadly bruised and wounded—it had had enough of the nomadic life." Montmain compared the troupe to a decimated cavalry squadron without new recruits. It was, he said, "broken physically and in morale." John Davis would never try the road again.[41]

Had these years of tour been a failure then, and was the company in decline? By no means. When one pauses to consider the problems of taking around fifty artists on tour in the years from 1827 to 1833, the wonder is that the endeavor succeeded as well as it did. In truth, it was an astonishing accomplishment, one that left a permanent imprint on the course of music in America. Boston, Philadelphia, and Baltimore got their first tastes of a regular opera company; and in the two latter cities, the success of Davis' production of *Der Freischutz* presented a sharp contrast to the costly failure of local productions of the same opera shortly before. New York, to be sure, had already encountered grand opera when Manuel Garcia's company played in the two seasons immediately preceding the visits of the New Orleans company. But it found the latter to be "fully equal to that we imported from foreigners," and it enjoyed six seasons of such opera in what otherwise would have been a barren period.[42]

Most impressive, however, is the sheer abundance of the musical feast laid before northeastern cities. In those six summers, the New Orleans players presented sixty-one different operas by twenty-four composers for a total of two hundred and fifty-one opera performances. New York got one hundred operas, Philadelphia one hundred and nine, Boston twelve, and Baltimore thirty. Operas by Isouard, Dalayrac, Boieldieu, Bochsa, Fetis, Cherubini, Auber, Weber, Solier, Gaveaux, Berton, Herold, Della Maria, Gretry, Mehul, Carafa, Rossini, Lebrun, Devienne, Spontini, Catel, Le Sueur, Mozart, and Halevy appeared, most of them for the first time in the Northeast. The most popular composers were Boieldieu, seven of whose operas were given fifty times; Auber, with seven operas played forty-three times; Rossini, with three operas played twenty-eight times; Isouard, with five operas played twenty-five times; Herold, with five operas played twenty times; Weber, whose single opera *Der Freischutz* played sixteen times; Dalayrac, with six operas played fourteen times; and Gretry, with four operas played eight times.

Among single operas, the most performed were Boieldieu's *La Dame Blanche* with twenty-four playings; Weber's *Der Freischutz*, sixteen playings; Rossini's *Le Barbier de Seville,* thirteen; Auber's *La Muette de Portici,* twelve; Isouard's *Joconde,* eleven; Auber's *Le Macon,* eight; Herold's *Zampa,* eight; and Isouard's *Le Rendezvous Bourgeois,* seven.

In any one summer, the most successful operas were *Zampa,* played eight times in 1833, and *La Dame Blanche,* played eight times in 1827. *La Muette de Portici* played seven times in 1831; *Der Freischutz,* six times in 1827; *Le Barbier de Seville,* five times in 1828; and *La Pie Voleuse (La Gazza Ladra),* five times in 1830. On the other hand, several operas appeared once, and then no more, apparently withdrawn as failure. Among these were Gasparo Spontini's *La Vestale,* Halevy's *Le Dilettante d'Avignon,* Cherubini's *Les Deux Journees,* and unaccountably, Mozart's *Les Noces de Figaro.* Rossini's *Le Comte Ory* appeared twice in 1831 and then only once again in 1833.[43]

But the greatest achievement during these years of travel was the simple perseverance of this unique opera company at home in New Orleans. From the fall of 1827 through the spring of 1833, the Orleans Theater produced a total of 367 opera performances, representing eighty-five operas by thirty-two composers. No fewer than twenty-seven new operas by twelve composers were introduced. As before, Boieldieu, thanks to *La Dame Blanche,* was the most popular composer—nine of his operas played sixty-eight times. Of these *La Dame Blanche* had fifteen playings, *Jean de Paris* had eleven, and *Le Petit Chaperon Rouge* had nine. Auber now ranked second, having eleven operas performed sixty-seven times. His most popular were *La Fiancee,* with twelve playings; *La Muette de Portici,* with ten playings; and *Le Macon,* with nine playings. The growing popularity of Rossini made itself evident with six of his operas being performed thirty-seven times—*Le Barbier de Seville* accounted for sixteen; *La Pie Voleuse* (*La Gazza Ladra*), nine; and *Le Comte Ory,* seven. Finally, Dalayrac remained popular with six operas played twenty-seven times. Other composers who had ten or more playings were Herold with nineteen (*Marie* accounted for eleven of these); Carafa with sixteen (*Le Solitaire* accounted for twelve); Isouard fourteen; Gaveaux thirteen; Mehul, Robert Bochsa, and Gretry ten each.[44]

Some interesting comparisons with the Northeast present themselves. Operas like *La Dame Blanche, Der Freischutz, Le Barbier de Seville, La Muette de Portici, Jean de Paris,* and *La Gazza Ladra* proved popular at home and on tour. Mozart's *Les Noces de Figaro* appeared only once in New Orleans as in New York. In contrast, Bochsa's *La Lettre de Change,* which played only once in the North, played ten times in New Orleans. But, for the most part, the operatic tastes of the North and of New Orleans were strikingly similar.[45]

James Caldwell's American theater on Camp Street had also been musically busy during 1827–33. Over one hundred performances of operas and near-operas took place, among them *The Beggar's Opera*. As in the Orleans Theater, Rossini was immensely popular. *Cinderella,* an English adaptation by Lacy of Rossini's *La Cenerentola,* played twenty times from its first introduction on February 18, 1833, to May 18, 1833. An English version of *The Barber of Seville* appeared six times on Camp Street, making the total for both theaters reach twenty-two. Likewise, an English version of Boieldieu's *Jean de Paris* played six times on Camp Street as well as eleven times in the French house. Thus on Wednesday night, March 17, 1830, one could hear *Jean de Paris* in English at the Camp Street Theater and on the following night compare it with the French rendering at the Orleans Theater. Mozart fared better in the American theater than he did in the French. His *Marriage of Figaro* appeared five times, and *Don Giovanni* was also produced.[46]

" . . . operas appear to amuse our citizens more than any other form of public amusement. . . ."

Chapter Seven

THE OPERA: SETTLING DOWN

*T*hus the fall of 1833 found a weary and discouraged group of musicians home once again in New Orleans. Nor would the season to come lighten their spirits much. As if to try them to the utmost, winter came that year with unprecedented fury. On January 3, four inches of snow fell, making streets, rooftops, and trees a vision in white rarely seen in the Crescent City. Even sleighs appeared in the streets, while delighted youngsters ice-skated in the Place d'Armes, on Rampart Street, and elsewhere. All this meant fun and frolic for many, but a disaster for the theater. Even dancing attendance fell off.[1]

The snow had barely melted when a new distraction appeared. Over on Camp Street, James Caldwell brought the well-known English singers, Mrs. Elizabeth Austin and John Sinclair, to his theater. Caldwell had already staged some English operas featuring Mrs. Knight, and with these additions he had a strong attraction. *Cinderella*, which had proved so popular last season, was frequently played, along with *The Barber of Seville, The Marriage of Figaro* (arranged by Bishop), *The Beggar's Opera, Guy Mannering, Rob Roy, John of Paris, Masaniello,* and *Fra Diavolo.*[2]

This was more ambitious opera fare than the American theater had yet presented, and in spite of a weak orchestra and poor support, Mrs. Austin, who was acclaimed as "superior to any . . . before heard in this city," drew many habitual patrons of the Orleans Theater over to the house on Camp Street. And as music lovers swelled Caldwell's attendance, they insisted that his orchestra be improved. At least two flutes, two clarinets, two horns, an oboe, and a trombone should be added, said one, demanding at the same time a change in conductors. "If the expense of maintaining a full orchestra cannot be supported, let it not at least be spared during the engagements of M. Sinclair and Mrs. Austin." [3]

Very soon came the good news that another horn and clarinet had been engaged, along with a new conductor who proved to be none other than that former favorite of the Orleans Theater, M. Paradol! Further additions to both the orchestra and chorus rounded out the support for Mrs. Austin, until it was "as perfect as possible." Among the additions was a prominent flutist from New York, reputed to be unsurpassed in the United States. By now, even that most partisan of French newspapers, the *Bee,* was forced to concede that the American theater was producing operas "in a style of taste and splendour," with an orchestra only a "little inferior to the Orleans Theatre." John Davis faced strong competition on Camp Street.[4]

Only one flaw marred the glowing picture at the American theater. The audience did not always behave in keeping with the new elegance of orchestra and singers. Perhaps the regular customers simply did not know how to take this more serious music. At any rate shouts, hurrahs, demands for repeated encores, and fights frequently made an evening at the Camp a memorable experience.[5]

Here was at least one thing at the American theater that the French could point to with scorn. Some American papers at first defended the behavior of their countrymen, arguing that decorum at the American theater was just as orderly as at any other, and accusing the French of criticizing the Camp Street audience simply because it was American. But when a swordsman laid open a doctor's head just outside the theater; when another man suffered a critical stab in the abdomen; and when the management felt compelled to employ armed guards inside the theater, it was plain that the French weren't merely carping. The *Louisiana Advertiser,* an American paper, soon admitted that frequent fights were a hazard around the American theater. And in April a man was stabbed to death in front of the theater.[6]

Of course the French press delighted in reporting "these nightly outbreakings" and the necessity for armed guards on Camp Street. In contrast, the French theater did not need nor would it tolerate such a guard, the *Bee* said smugly. The unkindest cut came from the editor of the *Courier* who charged that in the American theater although "one lifts his voice against the presence of the guard, and another complains that the parquette has been polluted by lewdness; yet not a syllable has been uttered against the sins of the stage." He was referring to *The Beggar's Opera* which he said "was voted a failure on all hands," but not criticized in the American press because of a conspiracy of silence among Caldwell's newspaper friends.[7]

Nevertheless there were many—even many French—who were satisfied with the performances at the American theater, and the engagement there of Mrs. Austin, coupled with the improved orchestra led by Paradol, hurt the French box office. When to this is added the discouragement of the troupe that had returned in the fall, plus the ice and snow in January, one sees that 1833–34 proved to be another hard time for the Orleans Theater. When the unhappy season ended, Guillaume Montmain summed it up. He considered the house—so full at times but often so deserted. Two of the lead singers, the conductor, the first oboe, and some others had gone back to France. He wished that New Orleans had a theater worthy of her, but the departure of the best of the company with little more than a *bon jour* or a *bon soir* to take home was discouraging. He doubted that replacements could be found. Montmain was a man of little faith—New Orleans was approaching her most brilliant years of opera.[8]

With stubborn courage John Davis managed to secure a new troupe for the season of 1834–35. New Orleans heard that he had even obtained some of the best artists in Europe. When the season opened on November 20, with six newcomers making their debuts in *La Dame Blanche,* the rejuvenated company lived up to these high hopes. Mme. St. Clair, who had so captured the hearts of New Orleanians for the past four years, was one of the few familiar voices to return. Her fans insisted that she was now better than ever, fully capable of matching Mme. Malibran anywhere. Heyman, the new tenor, seemed the best yet, and the entire company appeared to be better than it had been for many years. Davis had seemingly wrought another miracle.[9]

Of course wherever there is a theater, especially one as close to the people as this one was, there will be some dissatisfaction. A long letter appeared in the *Louisiana Advertiser* just before Christmas. Because it tells so much of costs, salaries, problems, and the position of the opera in the community, it is worth reproducing in part. The writer of this letter stated that he had frequently offered articles to editors who said they would be happy to have them. But the moment he mentioned that they were about the theater—a subject he claimed to know, not having missed a performance—he detected a coolness. Adverse criticism of the theater was not welcome. Had he considered, he would be asked, that there was but the one French theater, and that it was two thousand leagues from France? One editor laid down these rules for any article dealing with the theater:

You must agree not to say that St. Victor massacres all his roles by charging them to death. That Madame St. Clair has lost a part of her voice and that her playing is always cold, which does not however justify the administration in seeking to show ingratitude towards her after having so well profited from her good days. If you will not say that Victorin plays all his roles in the same manner, like an old clock striking always the same tone. That Mademoiselle Dupuis seems to believe that the freshness of her voice dispenses with the need of any soul in her playing.

If you do not tell me, above all, that Monsieur Davis maintains his dramatic omnipotence in order to foist on the public all the old, passe productions it pleases him to give. That if he wished to make some reasonable sacrifices, he would have been able to mount a better assorted troupe, and to give us something more than the shadow, the appearance of a chorus.

That he profited, as a tyrant, from the uncertain and isolated position of unfortunate actors so far from their country, in order to impose on them his caprices, and to take out on them the reproaches the public gives him. That in order to economize 100 miserable dollars a month, that it would cost him to reengage Madame Clozel, he prefers to give us a caricature of dramas.

Other editors, the letter went on, were all the same. One nearly wept, pleading how good John Davis was; how he gave the "greatest example of generosity in the memory of man" when he produced Meyerbeer's *Robert le Diable* at a cost of twenty thousand dollars, knowing full well it wouldn't draw over six thousand—thus sacrificing fourteen thousand dollars simply to please the public. However, the complaining writer did not contest these figures and before closing added that he wanted to thank the danseuse, Mme. Millot, for the pleasure she gave, and to thank and praise Heyman "for his excellent method, his fresh and pure voice, his profound art." [10]

Now here is a long grumble that really speaks quite well of the opera. Most of the criticism is directed mainly against Davis and the dramatic side of the company. Only the chorus comes in for any real complaint on the musical side—and then only regarding its size. True, the writer considers St. Clair's voice as beyond its peak, but one may doubt that. She was still young (this was only her fifth season in New Orleans), and she had been steadily growing in favor. Finally, the writer praises the singing of Dupuis and Heyman, as well as the dancing of Millot.

The criticism of the repertoire did find an echo in Montmain who also thought the season dulled by repeated playings of old pieces. But it is clear that Montmain too referred chiefly to dramas; and unlike the other writer, Montmain considered the chorus, as well as the orchestra, to be strong points of the opera.[11]

Possibly to relieve the dullness complained of, the management hired a tight rope walker to share the bills. "This," said Montmain, "is the sad state into which our theater has fallen, thanks to the indifference of the public, which prefers acrobats. The Orleans Theatre will die a beautiful death if it is not better sustained, and we poor French by birth will be reduced to hearing our tongue only in the legislature or the city council. What a beautiful prospect." [12]

It is noticeable that such laments over the public's indifference always seem to occur during the season; in retrospect the same critics claimed that Davis profited greatly. So too the French might carp at the quality of their opera, but when the Americans sought to challenge it, the carpers changed their tune. The sharp rivalry that developed between the two theaters over Meyerbeer's new opera, *Robert le Diable,* is a case in point.

On Camp Street the season had begun with the usual English operas such as *Cinderella* and *Rob Roy.* As 1834 ended, however, the theater engaged a fine bass singer named Reynoldson to take charge of all music, and especially to produce Italian and French operas. *Robert le Diable,* which had been introduced in Paris only three years before, was to be the first. This meant that the American theater was planning to be the first to give New Orleans the greatest French opera to date.[13]

Montmain cried out that he almost couldn't believe it. To think of the Americans attempting Meyerbeer's masterpiece with an orchestra of not over fifteen men! He fervently hoped the Orleans would make haste to produce this opera. Almost at once one finds a different tone towards Davis' company in the French press. A performance of Herold's *Zampa* at the Orleans was compared with the same opera as given on Camp Street. The former came out far superior in every respect, from the orchestra to the accommodations —"in short the *tout ensemble.*" And again, in reviewing *The Barber of Seville* at the Camp Street Theater, the *Bee* advised all who wished to "see and hear it properly done" to go instead to the Orleans.[14]

As soon as it became known that both theaters were rehearsing *Robert le Diable,* the Americans were animated by a strong desire to excel the long-superior French house. Their goal was to produce a *Robert* that would be "more pleasing and perfect" than the one being prepared by the French. The Americans intended especially to go all out for lavish scenery, and they were even willing to alter the plot itself if this would give greater scope to the efforts of the scenarist and mechanist. One scene, they claimed, would exceed anything ever witnessed "in this or any other country." [15]

On Monday, March 30, 1835, *Robert le Diable* was played for the first time in the United States in the theater on Camp Street, and the Americans had beaten the French in presenting a great French opera in New Orleans. As if this alone, plus the spectacular scenery,

New Orleans' love of opera was virtually unlimited. French, Italian, and American compositions were received with warm applause.

might not insure a full house, the Americans offered the added attraction of Daddy Rice, the father of American minstrelsy, who was then at the height of his fame. The music of Meyerbeer, along with "Oh! Hush" and "Jump Jim Crow," did indeed pack the theater.[16]

An American viewer was quick to praise the Camp Street effort. He found the scenery, machinery, and costumes all to be splendid. Only the orchestra might not be up to the rest, although it was better than he had expected; and this was more than offset by the great advantage of having Reynoldson to direct. Reynoldson had seen the opera in Paris directed by Meyerbeer himself, had heard it again in London, and had produced it as a drama in New York.[17]

The French critic, Montmain, saw the opera with different eyes and heard it with different ears:

A goodly number of French were there to assure themselves whether the masterpiece of modern French operas would be played as announced, that is to say, in a manner worthy of its high reputation. Great was their disappointment, not because they hoped to see it done as well as in Paris, when even London couldn't succeed at that, but they hoped at least that a piece so long in rehearsal, and staged at a cost, according to the notices, of little less than $10,000, would offer the public as agreeable an evening as possible. We will ask the true connoisseurs first if they believe an orchestra of 15 or 16 musicians suffices to play an opera which, at the least, demands about 40 and demands a skillful execution and not one gap in the instrumentation.

. . . We will not pass on the ineptness of the costumes because it is not this that should draw the major attention of the critic. We will only remark that, true or false, they did not enter much in the budget of expenses. For a piece of this calibre, if the costumes are not exact they should at least be fresh.

Montmain had kinder words for the scenery which in fact, he said, rated the most applause. Even so, some of it, he thought, would have been laughed at in Paris. And as for the singing, Montmain could only say "that it was truly pitiful . . . we defy any man of taste to show us a spot in the opera . . . sung as it should be, as it is in Italy, France or Germany." Montmain promised to return to *Robert le Diable* when it appeared at the Orleans Theater, that is, he ended despairingly, if it ever got to be played at the French house.[18]

The Americans were not perturbed. Whether it was the opera or Daddy Rice's "Jim Crow" that drew the crowds, the Camp Theater played *Robert le Diable* five successive days. Moreover, there were ardent defenders of the American production to answer Montmain specifically. One of these conceded a shortage of nuns in the chorus, but insisted that the scenery was excellent, the costumes not at all old, and that there were no soloists at the Orleans Theater any better than Mrs. Knight, Hodges, Reynoldson, and Thorne. The writer did admit that a production of *Robert* at the French theater might have better instrumental music, primarily because of certain advantages: a large organ and the fine orchestra. (*Robert le Diable* and *Zampa* were the first two operas requiring an organ on stage.) So a French production might have more taste in dress and "a greater supernumerary corps of ladies for nuns," but could not excel in other respects. Another American denied that this production cost any less than ten thousand dollars, and argued that it surpassed "anything of the kind ever before presented to the New Orleans public." [19]

Robert played three more times during April—thus making a total of eight showings on Camp Street—before the French presented their version on May 12, six weeks after the American premiere. It was now the Americans' turn to be critical. [20]

"We went," said one, "determined to be pleased, and desirous . . . to give the preference to . . . this theatre. We succeeded in our resolution but not in our wishes." Of course the French orchestra was unquestionably the better, but still an American liked to hear more wind and brass instruments. Aside from this, the French outdid the Americans only in the chorus and the nuns. All of the French lead singers were inferior except for Mme. St. Clair, who, this American had to admit, got better all the time. But the scenery, machinery, dresses, and decorations were not up to the American production; and the French, moreover, took too long between acts. [21]

A stranger reading the reviews might have thought that the French were speaking of an entirely different production. It was called nothing less than "an epoch in the French theater of New Orleans." They explained its failure to be first on the boards as simply due to the fact that the Orleans Theater wisely waited until the opera could be performed "in a manner, if not perfect, at least rational and dignified for a public rich and enlightened." The staging and scenery showed conclusively that M. Develle, the scenarist, ranked among the finest. And lastly, "What shall we say of the orchestra? Enriched with some additional talent it proved easily and fully that it merited the title accorded it by visitors of being the best in the United States." [22]

With *Robert le Diable* at long last on the stage of the Orleans Theater in what must have been a much more accurate and worthy production, the Camp Theater ceased its showings of that opera. It was enough to have been first, if not best, in giving *Robert le Diable* to New Orleans. The Americans did continue to offer the third act of the opera occasionally, for this contained a cloister scene which the Americans insisted was "more effective and better got up" than the one on Orleans Street. Any Creole ladies who doubted this were invited to come and see for themselves.[23]

During the remainder of the season, *Robert* played six more times at the French theater. Thus with the eight showings on Camp Street, an opera lover could have seen *Robert le Diable* fifteen times in less than three months. Though probably no one did.[24]

A year before, James Caldwell had retired from the active management of his theater on Camp Street, giving a five-year lease to Richard Russell and James S. Rowe. Caldwell now had larger plans. His success both in drama and in music prompted him to plan an ambitious new theater, one which would not only outdo the other two in size and splendor, but would be, indeed, the largest in the entire United States. What was more, this theater could, if he desired, enable him to challenge the pre-eminence of the Orleans Theater in music. It has been said that nothing less than this was his goal.[25]

On May 9, 1835, construction began on St. Charles Street. As the grandeur of the structure emerged, New Orleans swelled with pride. Here was not only a wonderful theater, exulted one observer after construction had been underway for four months, but Caldwell

. . . will have connected with it an arcade for dry goods and other stores; also a hotel, a restaurant, a bath house, and (we believe) a cigar divan, similar to those of London and Paris. He will have excellent boudoirs attached to the dress circle in the theater, with fine saloons—his baths will be about forty, of marble and tin—his restaurant will contain refreshments of all kinds at every hour till midnight—his hotel will contain about 100 separate rooms for single gentlemen—and his cigar divan will contain all the principal periodicals of the day, with chess and backgammon boards, liquors, coffee and cigars.[26]

High overhead was to be a magnificent chandelier, weighing at least 2 tons, and measuring 14 feet in diameter. The light would come from 250 burners, reflected by 23,000 pieces of prismatic flint glass. In all, Caldwell would invest more than $325,000 in his pleasure dome.[27]

Speculation was high about the orchestra to go with such a grand palace, the one certainty being that only the top professionals in the country would be engaged. At the time two great rivals, Alessandro Gambati and John T. Norton, were enlivening New York with a trumpet contest in Niblo's Gardens. When the news spread that both of these men would be coming, along with James Kendall on clarinet and Felippe Cioffi on trombone, as well as a host of others equally well known, New Orleans was happy. Her new orchestra would easily be the equal of any. And, said the *Bee,* "this in New Orleans is a matter of prime importance." It was especially pleasing for the American population of the city to anticipate at last an orchestra which would "be a good rival to that at the French theater." [28]

Caldwell's magnificent new theater, the largest in the United States, opened on Monday, November 30, 1835. Those who were able could reserve a season box for a mere one thousand dollars. The less affluent, or perhaps less ardent, could buy single tickets for one dollar and a half or one dollar, the same as at the French theater which had begun its season three weeks earlier. Since the other theater on Camp Street had opened on the nineteenth of the month, New Orleans now had three theaters presenting operas to a population of only about sixty thousand—twenty-five thousand whites, twenty thousand slaves, and fifteen thousand free colored. When one considers that Caldwell's new theater alone had room for four to five thousand spectators, it is clear that Negroes formed an essential part of the audiences. Thus the St. Charles reserved a section for free colored at one dollar a seat, as well as a section for slaves, who with their masters' written permission and fifty cents could gain admittance. In practice, only the latter requirement was crucial.[29]

On the opening night New Orleans' newest orchestra chose the overture to *Masaniello* for its introduction to the eagerly expectant audience, and later in the evening it played the overture to *Der Freischutz*. The next night saw the first full opera, Mozart's *Marriage of Figaro*, which was repeated two days later. This was all the delighted listeners needed to decide that this orchestra was "probably the best in the United States," with but one exception—the orchestra in the Orleans Theater.[30]

At least twenty-nine instrumentalists plus the conductor, whose name is given only as Willis, made up this ensemble that had pleased so much. There were ten violins, three cellos, two violas, two basses, two trumpets, one trombone, two clarinets, two flutes, two horns, and one oboe, harp, and bassoon. This was somewhat smaller than the Orleans Theater orchestra, and considerably smaller than an opera orchestra of today, but it is nevertheless impressive. The papers carried a complete roster of the personnel and their backgrounds, and soon instrumental solos by one or another of these musicians became a regular part of the St. Charles' programs. Especially did Norton, the first trumpeter, and Signor Cioffi, the trombonist, share billings with operas.[31]

In this respect the third orchestra in town, that on Camp Street, could compete. That other renowned trumpeter, Gambati, had indeed come to New Orleans, but to Camp Street rather than to the St. Charles. Apparently no single orchestra was yet big enough to hold both rivals. Soon the contest between the two which had started in New York was resumed in New Orleans. Each trumpeter soloed often on the stage of his respective theater, featuring the same songs played in their New York battles. Each artist was the yardstick by which the papers judged the other's skill. Interest in the contest was heightened by the fact that Gambati was using the new chromatic valve trumpet, while Norton used a slide trumpet.[32]

Thus Norton's trumpet and Cioffi's trombone at the St. Charles Theater and Gambati's trumpet at the Camp Street Theater became frequent feature attractions. New Orleans seemingly couldn't get enough of their brass blowing. Even the other "heroes" in the orchestra, as all the instrumentalists were now fondly called, applauded as vigorously as the audience in demanding encores. And a popular ballerina, dancing a new ballet to music by Weber, found herself accompanied chiefly by Cioffi's solo trombone.[33]

Other instrumentalists were also featured in the two American theaters. Flute, clarinet, and harp players left the orchestra from time to time to take the stage, in spite of some grumbling that their place was in the orchestra. And that is where they remained in the more reserved Orleans Theater which rested content in the knowledge that its orchestra was "the very best in the country in numbers, discipline and efficiency." [34]

On the whole, Caldwell's new theater prospered in spite of vigorous competition from the two older theaters. An attraction like the French dancer, Mlle. Celeste, drew nightly gates in the neighborhood of $2,500. Encouraged by his success, Caldwell now prepared to challenge the Orleans Theater more directly. While it is true that he had produced during the past decade a number of operas that were fairly creditable for the time and place and were the object of much American bragging, the galling fact remained that in all honesty the French productions were really far superior. Nor did it seem likely that any American-English company could be assembled that would have the calibre and repertoire necessary to threaten the pre-eminence of the French.[35]

It was great good news therefore to the American side of New Orleans when Caldwell announced that he was going to bring a well-known Italian opera company to his St. Charles Theater. Currently playing in Havana, the G. B. Montressor company had just completed successful runs in London and New York. But for New Orleans Caldwell let it be known that he would augment the company with additional talent from the Havana Opera, while his musical director, James G. Maeder, advertised for twenty-five more instrumentalists plus an equal number of men and women choristers. It was said that the cost of all this would be at least twenty thousand dollars. The *Bee* proudly noted that in Paris it "required the wealth of the French government to maintain an Italian Opera," in London the wealth of the nobility, and in New York the wealth of the wealthy. Here in New Orleans one man alone would take the risk, but the paper assured this brave man that a grateful populace would more than compensate him.[36]

Caldwell shrewdly invited members of the press to rehearsals, a generosity that was promptly repaid. "Anything we could say would appear exaggerated," wrote one; "even so we cannot refrain from praising Mme. Pedrotti, prima donna, Montressor, primo tenore, and M. Antonio Rosa, primo basso cantante." [37]

Bellini's *Il Pirata* was chosen for the Italians' initial offering on Sunday, March 6, 1836. Although the Orleans Theater played Herold's very popular *Le Pre aux Clercs* that same night, the gate at the St. Charles ran over three thousand dollars. The first impression of those whose ears were long accustomed to English and French operas was that there was "too much instrumentation and noise." But that impression soon changed, and it became clear that "Caldwell and his Italian opera company have taken the town by storm." *Il Pirata* played eight times; Rossini's *Otello* and his *Zelmira* four. The biggest success was Bellini's *Norma,* given ten times, while his *La Straniera* played only twice.[38]

For those Americans who had resented French superiority in opera it was a happy time. They exulted in Pedrotti, proclaiming her the very best cantatrice ever heard in New Orleans, and they marveled that until Montressor, they "had never known the power of a pure tenor." When the Italian engagement ended, they wondered if New Orleans would ever see its equal again. Such jibes at the French company were natural, but to pretend that the St. Charles had presented the first legitimate opera in New Orleans and that "the continuance of Grand Opera in this city" depended on a return of the Italians was simply absurd.[39]

English operas were not displaced at the St. Charles Theater during the Italian stay. Normally the Italians sang on Sundays, Wednesdays, and Fridays, leaving the other nights for the Americans. Thus the spring of 1836 saw a wealth of opera in New Orleans. On one Tuesday night in April, for example, a person might attend the St. Charles Theater to hear Mrs. Gibbs of the Drury Lane Theater sing Rossini's music in *Cinderella;* or if he preferred Bellini, he could go to the Camp Street Theater where Miss Russell was starring in an English version of *La Sonnambula.* At the Orleans Theater he would find Auber's *Le Cheval de Bronze* that evening.[40]

The following Wednesday night he could choose between Bellini's *Norma* sung at the St. Charles by the Montressor company or the same composer's *La Sonnambula* on Camp Street. In the single week of April 18–24, fourteen performances of nine operas were available. Four companies, two of which were unsurpassed in the United States, operated in three theaters, one of them the largest in the country. Certainly no other city in America, and probably no other of like size in the world, offered so much. Operas, said the *Bee,* ". . . amuse our citizens more than any other form of public amusement—except balls." [41]

The presence of so much talent made possible various extraordinary combinations such as the one Gambati, the trumpeter at the Camp Street Theater, arranged for his benefit—and for the performance of which he chose the Orleans Theater. Here the soloists from the Italian company were accompanied by a super-orchestra made up of the best musicians from all three theater orchestras.[42]

New Orleans was intoxicated with such music and hoped to stay that way. When it heard that some of the St. Charles' musicians were dissatisfied and threatening not to return next season, the city took Caldwell to task for not being aware of these grievances. He was urged to deal directly with his musicians rather than through underlings since he could never replace such valuable musicians. And when word got around that Caldwell was thinking of making an Italian company a permanent feature at the St. Charles, citizens immediately volunteered to help find ways and means. They hoped to make New Orleans "the metropolis of beaux arts in America." [43]

Quick to take advantage of these sentiments, Caldwell opened a subscription list for next season's Italian opera while his Montressor troupe was in full swing. In early May he threatened that unless the list was shortly filled there would be no return engagement. Warning that Havana was also filling a subscription for the same company, the *True American* asked, "Shall New Orleans, for the sake of a few thousands, be deprived of the most agreeable and refining amusement?" The paper trusted not; "but what is done must be done quickly, or they go to Havana." On May 30 Caldwell gave a "last notice" to all who desired to retain the Italian opera, calling the supporters to meet in his theater that day. They came and formed a citizens committee sworn to make "every effort to second the zeal and devotion of Caldwell." [44]

In return, Caldwell promptly pledged to bring back Italian opera with "such a corps and ballet as was never seen in this country." He was pleased by the sale of nearly all the boxes in the first tier, but he cautioned that seats in the parquette should be secured "at once." He claimed that he had lost over ten thousand dollars on the Montressor engagement and that, understandably, he wanted some assurance before bringing another troupe to his theater.[45]

Actually it is doubtful whether all this was anything more than the tactics of a good promoter. When the Montressor company finished at the St. Charles on May 27 with Rossini's *Zelmira,* only Pedrotti and Montressor departed for Havana. The rest of the group remained at the St. Charles to play *Il Barbiere di Siviglia* for three successive days beginning May 29.[46]

Evidently Caldwell had made all arrangements to hire the singers some time before. They needed only the addition of a basso to sing Bartolo, and Caldwell had seen to that, too, in the person of one Orlandi whose performance as Bartolo New Orleans greeted as "without equal in this country." Furthermore, it turned out that Caldwell had also made all plans to summer the Italians in a theater that he owned in Louisville, Kentucky.[47]

As for losing money, not only do the above actions seem to belie this, but Montressor himself put the total cost at not over twelve thousand dollars, although his estimate may have excluded the costs of the orchestra, since Montressor brought with him only a conductor, Signor Commi. The *Bee* gave the nightly cost as around nine hundred dollars, which would bring the total to a little over twenty-four thousand; and with receipts running as high as two to three thousand dollars on some nights, this paper asked how Caldwell could have lost money.[48]

With a production of Adolphe Adam's *Le Chalet* on May 17, the Orleans Theater closed its season. It had continued to grow and to sink roots despite Caldwell's efforts to usurp its place. In the three seasons since ceasing its summer travels, it had played one hundred and sixty-six nights of opera, encompassing forty-four operas by eighteen composers. One of the composers, it is worth noting, was a local musician, Gregorio Curto, whose *Le Nouvel Hermite* appeared on May 16, 1834. Auber had taken first place in popularity, with ten operas playing forty-three times: *La Muette de Portici* accounted for ten performances; *Fiorella* and *Le Macon*, six each; and *Fra Diavolo*, five.[49]

Herold was the second most popular composer, with five operas playing thirty times. His *Le Pre aux Clercs*, played eleven times; *Zampa*, seven; and *La Medicine sans Medicin*, five. Boieldieu had slipped back somewhat, with five operas playing seventeen times, *La Dame Blanche* and *Jean de Paris*, accounting for six each. The sharpest drop in popularity was Dalayrac's, who had but three operas played six times. Four of Rossini's operas played twelve times, of which *Le Barbier de Seville* accounted for five.

By far the most popular single opera during these three seasons was Meyerbeer's *Robert le Diable*, given twenty times at the Orleans Theater and thirteen times at the Camp Street Theater. Other single operas playing five or more times were Louis Lebrun's *Le Rossignol* (five); Weber's *Der Freischutz* (six); and Adam's *Le Chalet* (seven).[50]

Although the French opera had more than held its own against Caldwell, it faced the prospect of more Italian opera at the St. Charles in the season to come. Furthermore, a newspaper reported having been shown a letter from Caldwell in which he offered fifty thousand dollars to the greatest prima donna of them all—Mme. Malibran herself. Whether or not Caldwell had really sent such an offer, John Davis felt compelled to make every effort toward strengthening his company. He sent his son to France in search of new talent. There John, Jr., enlisted every Louisianian residing in Paris to attend the auditions and to consult over the choices, in order, he wrote his father, to avoid any reproaches later. By summer's end they had agreed on many "excellent acquisitions in the chorus and orchestra," but they were most excited about the new *premiere chanteuse*, Mlle. Othman. Word from Paris described her as a young woman whose voice was pure, full, and well timbered; whose face was pretty; and whose figure was tall, majestic, and, to say the least, very agreeable.[51]

"The next season," predicted the *Bee,* "should be our most brilliant up to now." [52]

"We have now, in this place, what no city in America, and few cities in the world can boast of. . . ."

Chapter Eight

THE OPERA: MATURITY

The approaching season of 1836–37 did indeed promise much. Caldwell's Italians, led by Antonio De Rosa, had summered successfully in Louisville and would be back at the St. Charles Theater. Davis' company was looking forward to an infusion of talent from France. The smaller theater on Camp Street made plans, too, which included such operas as *Cinderella, La Sonnambula, John of Paris,* and *The Marriage of Figaro.*[1]

All three theaters set opening dates in November, but a hitch soon developed in the preparations at the Orleans. Mlle. Othman, the young lady with the beautiful voice (and figure), embarked at le Havre on September 2 along with the other newly hired performers, but Davis had no way of knowing just when they would arrive. They were still at sea when the St. Charles opened on November 14; nor had they yet made port a week later when the Camp Street Theater followed suit. Not wishing to be left too far behind, Davis decided to begin his own season on November 24 with the forces on hand. His only thought, he said, was purely "for the convenience of the public and the employ of actors who have been out of employ for six months."[2]

Notwithstanding Davis' proclaimed concern, at least one indispensable actor viewed things in a different light. Insisting that his engagement was due to begin only when the rest of the company arrived, M. Victorin flatly refused to play, forcing Davis to cancel his opening with regrets for the "caprice" of one man. At once the *Bee* responded with an editorial supporting Victorin and strongly criticizing Davis:

No M. Davis . . . [Victorin] didn't refuse to play, but you refused to pay him. . . . To please the public you permit them to carry you silver, to be useful to your pensionnaires you charge them extra work. Eh! Monsieur Davis, are they to give you free a double task? Victorin, your *pensionnaire* and our friend for eight years, has he amassed some treasures from your munificence, as you, thanks to his talent, have gained land, houses, slaves, and the rest? No—he has nothing but a family to feed, nothing because you M. Davis have limited his circle of well being.

Today you offer him work as an alms, your heart seems touched by the privations imposed on him and his comrades these past months when the theatre was closed; why M. Davis do you not recompense them in a fashion to free them from these privations? . . . You exploited Victorin and he didn't complain. You propose to exploit him further and he refused, because he owes it to his family. And you accuse him of depriving the public of amusement. At least leave him the only wealth he has acquired, the friendship of all.[3]

All reproaches were laid aside, however, when on December 2, word spread through the cafes, salons, and exchanges that the ship *Ernest,* with the new talent aboard, had at last made port. Runners announced the good news to "mamas, sisters, aunts, cousins, to all the members of large and small families." A crowd soon gathered at the dock to assist the recruits in debarking as rapidly as possible. Helped ashore that day were no fewer than thirty-six singers and actors plus twenty-one instrumentalists. Their coming gave New Orleans a resident company more complete than it ever had been.[4]

And this was just in time, because no sooner had the French reenforcements arrived than Caldwell hastened to present on Sunday, December 4, his first Italian opera of the season, Rossini's *La Cenerentola.* By the end of February the Italians had performed nine times, giving three more Rossini operas—*Il Barbiere di*

Siviglia, L'Inganno Felice, and *Il Turco in Italia*—and introducing as well Luigi Caruso's *Monsieur de Chiffone.*[5]

As before, the Italian group shared the stage with the regular English-American company and were accompanied by the house orchestra which was again improved by the importation of instrumentalists such as E. Krakamp, formerly first flutist at San Carlo in Naples.[6]

In order not to fall too far behind, the Camp Street Theater had also put together an orchestra which "was much more effective than usual." And with well known singers of good reputation such as Charles Hodges and Mrs. Edward Knight for the leads, the Camp Street Theater could present a creditable showing, permitting New Orleanians to hear passable operas without going near either of the major theaters.[7]

Not wanting to lose any more time then, Davis scheduled the first performance of the long awaited Mlle. Othman for Tuesday, December 6, just four days after her arrival. This was rushing the newcomers too much, however, especially after their ocean voyage of three months; and Davis was compelled to postpone introducing his new company until Friday, December 9. Then, at last, New Orleans got to see the finest company it had yet known in a performance of Auber's five-act grand opera, *La Muette de Portici.*[8]

Success was immediate. Mlle. Othman fulfilled her advance notices both musical and physical, while the orchestra "surpassed, if possible, its reputation." French partisans were relieved to be confident once more of continuing to outdo the best their American rivals could offer. Supremacy was sweet—particularly when the same opera happened to play at both theaters. Thus when Mlle. Othman sang Rosine in *Le Barbier de Seville* only four days after Caldwell's Italians gave the same opera with Mme. Marozzi as Rosina, adherents of the Orleans Theater understood more than the mere words conveyed when they read in their newspaper: "Never has our stage heard a voice more agreeable, nor method more gracious . . . such delicious music, sung with so much superiority." [9]

And once the French company got underway, the Italian offerings at the St. Charles played to a "beggarly account of empty boxes"—a fact that afforded the French further gratification. They suggested that the Italians, too, ought really to be playing at the Orleans Theater where they would find an "overwhelming house." [10]

But Caldwell was not ready to give up yet. First he brought in several additions to his already commendable orchestra. Then, at the end of February, he disbanded his Italian company. What Caldwell had in mind was bringing to New Orleans the finest Italian opera company in the western hemisphere, currently playing in Havana under the direction of Francis Brichta. [11]

In the meantime, Caldwell kept the French on their toes by introducing Auber's operatic ballet, *Le Dieu et La Bayadere*. For the lead he engaged Mlle. Celeste, a ballerina of considerable fame in Europe and in America. To assist her were two dancers imported from the Havana Opera House, Signori Marietta and Eliza, plus the best of the singers from the St. Charles, including Mme. Thielmann. Opening on Tuesday, March 21, 1837, *Le Dieu et La Bayadere* gave a foretaste of things to come at the St. Charles by drawing so well that it played nine times during the eleven days left in March. [12]

Caldwell's renewed challenge precipitated a crisis in the management of the Orleans Theater. About a year before, a company had been incorporated to raise $100,000 for the French theater, and had taken title to the building. In December, 1836, the capital was increased to $600,000. Now the shareholders, who were increasingly restless under the one-man control of John Davis, forced him to step aside. Toward the end of March, 1837, they met to accept an amendment to their charter, already passed by the state legislature, which granted voting rights in proportion to shares. They then announced that the Orleans Theater Company would take over the administration of the theater on April 15. In preparation, they bought all of Davis' stage properties and contracts. On April 3 the new company elected six directors and a secretary, J. A. Durel, who had already been serving in that capacity. Durel promptly served notice that the first act of the new management would be to end all free passes and admissions on credit. The new company meant business. [13]

On the whole, this change met with approval. *Le Moqueur,* a new local journal devoted to music and opera, pointed out that in Paris from 1820 to 1827 opera had cost the government immense sums, and argued that a company would "be able to undertake expenses that a single director couldn't without risking his future." [14]

But it was not without some pangs that the city witnessed the departure from the French theater of the man who had built it. As the date of transfer drew close, *Le Moqueur* commented sadly on the irony of the event: "At the moment Caldwell began his company from Italy, Davis finished with his company from France." *Le Moqueur* hoped that this would not be his last battle.[15]

His withdrawal from the theater that he had built and controlled for eighteen years was in fact, however, Davis' last battle. He retired to Mandeville, a small summer resort across Lake Pontchartrain; and there, two years later on June 13, 1839, he died. He had been ill a long time, and perhaps this is why he relinquished the direction of his theater without more of a fight.[16]

Davis' death marked twenty years, almost to the day, since he had arrived in New Orleans in the wave of Dominican refugees who departed from Cuba in 1809. During most of those years he had been a highly successful businessman, and he was also a veteran of the great battle of New Orleans. But it was not for these things that New Orleans, a city noted for lavish funerals, gave Davis one that was among "the largest ever known in this city." A grateful populace turned out in an "immense crowd," and numerous companies of the Louisiana Legion marched in the procession. At the St. Louis Cathedral a special requiem composed for the occasion was sung by the entire company from the Orleans Theater. New Orleans was honoring this day the man who had raised its theater "from a wretched condition to prosperity and excellence." [17]

And this was only proper. When Davis retired from music in April, 1837, he left as his legacy an opera theater that had grown into an institution. Other hands would now support and guide it, but if any one man had been indispensable in bringing the New Orleans opera house to maturity, that man was John Davis. Indeed his contribution to opera elsewhere in America has never been adequately recognized. The six tours of the Northeast that he made with his entire company were prodigious feats that enlightened what would otherwise have been bleak years. The influence of these tours is immeasurable. But it was in New Orleans, of course, that he made his great contribution. Even the arrival of a top notch Italian company, imported expressly to challenge the company he had built, was really more a credit to him than to Caldwell.[18]

The Italians arrived on April 1, 1837. Delighted auditors needed only to hear the company in rehearsal to pronounce it "of unsurpassed magnificence," the best that ever left Italy. Francis Brichta, manager of the company, brought with him from Havana the soloists and chorus, the conductor Signor Luigi Gabici, and three string instrumentalists to play first viola, cello, and bass in the orchestra already at the St. Charles. Brichta planned to give operas by Bellini, Ricci, Rossini, Donizetti, and Mercadante.[19]

On Tuesday, April 4, the Italians made their debut. They chose Bellini's *I Capuletti e Montecchi;* their success was instantaneous and unreserved. There could be but one opinion, said the *Bee,* which was that the "most ardent expectations" were completely realized. The "highest order of talent," individually and collectively, was now in New Orleans.[20]

As the full impact of their musical wealth sank home, New Orleanians burst with pride. "We have now, in this place, what no city in America, and few cities in the world can boast of," wrote one; "strong companies in the English, French, and Italian languages, and what is more they are all extremely well patronized." A trio of enthusiastic men who called themselves the "Tribunal of Three" flatly asserted: "The opera . . . at present in New Orleans is unexceptionally the best which has ever been . . . in America."[21]

Equal praise was bestowed upon the audience. Almost daily New Orleanians were reminded that their city could "support more theaters than any other city of its size in the world"; that it should feel proud to display such "relish . . . for the masterpieces"; and above all that it alone "formed a bright exception to the tasteless apathy and soullessness which have characterized reception of Opera in every other city in the United States."[22]

Only one thing more might conceivably be needed to overflow

the cup and that was an escapade or two, a touch of those delightful whims of behavior that often accompany and enliven such a gathering of talent. They were not long in coming. On Thursday, April 6, just two days after the Italians' grand opening, the St. Charles filled with people come to hear Bellini's *I Capuletti e Montecchi.* The orchestra finished the overture and began the first act. Suddenly the manager discovered that his Juliet, Signora Teresa Rossi, was nowhere to be found. With the opera underway and the house full, there was only one thing to do—go on with the show. But since there was no understudy for Juliet, the part was simply cut. New Orleans had the unique experience that night of hearing Romeo without Juliet.[23]

Signora Rossi's disappearance provided a field day for excited and romantic rumors. One recalled that Montressor had had a long feud with the departed Rossi, and that he had left New Orleans last year vowing that he had friends who would avenge him. Another had it that Montressor's feud was rather with Signora Clorinda Corradi-Pantanelli, the contralto who sang Romeo, and that Montressor had himself lured Rossi away in order to injure Pantanelli. Yet another held that Rossi had simply been abducted by persons unknown. In the end it turned out that Rossi had actually eloped to Mexico with the *primo basso*—an escapade which, according to the *True American,* only proved the degeneracy of Italians.[24]

Incredible though it seems, a week later, the prima donna of the Orleans Theater, the shapely Mlle. Othman, likewise disappeared. There was a "sad monotony" to these flights, commented the *Bee.* "Who," the paper wanted to know, "could have foreseen such a catastrophe?" At the Camp Street Theater Charles Hodges, tenor, promptly sang the soprano title role in Rossini's *Cinderella,* gracefully accepting for his efforts a bouquet of cigars interwoven with mint. "Hodges knows," surmised the *Picayune,* "they are wanting Prima Donnas at both the other theaters, and is evidently trying his hand for an engagement." [25]

Mlle. Othman's flight was a direct result of the change in management at the Orleans Theater. She contended that John Davis had no right to sell her contract to anyone and no longer considered herself bound by it. As *Le Moqueur* put it, Mlle. Othman and some other players deeply resented being sold like machines and refused to consider themselves employed by the new company. While the others didn't depart with Othman, they sulked, playing with obvious boredom and actually leaving a performance at times to stroll in the sun or for some equally trifling reason.[26]

Meanwhile at the St. Charles, Alfred Boucher, first cellist, walked out in a huff of resentment over sharing honors with the cellist imported from Havana with the Italian opera.[27]

That all these trials were quickly overcome indicates the solid place opera had now attained in New Orleans. Within a week of Signora Rossi's departure on her unannounced honeymoon, Signora Papanti took her place. In addition Signora Marozzi, who had so pleased everyone last season, and Signor Fornasari, "the best bass singer in this country," joined Caldwell's company.[28]

The French company, of course, couldn't so easily replace its errant prima donna. That would have to wait until next fall. Nonetheless, the large repertoire of the Orleans company allowed it to carry on by avoiding operas that required a Mlle. Othman.[29]

But the honors, for the time being, belonged to the St. Charles Theater. Here on the night of April 21, the English and Italian companies appeared together in a double bill of Auber's ballet, *Le Dieu et La Bayadere,* and Bellini's opera, *Norma.* Such an "unparalleled" night of music, beginning at seven and ending well after midnight, had hitherto been known but rarely even in the greatest opera houses of Europe. It gave New Orleans considerable right to contend that she was writing "a bright page in the musical history of our country." [30]

Most of all the city delighted in the singing of Signora Pantanelli in such operas as *Norma, Donna Caritea,* and *Il Barbier di Siviglia.* This young girl, already recommended by Rossini himself, steadily improved during her stay in New Orleans. By June her enthusiastic followers insisted that since the recent death of the great Maria Malibran, Pantanelli had no rival and would soon be as famous as Malibran. Nor did they confine their admiration to words alone. When Pantanelli sang in Donizetti's *Parisina,* her fans completely filled the stage with bouquets, one of which carried a votive offering of five hundred dollars—a considerable sum in those days.[31]

And there were other ways to display enthusiasm. One Sunday night in May at the St. Charles Theater "the most curious finale" to *Semiramide* ever "performed in this or any other country" transformed the Italian opera to the "Italian Uproar." Let one who was there tell the story:

> The last scene of the opera, from some unknown cause, was *suspended* by the Italian troupe, and another scene was appended by the audience, which Rossini never intended, nor ever imagined could take place.
>
> The house was a very good one. . . . At the conclusion of the scene where Assur fancies he encounters the ghost, down went the green curtain, before the last scene had been performed. The *falling* of the green curtain was the signal for *raising* a most tremendous racket, by those who had paid their $1.00 and $1.50 to witness *Semiramide* entire. The house commenced operations with the celebrated tramp march so well known in this city by frequenters of the theaters. . . . the pit became uproarious. The backs of the seats received a succession of whacks from the canes of those who were provided with them, and those who had not used feet and tongues to the utmost of their power. By this time one or two of the backs of the pit seats were torn down. Fornasari made his appearance, bowed, said nothing, and retired. . . . The audience, finding they were to be kept in ignorance, now became tumultuous. Such a din we have rarely heard. Hissing, howling, whistling, kicking and screaming . . . [then] the gas lights were all extinguished. . . . T'was the signal for the demolition of everything they could lay their hands on. Chairs and canes were thrown towards the splendid chandelier—the pride of the St. Charles—and for some time its destruction appeared inevitable. . . . The drapery around the boxes was torn, the cushions in the pit ripped open, and chairs were flying in all directions.[32]

In short, here was one of those superb donnybrooks that gladden the hearts of participants and give everyone a topic for days of delightful talk. As one box seat customer shouted, while hurling three chairs on the stage, "Three cheers for the opera!" The French too could cheer from a distance—the riot confirmed their conviction of superior breeding. *Le Moqueur* smugly lectured: "The Americans, who pass for such great innovators . . . should take a little less pains in perpetrating their savage ways." [33]

What most had touched off these "savage ways" was a strong sus-

The theater on St. Philip Street, which had been the Salle Chinoise in which Tessier held his quadroon balls, opened in 1808. The Orleans Theater opened in 1815 and burned down a year later.

Old American Theater which opened in 1824. It was located on Camp Street in the American district of New Orleans.

Auguste TESSIER, a l'honneur de prévenir le Public qu'il est Locataire de la Maison en Ville, appartenant à M. Bernard COQUET, & de la Salle de BAL, depuis le premier du courant.

Il se propose de donner BAL deux fois par semaine aux femmes de couleur libres, où les hommes de couleur ne feront pas admis; il a différé de faire l'ouverture des Bals jusqu'à Samedi 23 du courant, pour a- le tems de joindre à l'agréable hofes utiles & néceffaires en pa- ...as; on y trouvera toutes fortes ...fraichiffemens, Confommés &c. &c. &c., & même de quoi ...s foupers & déjeûners.

...même époque fa Maison ...à toutes perfonnes qui ...s la journée, prendre ...s & faire une par-

Auguste TESSIER, a l'honneur de prévenir le Public qu'il est Locataire de la Maifon en Ville, appartenant à M. Bernard COQUET, & de la Salle de BAL, depuis le premier du courant.

Il donnera BAL tous les Mercredi & famedi aux femmes de couleur libres, comme il l'a annoncé; & il ofe fe flater, quelque fatisfait qu'on ait été au premier Bal, qu'on le fera encore plus aux autres. On y trouvera toutes fortes de Rafraichiffemens, Confommés, Vins, &c &c., & même de quoi y faire des foupers & déjeûners.

Sa Maifon est, & continuera d'être ouverte à toutes les perfonnes, qui voudront, dans la journée, prendre des Rafraichiffemens & faire une partie à des jeux permis.

Il y fera fervir des Repas, en étant prévenu à tems, & louera fa Salle à qui voudra donner une Fête particulière.

Ce fera aux perfonnes qui l'honoreront de leur préférence à juger de la propreté & de la diligence qu'on mettra en les fervant.

This newspaper advertisement, dated November 23, 1805, is the first announcement of a ball held for free women of color and white men only. Negro men were specifically excluded.

Tessier's second advertisement indicates that this type of ball had proved successful. In this announcement, the exclusion of colored men is tacitly assumed.

Interior of the St. Charles Theater, opened in 1835. This magnificently decorated hall was the largest in the United States.

In 1840 with a population of slightly over one hundred thousand, New Orleans could boast three active theaters. Pictured here, top to bottom, are the Orleans, the New American, and the St. Charles.

picion that the Italians were simply lazy or anxious to get home, and that they cut the opera thinking the audience wouldn't know the difference. Two days later when *Semiramide* was again scheduled, Caldwell himself was obliged to take the stage to give personal apologies and assurance of a complete performance—since a large portion of the audience had come prepared to riot properly over the least omission. One suspects that some customers that night were disappointed at hearing *Semiramide* "played and sung to the full extent." [34]

The elopement of his prima donna and primo basso after one performance and the extensive damage to his theater at the hands of the rioters should have been misfortune enough for any producer —at least in one short stretch. But Caldwell's time of troubles was far from over. As June approached, his orchestra seemed to be melting away: four violins, two clarinets, a trumpet, horn, and flute took their leave. Caldwell hastily secured the popular trumpeter Gambati from the Camp Street Theater, but he couldn't replace the others. And, rightly or wrongly, the Italians and the patrons blamed Caldwell for this second disappearing act at the St. Charles. Almost daily the Italian manager Brichta carried the complaints of singers and conductor to Caldwell, only to be informed testily that the Italian opera must go on—with no orchestra at all if necessary. [35]

At the same time word spread that the Italians would shortly move over to the Orleans Theater, a prospect that hurt attendance at the St. Charles and drew heated denials from Caldwell. Actually both theaters were seeking to extend the Italians' stay, a contest that seemed settled when Brichta announced twelve further dates and several new operas for the St. Charles. But it was a false peace. [36]

On Monday, June 5, Pantanelli sang to a full house in Donizetti's *Parisina*. It was her benefit night and she expected, in addition to a shower of gifts, to receive a portion of the receipts. Pantanelli sang *Parisina* again the next night but absolutely refused to go on stage for a third performance on Wednesday until she got the money she claimed was due her from Monday. Caldwell flatly refused, arguing that his contract was with Brichta only, and charging that Brichta had advertized a benefit for Pantanelli merely to insure a good house. When Pantanelli proved just as stubborn, Caldwell turned off the lights and canceled the performance. And that was the end of Italian opera at the St. Charles Theater.[37]

The argument lingered on, however. Brichta published a long letter in which he accused Caldwell of continually haggling over and reneging on terms; of "brutality and coarseness"; and of having strongly "wished to God" that the ship bringing the Italians had sunk. It was only the final insult, said Brichta, when Caldwell shut off the lights before the Italians had a chance to dress.[38]

Caldwell answered by charging bad faith and temperament, declaring that he had "known nothing but trouble, annoyance, and loss since . . . [his] first unfortunate introduction of the Italian Opera." All he could honestly say it had brought him were "some enemies as unsought for as unjust." He swore never to touch the stuff again.[39]

With suspicious alacrity the Italians moved over to the Orleans Theater. Indeed, the first announcement of their impending shift appeared on the very day that Pantanelli refused to go on at the St. Charles. Those who had bought tickets for scheduled performances at the latter theater were promised that their tickets would be honored at the Orleans. All of which lent considerable weight to Caldwell's charge of chicanery. Be that as it may, it must surely have been galling to see the company he had imported as a challenge to the musical supremacy of the Orleans Theater end its stay in that house.[40]

On Saturday, June 10, the Italians commenced their run at the Orleans with *Norma*. Hard-core, loyal patrons of the French theater were delighted with their acquisition, insisting that "this will be the first time that Italian opera will be truly played in New Orleans." They argued that although the opera might have been heard at the St. Charles, it could not really have been seen, since half the scenery was lacking there, and much of what was used clashed with the story settings. Not only would the Italian operas now be staged with proper scenery, but with fitting accompaniment as well. The Orleans orchestra, always considerably superior to that at the St. Charles, gained further strength with the addition of some of the better of Caldwell's instrumentalists such as the "inimitable Cioffi" and his trombone. Thus with an orchestra that was surely the "best . . . ever . . . congregated in the United States," the Italians could at last show themselves at their finest.[41]

And indeed, to those numerous French who had steadfastly refused to attend the St. Charles Theater, the Italian opera was a revelation. Every part of it surpassed their previous experience. Even the small Italian chorus of but six men and three women seemed to outdo the French chorus of thirty voices. *Le Moqueur* soon analyzed the reasons for this: first, the Italians sang harmony whereas the French usually sang unison; second, the Italians were truly choristers, while many of the French were simply actors called upon to fill out the chorus; and third, the French sang too much through their teeth.[42]

Above all, Pantanelli conquered the French more completely, if possible, than she had the Americans. Her *Norma* so overwhelmed the critic of *Le Moqueur* that he found himself unable to write about it. Her part in *Tancredi* was "sung as it could scarcely be sung even in Paris or Naples." She was "the city's favorite, the ladies admiration, the divine Pantanelli," without question the best ever to sing in America. Taken all in all, orchestra, conductor, chorus, and soloists, New Orleans was happily certain that only in Paris could "such an assembly of talent" be found.[43]

In spite of the onset of summer heat which made the poorly ventilated Orleans Theater extremely uncomfortable, attendance was so high that the Italians were encouraged to extend their visit well into July. And of course the French chided the Americans about the full houses at the Orleans which they attributed to better taste and lesser parsimony. Finally on July 14, the Italians played their last opera in New Orleans, *Il Barbiere di Siviglia*.[44]

If Italian opera left Caldwell only unpleasant memories, it left New Orleans a better place musically. The Italians helped greatly to complete the revolution in taste that had begun a few years before with such operas as Boieldieu's *La Dame Blanche* and Meyerbeer's *Robert le Diable*. Now, after hearing operas like *Norma* for two seasons, New Orleans could no longer rest content with "the flourishes and obbligatos of genteel vaudeville" which characterized so much of the earlier opera. The administration of the Orleans Theater was advised to keep in mind that "the time of the tra la la's has nearly passed." As the *Picayune* put it a little over a year later: "The Italian opera . . . awakened and continued a most polished taste among us." [45]

Although Caldwell had vowed never again to have anything to do with Italians, his regular company was constantly striving to produce better operas. Toward the end of the season just passed they had staged the first two scenes of Halevy's *La Juive* and were planning to give the whole opera during the coming season.[46]

If the Orleans Theater now were to fail to present the best in current operas, Caldwell would be tempted to challenge its lead again. But the new administration promised to overcome all obstacles and began by having the theater repaired and remodeled during the summer.[47]

Next they sought a singer capable of competing with the memory of Pantanelli. Mlle. Othman was back in New Orleans, perhaps because she heard that the company was willing to pay ten thousand dollars for a prima donna. But Othman had walked out once before and might walk out again. In the end her flight proved fortunate, for in her place New Orleans got its finest prima donna, Mlle. Julie Calve. In short order this little soprano made the city forget all who preceded her and find deep satisfaction in possessing one of the truly excellent singers of the day. With her arrival in the fall of 1837, the opera in New Orleans was reaching maturity.[48]

It is of course difficult to evaluate a singer who sang so long before recording was possible. All we can do is take the words of those who saw her and who were competent to judge. One of these, himself a widely traveled and experienced performer, heard Calve in her prime and wrote:

The exquisite singing and acting of the little piquante Prima Donna, Mademoiselle Calve, have made the French opera in New Orleans very popular. Her voice is one of the most pleasing I have heard for a long time: considerable in extent, pure in quality, and round in tone. . . . Her *sostenuto* in pathetic music is also admirable, and her general style full of intensity, of feeling, and vigour.[49]

Besides Calve, there were sixteen male and twelve female singers and actors new to the company. The season began on November 9, but Calve didn't make her debut until November 21, at which time the twenty-year-old girl sang in *Le Barbier de Seville*. Her success was immediate and overwhelming. The first *cavatine* drew a "burst of applause rarely heard in New Orleans," and by the third act the applause was frenzied. Sober second thoughts only augmented this initial response, praising unreservedly both her voice and schooling. "For New Orleans," said the *Bee*, "this was the most beautiful day ever risen." [50]

Inspired by their bright new star, the Orleans company developed an esprit de corps during this successful season that kept the organization virtually intact throughout the summer. By appearing in concerts, ballrooms, museums, panoramas, and summer gardens, the performers held on until the new season could begin. And when fall did come it brought with it several important additions. A new conductor and assistant conductor, two more women soloists, another bass, a tenor, six choristers, two violins, a cello, and a bassoon all arrived on the ship *Garonne* at the end of October.[51]

Eugene Prevost, the new conductor, was to prove an even more important acquisition, possibly, than Julie Calve. Not yet thirty years old when he came to New Orleans, he had already won the first and second grand prizes in composition from the Paris Conservatory, had produced his own operas, and had been conductor of the theater in Le Havre for three years. He would conduct the French opera in New Orleans for almost the next thirty years and compose much music of all kinds, including operas. (It was Prevost who composed the requiem for John Davis in 1839.) [52]

Also there was Mme. Bamberger, wife of the new cellist and one of the two added women soloists. As time went on, she steadily gained in skill and popularity until her growing challenge to Calve caused an open feud, to be described presently. The other newcomer, Mme. Ellerman, feuded much sooner. She stayed not quite two months before she quit in anger because, so it was said, she was jealous of Calve.[53]

Opening on November 6 with *Le Barbier de Seville*, the improved company lived up to all expectations. There was "no marring by an imperfect orchestra or poor singers," and the best compositions available were played with "taste, skill and feeling not often surpassed." As for Calve, "we doubt that it is possible to be more perfect than this singer, even as an actress." Taking a guest to the French opera that winter was said to be the highest compliment a host could pay.[54]

A highlight of this season came at the beginning of January, 1839, when Eugene Prevost conducted his own two act opera, *Cosimo*. To show their pleasure in having an opera composer in their company, patrons at the second performance of *Cosimo* sent up a wreath of flowers containing a diamond breast pin worth six hundred dollars. "He deserves it," stated one editor, "for if there ever was an opera . . . which shows genius and judgement, it is the *Cosimo* of Mons. Prevost." This little opera-bouffon was given four times that season, and themes from it were played at the society balls.[55]

Another peak was the American premiere of Meyerbeer's most successful opera, *Les Huguenots,* which had been introduced in France only three years before the Orleans Theater staged it on April 30, 1839. Those who heard it that first night were astonished. They were not prepared for what seemed to them "strange melodies" and "lush instrumentation." Nor were they used to giving sustained attention for a full five hours. A numbed bewilderment was more in evidence than any enthusiasm at the first two performances of *Les Huguenots*. As one put it, "the coldness with which the public received this work is remarkable." [56]

A growing reputation for musical taste was at stake, however; and a determined audience, plus enthusiastic singing and the zeal of the orchestra, persevered to turn coldness into triumph. By the third playing "a durable success was assured." This five-act, five-hour opera was performed no fewer than eight times in five weeks, while music stores sold Meyerbeer's opera suitably arranged for piano alone, or for voice and piano, or even for guitar.[57]

Les Huguenots serves well to mark the point reached by the New Orleans French opera in 1839. Meyerbeer used "an elaborate and ingenious orchestration that may well have caused managers to complain on account of all the extra instruments involved." In ad-

dition he required "gorgeously spectacular settings." Develle, the
scenarist at the Orleans Theater, painted six new scenes for *Les
Huguenots,* each of them separately titled and advertised in the
newspapers. To play and to stage such an opera was accomplishment enough; to make it popular was a triumph.[58]

When the 1839–40 season opened on November 7 with Halevy's
L'Eclair, all were glad to see Julie Calve back for her third season
and the composer-conductor, Eugene Prevost, again on the podium.
And connoisseurs began more and more to notice a young girl who,
although shy and inexperienced, was rapidly developing into an excellent singer. She sang in Donizetti's *Anne de Boulen* on December
12 and 17, but it wasn't until the third performance at the end of
January that the name of Mme. Bamberger was placed on the bill-
ing with the name of Mlle. Calve.[59]

Thereafter Mme. Bamberger received increasing attention. For
example, in a review of *Anne de Boulen,* after giving Calve the
lion's share of praise for her playing of Anne, the writer went on:
"Mme Bamberger in the role of Jane Seymour is a worthy rival of
Mlle. Calve, although we have not the least wish in the world to
establish the least comparison between these two! As much as the
singing of the one is firm, pure, correct, and arresting, is [that of]
the other uncertain, hesitant and inexperienced. But Mme. Bamberger has certain cordes [tones] in her voice of a beauty so
marvelous, she studies so conscientiously, she has progressed so sensibly, that we hope to see a very distinguished cantatrice. Her applause last Thursday was calculated to make her lose some of her
timidity." [60]

Of course if such commendation was intended to lessen Bamberger's timidity, it was also bound to excite Calve's jealousy. And
strong disavowals of any slightest wish to bring about the least comparison between these two most likely would accomplish just that.
Was it mere coincidence that the first faint criticism of Calve appeared this season? After praising her voice, her looks, and her
performance as usual, the *Bee* wondered "if she might not be neglecting her daily exercises," and if she were not "counting a little
too much on the inspiration of the moment." "Why does she rest

content and not work for perfection?" the *Bee* wanted to know.[61]

Whether spurred by such comments or motivated simply by the desire to keep ahead of Bamberger, Calve decided not to rest content. Although the end of the season found her still acclaimed as "unsurpassed," she went back to France for more study. When she returned in late November of 1840, she was assured that she was "still the pearl of our theatre." But Bamberger was also back at the Orleans, still studying, still progressing; and if she was not yet a pearl, all she needed was a bit more polishing. When she shone enough to distract from Calve's lustre jealousy was inevitable.[62]

The clash came suddenly in March, 1841. In the words of a witness:

It had become an every-night fashion to summon Mademoiselle Calve before the curtain after her performance, and to shower all kinds of bouquets and garlands upon her. . . . After having held undisputed sway over the hearts of her admirers for a considerable time, an attempt was made by a few to get up a little excitement in favor of Madame Bamberger, which eventually succeeded in working up the sympathies of the audience so far as to cause that lady to be led out to receive a portion of the applause. On these occasions, as soon as a bouquet was thrown upon the stage, the countenance of Calve was seen to undergo a dreadful change: her eye would flash fire and defiance, her lips quiver, and her every fibre swell with passion, lest her less-gifted rival should dare to appropriate any portion of the spoils to herself. A beautiful wreath was once thrown so ostensibly at the foot of Madame Bamberger, that she, in spite of her modesty, and that excess of timidity which had rendered her passive under the most aggravated cases of insult, ventured to lay her hand upon it. Calve no sooner saw this, than, enraged at her audacity, as well as out of temper with the audience, she indignantly flung her pretty cargo of flowers upon the stage, and bolted off in divine disgust.[63]

At Calve's next appearance two nights later "everything was confusion, noise and discord." Chastened, she tried to apologize, but the din was so loud that neither her apologies nor her singing could be heard. To add to her distress, the audience literally showered Bamberger with bouquets and applause. As one wit remarked, "The opera is out of tune at the French Theatre." Calve ultimately made her peace with the patrons, but she must henceforth acknowledge—and be gracious about—Bamberger's rivalry. Young gallants and opera buffs eagerly chose sides and filled Jackson Square on Sunday afternoons "discussing the rival claims of Calve or Bamberger, the favourite prima donnas of the Opera." [64]

For those seeking more than feuds, the season brought ample rewards. Auguste Nourrit, a new tenor making his debut in *Robert le Diable,* became almost at once another singing idol. The orchestra and chorus were compared favorably with those of Drury Lane and Covent Garden by a visiting actor. And the foremost ballerina of her day, Fanny Elssler, came to New Orleans in 1841 to appear during March in the St. Charles and during April in the Orleans. Dancing in *La Sylphide* by Salvatore Taglioni and other such ballets, she filled both theaters at advanced prices. (Her benefit night at the Orleans brought her close to five thousand dollars.) [65]

Most of all it was the repertoire that bespoke maturity. In just the five seasons since the fall of 1836, the quantity of music performed was astonishing. The French company in the Orleans totaled three hundred and sixty-four performances of sixty-five operas by twenty-seven composers. Among these were sixteen premieres. The Brichta Italian company, imported from Havana by Caldwell in 1837, gave thirty performances at the St. Charles and fifteen more at the Orleans, showing in all eight operas (five of them premieres) by five composers. Together with the De Rosa company that preceded the Brichta troupe, the total of Italian performances in 1836–37 reached fifty-four, of which seven were premieres. Moreover, English companies at the St. Charles played Auber's ballet, *Le Dieu et La Bayadere,* forty-one times, first as a vehicle for Celeste and then for Fanny Elssler. Auber's *La Muette de Portici*—the English called it *Masaniello*—was played ten times; his *Gustave III* nine times; his *Fra Diavolo* six times; and his *The Pages of the Duke of Vendome* twice.

Halevy's *The Jewess* played thirteen times; Bellini's *La Sonnambula* ten times; Rossini's *Cinderella* fourteen times and his *Barber of Seville* three times; Boieldieu's *John of Paris* eight times; Mozart's *Marriage of Figaro* twice; and Weber's *Der Freischutz* once. In addition, English companies at the Camp Street Theater gave *Cinderella* seven times; *Le Dieu et La Bayadere* twice; and *John of Paris* once.

Thus these five years saw at least five hundred and forty-nine opera performances, to say nothing of a considerable number of ballets on the order of *La Sylphide* and *L'Hirondelle*, and an even greater number of English musicals—especially those with music by Sir Henry Bishop.

Auber was by far the favorite composer during this half decade. The French company gave one hundred and fifteen performances of thirteen operas by Auber, four of them premieres. Of these the most played were *L'Ambassadrice* which played twenty-two times; *Le Domino Noir* twenty-one times; *La Muette de Portici* twelve times; *Fra Diavolo* ten times; *Le Dieu et La Bayadere* ten times; and *Gustave III* nine times. When to this is added the seventy English performances already mentioned, New Orleans heard Auber's operas and ballets one hundred and eighty-five times in five seasons. On April 5, 1838, *Gustave III* was played simultaneously in both the Orleans and the St. Charles.

Adam was next in popularity for French operas alone, although Rossini and Boieldieu ranked higher in the city as a whole. Of Adam's operas, seven were performed forty times, four of them premieres. Among these, *Le Chalet* played sixteen times, *Le Postillon de Longjumeau* twelve times, and *Le Brasseur de Preston* eight times.

Of Rossini's operas, five were performed twenty-five times. Accounting for most of these performances, *Le Barbier de Seville* played ten times, *La Pie Voleuse* nine times, and *Le Comte Ory* four times. But in addition, Brichta's Italian company sang *Semiramide* five times at the St. Charles and twice more at the Orleans; *Tancredi* three times at each theater; and *Il Barbiere di Siviglia* four times at the St. Charles and three more at the Orleans. Besides these performances, De Rosa's earlier Italian company gave Rossini operas seven times at the St. Charles, while English companies gave another twenty-four performances at the St. Charles and the Camp Street theaters. In all, ten of Rossini's operas accounted for seventy-six performances.

Boieldieu remained popular. His operas, eight in all, were given thirty-nine times at the Orleans with *La Dame Blanche* being given ten times and *Le Nouveau Seigneur du Village* eleven times. *Jean de Paris* was played only twice in French but was given nine more playings in English.

Other composers playing ten or more times were Meyerbeer with two operas played thirty-four times; Herold with four operas played twenty-five times; Halevy, whose *L'Eclair* played sixteen times (and whose *The Jewess* played thirteen times at the St. Charles); and Donizetti with ten playings of *Anne de Boulen* and three of *Lucie de Lammermoor*. Donizetti's *Parisina* was also given by the Brichta Italian company in a total of four performances. Brichta's company gave two of Bellini's operas, *Norma* and *I Capuletti e Montecchi*; each was presented six times at the St. Charles and twice at the Orleans. There were also ten performances in English of Bellini's *La Sonnambula*.

The most popular single opera continued to be Meyerbeer's *Robert le Diable*, played twenty-six times, followed by Auber's *L'Ambassadrice*, twenty-two times, and his *Le Domino Noir*, twenty-one times.[66]

Thus in the spring of 1841 New Orleans could look back on a half century in which opera, after a decade or so of extremely precarious existence, had slowly rooted and grown into a permanent institution without parallel in America. Occasionally other American cities—notably New York—had a season or two of opera which invariably ended in financial disaster. In these sporadic efforts one or two singers were sometimes superior to, or at least better known than, the soloists in New Orleans, but the ensemble was always greatly inferior. And no other American city could come close to New Orleans in supporting, year after year, a consistently well rounded, steadily improving opera and orchestra. No matter what crises arose, financial or otherwise, a constantly developing musical taste combined with French pride and civic pride to surmount all obstacles.[67]

More new operas had been introduced to America in New Orleans than in the rest of the country put together, and Davis' company had kept opera alive in the northeastern cities for several years after Garcia's introduction of Italian opera in New York in 1825. If, in these early years, New York had an occasional Garcia, New Orleans too had visits from singers like Montressor and Pantanelli, as well as from dancers such as Celeste and Elssler. And with the coming of Calve and Nourrit to the Orleans company, New Orleans no longer needed to concede anything in the way of individual stars.[68]

So it was that by the close of its first half century, opera in New Orleans had grown to full maturity and achieved the status of an institution. For the next sixty years most of the great French and Italian operas would be beautifully staged in the Orleans Theater and in its successor, the French Opera House. Even in the two decades of its old age before it was destroyed by fire in 1919, its productions were such as to kindle new enthusiasm and to revive superb memories.

". . . after a good house one night we can invariably expect a poor house the following."

Chapter Nine

THE OPERA: GROWING PAINS

*D*uring the period when opera was being established, New Orleans had little more than eight thousand residents. Not until 1830 did the population grow to thirty thousand, and by 1840 when the opera reached maturity the city contained only a little over one hundred thousand residents. At all times a substantial proportion of that population was Negro, and only a limited portion of the whites had the means to attend opera frequently. "Experience has shown that after a good house one night we can invariably expect a poor house the following." This resigned statement, made in 1838, well summarized a hard fact of life for the opera during its years of growth. And besides a want of sufficient population there were many other obstacles that made life for the opera hazardous.[1]

Weather could be a deterrent. The extreme heat of the New Orleans summers early taught the various opera promoters that they could not hope to remain open during that season. But heat in New Orleans was not confined to the summer months, and unless the opera season was to be impossibly short, there was frequently the danger that a hot night would deplete attendance. On such nights the spectators must have been very uncomfortable as they sat in a fairly small enclosure under the oil lamps that provided the only light. Moreover the fumes from those lamps were extremely unpleasant. Thus as early as May the diminishing public would be promised that all doors and windows in the theater would be left open. Or the management promised to use an oil that made less smoke and smell. The lamps too were replaced with *quinquets* such as were used in the best theaters in France. Later, of course, gas lights helped greatly to eliminate fumes and to give better light, but they were no less hot. And so throughout this first half century of opera the heat was frequently blamed for poor crowds. Sometimes as few as five or six yawning spectators constituted the entire house.[2]

Cold was not as damaging to the box office as heat if only because it came less frequently, but it too could injure the night's receipts. In January, 1834, three to four inches of snow fell and remained on the ground for several days. A winter like this was unusual, but cold spells were common and, said one observer, during such weather "even his beloved Opera . . . cannot tempt [the creole] . . . to his loge." Instead he hugs "a blazing grate of Pittsburg coal." Women especially were absent from the opera during the cold.[3]

Almost as damaging as extremes of temperature was a steady rain or a sudden and heavy shower. Street travel was difficult at best and close to impossible in wet weather. The hoped-for receipts of a given performance could simply be washed away by a shower. On one occasion in the ordinarily good month of December, rain caused such poor attendance at the Orleans that a concerned supporter of the opera publicly prayed never again to "witness such a vacancy."[4]

Such uncertainty at the box office set up a vicious cycle in which a room too scantily filled at curtain time caused a delay of the performance in the hope that a few more patrons would arrive. The spectator sat wondering whether or not there would be a performance. "Finally," wrote one, "little by little the number became considerable, but still not enough to pay expenses." At this point the orchestra began to play, but instead of the awaited overture the audience might hear "The March of Washington"—a further stall for time and all the more distasteful because everyone was thoroughly tired of this march. On the other hand, the uncertainty of curtain time, and the possibility that the curtain might not be raised at all, was in itself a cause of poor attendance. Thus it was not uncommon for the managers to give assurance of a prompt start at the advertised time—"crowd or no crowd." [5]

Late curtains not only annoyed those who sat waiting but could cause the opera to finish so late as to provide a real inconvenience to the audience, especially to those who lived any distance from the theater. Consequently the management was often forced to promise that it would take "the most certain means . . . to ensure an early termination to the performances." There were times when the mayor himself ordered a precise curtain time. [6]

The vexations of a late curtain persisted, however. Even in 1834 one annoyed patron counted but two orchestra members ready to play ten minutes after curtain time. And he noticed another delay between the end of the overture and the rise of the curtain. As long as there was any hope of more customers it was only human to stall a little. [7]

Weather and uncertain starting times were not the only brakes on attendance. Yellow fever and cholera made almost annual visits to New Orleans, frequently lasting past summer into the opera season. At best, a lingering plague kept customers away and led to measures like half price admittance after 9:00 P.M. At worst, it caused the theater to be closed completely for a period, which added the complication of arrears with the subscribers. The observance of Lent also kept many French Catholic families away from the theater, excepting on St. Joseph's Day, and in some years caused the theater to shut its doors during Holy Week. [8]

Perhaps the greatest obstacle to achieving satisfactory attendance was the effort to divide what was, after all, a limited number of customers. Almost from the beginning, dissident artists or rival promoters attempted to run competitive operas; and as time went on, such efforts intensified rather than diminished. Thus on a Tuesday night in 1836 those who contemplated attending an opera could choose among three. At the Orleans Theater was *Le Cheval de Bronze;* at the St. Charles, *Cinderella;* and at the Camp Street Theater, *La Sonnambula.* A fourth fine opera company, an Italian troupe, was also in town, but it was not playing that night. Perhaps some kind of peak was reached in the following opera season when on a Thursday night the St. Charles and the Orleans each offered *Jean de Paris* by Boieldieu, while the Camp played *The Marriage of Figaro,* and then on Saturday the Camp and the St. Charles offered *Jean de Paris*—four performances of *Jean de Paris* by three different companies on a single weekend.[9]

Far from deploring such a drain on the public's ability and desire to attend all the offered attractions, those who commented did so with pride. One said his only regret was that there was not another American theater. At the same time, John Davis had to resort to the extreme of offering to sell his Orleans Theater in order to discourage proponents of yet another French theater.[10]

The arguments he and his son made on this occasion well illustrate the real situation. They pointed out that the public was of limited size; that the heat and poor climate forced the theater to close four months each year; that in those months if the troupe went on tour the costs of travel and the rent of theaters absorbed the receipts; that, in short, supporting two French theaters was an impossibility. Hence came the Davises' offer to sell with the hope that "our successors will work as we have . . . for sixteen consecutive years." [11]

Of course to some extent rivalry might stimulate both endeavor and attendance. It was not unusual to see a comment that an opera like *The Barber of Seville* was "lately performed indifferently well at the American Theatre. . . . But those who wish to see and hear it properly done, should attend the Orleans Theatre this evening." Such statements were not advanced by the theaters themselves but rather by their champions in the several newspapers of the city. The theaters, however, undoubtedly shared in these partisan claims and were stimulated to do their utmost to make them good. When, for example, it became known in the spring of 1835 that both the American and the French theaters were contemplating a production of Meyerbeer's *Robert le Diable,* the managers and musicians at the Camp Street Theater freely admitted that they were "excited by a spirit of emulation and rivalry in their efforts to excel the production of the opera at the French theatre." Lovers of music were invited to attend both theaters to compare productions, and indeed more of the French than usual attended the Camp and vice versa.[12]

More often than not, the choice among theaters presented to the New Orleans public meant only that there were too many seats for too few patrons. This effect was heightened by a national feeling that kept a number of French and American families from attending each other's theater. On one occasion, when two well-known French dancers appeared at the American theater for a long run, several French families expressed strong disappointment at being denied an opportunity of seeing these dancers. And they blamed John Davis for their loss—he should have engaged the dancers for the Orleans Theater, the only one, apparently, that these families felt they could attend. For its part, the American theater urged Americans to show "a little national feeling," by sticking to their own theater where they were promised "more really national entertainment than . . . at any other place in this city." [13]

Thus it happened that if an especially good performer or troupe visited one of the theaters in New Orleans, the others sought to engage the same act for the benefit of its own exclusive customers. Celeste and Constance, the two French dancers mentioned above, were finally brought over to the Orleans by Davis. One year the American theater went so far as to engage the complete corps de ballet of the Orleans Theater for four appearances on the American stage. The most spectacular of such steals occurred when the Orleans Theater succeeded in engaging the entire Italian opera company that James Caldwell had brought to New Orleans for his St. Charles Street Theater.[14]

This practice could hurt attendance. The expectation that a particularly good show would be made available at one's theater of national preference made it easy to resist any temptation to attend the rival theater. At times the management made vigorous attempts to deny any possibility of waiting until a current attraction came to one's favored theater. Such denials were of little avail. On one occasion the American Camp Street Theater brought Madame Feron to the city for the first time. This singer enjoyed at the time a high reputation both abroad and in the North, for she had sung at the

San Carlo in Naples; at La Scala in Milan; with the Italian opera in
Paris; at Drury Lane in London; and at the Park Theater in New
York. Mme. Feron proved no disappointment to New Orleans when
she opened there in March, 1830, in Rossini's *Barber of Seville*.[15]

But the famed cantatrice didn't fill the house as had been hoped,
and the management knew what to blame. "A report is spread
about that . . . [Mme. Feron] . . . is engaged at the Orleans."
This the American vehemently denied, warning those who wanted
to hear her to do so right away. Such denials and warnings were
repeated for over a week, at the end of which time the management
was still insisting that "those who have been waiting better see her
now while they can." But those unconvinced ones who had been
waiting duly received their reward when Mme. Feron opened at the
Orleans in April, again singing Rosina in *The Barber of Seville*.
This was just what they had known she would do.[16]

If this kind of national partisanship could hurt the box office, it
could also provide a strong nucleus of loyal attendance, especially
in the French theater which, after all, persisted as the site of good
opera. Virtually from the time when the Americans bought Louisiana from the French, the major rallying cry of support for the
French theater was based on national feeling. Frenchmen were reminded several times annually of their duty to attend their theater.[17]

Others beside patriotic Frenchmen had to be drawn to the opera,
however, if it was to survive in New Orleans. One reliable stratagem
was to involve amateurs in one way or another with the productions. Everyone knows that parents and friends will come to see
children perform. Since the dancers in the opera usually taught
dancing in the city, it was easy enough to arrange an occasional appearance of children. Thus an opera by Isouard might be followed
with a dance by five local children—an attraction the success of
which warranted repetition. Or a ballet like *La Fille Mal Gardee* by
Dauberval might be followed by a "Great Chinese Divertissement"
in which the regular dancers of the company danced with eight of
their pupils. The aid of amateur dancers, both children and adults,

either in an opera or on the same bill with it, was freely resorted to during the first three decades of the opera's growth.[18]

Amateur singers also appeared with the professionals, though not so frequently as did dancers. To place an amateur singer in an opera could tax the endurance of the audience too far. On one occasion in June of 1808, an amateur sang the role of Valere in J. P. Solier's opera *Le Secret*. Twelve days later the opera was repeated —but with the promise that a professional would sing Valere. It was explained that last week's casting of an amateur in this role was an accident. On the other hand, an amateur sucessfully sang a male lead in Paisiello's *Barber of Seville* in 1819, or at least this performance and others like it were not subsequently referred to as "accidents." In the chorus amateur singers could be of real aid to production as well as to attendance in the early years of the opera.[19]

Perhaps the greatest service rendered to opera by amateurs during the formative period occurred in the pit. There were too few professionals to make anything like a full orchestra; accordingly the addition of a few competent amateur instrumentalists was welcomed. Especially was this true as the operas performed began to tax the resources of too small an orchestra. As early as 1810 the orchestra of the St. Peter Street Theater was augmented by amateurs for the premiere of Antonio Marcel Lemoine's opera *Les Pretendus*. Their talent, said the *Moniteur*, "will contribute to render, in all its perfection, the execution of the delicious music." Again, for the premiere of Paer's *Le Maitre de Chapelle* at the Orleans Theater in 1823, amateurs swelled the orchestra. A few weeks later the enlarged orchestra made an encore appearance during which it played a symphony composed by a local artist and dedicated to the Louisiana Legion. Presumably this program filled the theater with the members of the Legion as well as with the friends and families of the amateurs. At any rate, the symphony was repeated with another opera in the following week. Until the early 1830's the orchestra at one or the other of the two theaters was, on occasion, "greatly improved by the aid of a number of amateurs." [20]

A greater orchestral treat occurred when the musicians of both theaters combined with amateurs to enlarge the orchestra as much as possible. Such an aggregation played at the Orleans Theater in 1826 when the Philharmonic Society, a recently organized group of amateur musicians, together with the Camp Street Theater instrumentalists, added their combined talents to the French theater orchestra. Again in 1833 the Camp Street orchestra was greatly expanded by musicians from the Orleans Theater plus several other professionals and a number of amateurs.[21]

After the St. Charles Street Theater opened in 1835, such combinations were no longer necessary. Thereafter both the Orleans and the St. Charles orchestras were generally adequate in size and quality. Indeed, the St. Charles orchestra was vaunted as "probably the best in the United States," excepting, of course, that of the Orleans. By this time, too, the operas being produced were increasingly complex and demanding, and the standard of performance had risen steadily.[22]

Enlisting amateurs was only one of the means used to draw customers. Another was outright psychological pressure. In the space of a single year, prospective patrons were warned that the city couldn't hope to attract artists of high caliber unless the receipts proved more encouraging; that they might never hear a certain singer again unless she was better supported; that they couldn't expect the best performances in a partially filled house; and that not to attend would be to show ingratitude, or worse, to display poor taste.[23]

Sometimes, during the early years, the plot of a forthcoming opera was published in advance. Later when an important new opera such as *Robert le Diable* was in rehearsal, management went further, using a full column of newspaper space to give a serial presentation of the historical background of the characters and setting, and descriptions of incidents and scenes from the opera itself. Seldom though did the French management resort to ballyhoo like that used by the American when it described one operatic offering as a "Celebrated, Tragical, Comical, Melodramatical, Operatical, Farcical, Olopodridical, Pantomimical, Romance." [24]

In a day when travel was difficult and cameras unknown, the opera could be expected to attract many who were curious about faraway places. Scenes were often given precedence over scores in the newspapers. Siberia; "Kamchattka covered with snow"; "a picturesque scene in Germany"; an exotic slave market; the ruins of Athens with "handsome monuments of antiquity"; Zurich Lake; Mont Parnasse; or simply "a great picture" were strong inducements to attend the opera. Meyerbeer's *Robert le Diable* was an important opera long and eagerly awaited in New Orleans, but its initial attraction was heightened by "a scene embodying Martin's masterly picture of Pandemonium . . . likely to prove one of the most splendid scenic effects ever witnessed . . . in this or any other country." A music critic might lament that the operas were relying so much on extravagant scenery and then go on to say, "However, I am persuaded that the beauty of the scenery, and the execution of the machinery . . . are alone enough to draw a large number to more playings." [25]

New decorations and new costumes were frequently employed to freshen interest in a familiar opera—an important consideration when the repertoire was limited. Best of all was to acquire new scenery resembling as closely as possible that used for the same opera in France. But merely a new front curtain depicting Harlequin's mantle and coronation with "two representations of Fame" or even new red lights from Paris could bring out an increased crowd.[26]

The French and American theaters were rivals in scenery as much as they were in orchestras. And here too the local press awarded palms to its own. "No two theatres in the Union produce in their respective lines (consulting, as they are obliged to do, national prejudices) so great a mass of valuable and splendid scenery as do the two elegant theatres of our city." [27]

But perhaps the surest way to keep customers coming to the operas was simply to couple the principal performance with other attractions. Light musical comedies of one or two acts, called vaudevilles, were the most common of these. Seldom was an opera scheduled without at least one vaudeville. Occasionally, if an opera was very long, as in the case of *La Dame Blanche,* it was presented alone. But after six playings of this opera, a vaudeville had to be added as a companion piece.[28]

More than vaudeville was needed, however, and a steady procession of bizarre acts were paired with stately operas. A horse act; M. Sacosky, the strong man; Mrs. Champciaux who rendered Spanish dances with castanets and Chinese dances with the tambourin—all on a tight rope; jugglers; lecturers on physics; an automation trumpeter; hydraulic experiments; burlesque; duels, Tyrolian minstrels; a "Trestigiator, Mimic and Angostemith" who gave representations of the wonders of art and nature; and a gruesome team consisting of an anaconda and a boa constrictor—all shared the bill with operas at one time or another.[29]

Those who went to the Orleans in 1827 to hear the opera *La Vieille* by François Fetis were subjected to a "phantasmagoria" in the first scene of which a skeleton, beating the call of the dead on a drum, came from the distance and kept approaching the audience. This cheerful sight was followed by the tomb of Louis XVI, then assorted Egyptian mummies, and finally a view of Dr. Young stealing a grave for his daughter and burying her. Little wonder that a critic found the opera to be "extremely cold" and the chorus singers "badly indifferent." Who wouldn't be? [30]

Acrobatics on the tight rope proved a durable favorite as a companion piece to opera. In the beginning of April, 1833, the Ravel family of ten "rope dancers" began an engagement which lasted over six weeks, during which time they performed with various operas. When the Ravels at last departed, one relieved critic made much of the first opera played without them—not because the presentation was good but because it marked the end for a time of "these interminable representations of tightrope." [31]

Yet another tightrope artist was Herr Cline who performed at the Orleans in 1830. He first appeared at Caldwell's Camp Street Theatre but had had an uproarious quarrel with Caldwell in which each came on stage to plead his case with the audience until that abused group forced the show to continue. Herr Cline was thereupon hired by the Orleans Theater where he lent drawing power, if not dignity, by dancing a *pas de deux* with his grandmother on the high wire and by climbing sixty feet "to paradise." The Camp Street Theater promptly objected that the "dwelling of the Gods" could not be reached in the rival abode, for "at this height, in the

Orleans Theatre, dwell the goddesses of fraility [sic]." But this statistic, if accurate, could only enhance the excitement of the climb. Certainly Herr Cline continued his visits to Paradise and the nymphs in the balcony at the Orleans off and on for the next five years. "This is the sad state into which our French Theatre has fallen," wrote one dejected music lover, "thanks to the indifference of the public which prefers acrobats." [32]

The protesting critic might have taken comfort from one practice fortunately lacking at the French theater. At least there an opera, although it might be sandwiched in between an acrobat and a burlesque, was performed with as much integrity as possible. Such was not the case at the American theater where it was often thought desirable to include currently popular numbers within the very body of whatever opera was being played. When Mme. Feron sang *The Barber of Seville,* she was obliged to omit a substantial portion of Rossini's music in favor of songs like "The Arab Steed," "Trifle Light as Air," or "An Old Man Would Be Wooing," while in Mozart's *Marriage of Figaro* she was compelled to sing "The Light Guitar," "Should Be Upbraid," "Come Prithee Kneel to Me," and "Bright Eyes." In the same vein, Boieldieu's *Jean de Paris* was advertised with the promise that in it the customer would hear "Love Among the Roses," "The Knight of the Golden Crest," "All's Well," and other songs plus, either as reward or punishment, a number of solos and choruses "belonging to the piece." Perhaps these latter were included in order to identify the opera to the listener.[33]

Subscribers to the Orleans Theater at times got not only an opera but a concert as well. A typical concert at the Orleans included an overture, a clarinet solo, an air and variations on the guitar by the wife of one of the orchestra members, a vocal solo, and a violin and viola duet—all preceding the opera. One concert was rendered by an Italian couple newly arrived from Portugal who hoped to acquaint the city with their abilities as singers and teachers of singing. On another such occasion, M. Lewis and his five children performed upon two pianos, harp, violin, cello, and bass. The Lewis family gave four concerts with four different operas at the Orleans.

Now and then an instrumentalist of the orchestra played a concert solo at the French theater, while at the St. Charles the appearance of a lone virtuoso became a commonplace occurrence. There trumpet, trombone, flute, and clarinet solos accompanied nearly every show—not excluding even the Italian opera.[34]

By spicing the fare the theaters of New Orleans sought to increase the public appeal of operas. So famed a personality as Daddy Rice, the black-face entertainer, might appear on occasion to do his "Jim Crow" and "Oh Hush," sharing the bill with Meyerbeer's *Robert le Diable*. Or, in less spectacular fashion, the French theater company after singing *William Tell* might make a quick change into the militia uniforms of the various companies of the Louisiana Legion and sing songs dedicated to the soldiers. In either case the object was the same.[35]

On the whole this variety, though born of necessity, was probably a healthful practice. Facilities for entertainment were few, and there must have been a great many people who endured the opera in order not to miss the other attractions. Who can tell how many of these people became sincere opera lovers? Familiarity is a necessary breeding ground for appreciation in any art. So too the involvement of amateur and professional local talent, on the stage and in the pit, was bound to promote a feeling of kinship and loyalty to the resident company, thus providing an important base of support. Ultimately, of course, opera must rely primarily upon its intrinsic merit in order to survive, but the initial task of developing a hard core of devotees cannot always be trusted to merit alone. The extra-operatic attraction, tasteless as it may have seemed in some cases, performed valuable service as midwife until, by 1840, a strong and genuine tradition of opera appreciation had been born.

The spectre of insolvency hovered always close about the French company during its early years, causing concern with matters as trivial as the sale of cut-rate tickets and matters as serious as heavy debts. Trouble over tickets had its origin in the policy of selling subscription passes for a season. A minimum of subscriptions had to be sold each year in order to guarantee some stability of income, and every effort was made to sell as many as possible.

Ideally, of course, if all seats could be sold by subscription, income would be assured and ample. But only a portion was sold in this way which meant that the difference between a solvent and an insolvent season rested upon the door sales of the unsubscribed seats. The obstacle was that many of the subscribers were as zealous in selling their own tickets when not in use as was the theater in selling its own. The more venturesome or avaricious made it a custom to go to the streets around the theater or even to the theater door to sell their passes, in spite of warnings that "proper steps" would be taken against such practices. By the second decade of the nineteenth century this difficulty had dwindled away only to be replaced by another irritation. Certain subscribers fell into "the habit of demanding tickets on credit" while developing at the same time a reluctance to pay up. There were enough of these delinquent patrons to force the management periodically to threaten legal action. Unlike the earlier trouble, this vexation was not outgrown. In 1840 there were subscription arrears that dated back three years.[36]

Perhaps as many as half of the shows in a given season were nonsubscription. On these nights all the seats in the house were for sale. When a subscriber came to these shows, however, he naturally wanted his own seat or loge and would most likely be offended if it were not held for him. But what if he chose not to attend? All the management could do was request that subscribers give advance notice when they did not intend to come so that their seats might be sold. Even had there been telephones this policy would have been far from satisfactory.[37]

Nor were these matters of small importance—the Orleans Theater needed every penny. By 1830 the municipal corporation had advanced more money to John Davis, for the support of his theater, than he could repay. To make matters worse, his debt was the subject of a bitter dispute in the city council between the American and the French members. The Americans were inclined to be less lenient than the French in the matter of Davis' arrears. The council finally agreed to a partial settlement of eighteen thousand dollars but only because the mayor convinced the members that this was the most that could be hoped for. Even so, Davis requested twelve years in which to complete payment.[38]

Fortunately for the continuance of opera in New Orleans, the theater had recourse to various other sources of income. Balls were prime contributors, directly and indirectly. Opera could never have gotten a start without the assistance of ballrom proprietors, and the Orleans Theater could not have existed without its own profitable ballroom. Balls were sometimes used to draw people to the opera—a ticket to the opera entitled the holder to attend the ball free or at most to pay only fifty cents if his seat were in the pit. Maskers attending fancy dress balls often rented their costumes from the Orleans Theater wardrobe, thus supplying another bit of revenue to the hard-pressed management.[39]

The Orleans orchestra received directly the proceeds from a series of Saturday balls in 1837; and since balls were frequently given in conjunction with a concert, the singers also were able at times to share in the proceeds. Much more often though the balls served to augment the income of many orchestra members hired to play for them. In addition to the promise of good music, an orchestra composed entirely of instrumentalists from the Orleans Theater lent cachet to a ball. Even having an orchestra directed by one of the Orleans musicians enhanced the drawing power of a ball.[40]

Balls were not an unmixed blessing, however. Even the great Junius Brutus Booth played to an empty house on a night when there were numerous balls elsewhere to entice those in search of entertainment. As ballrooms of the less reputable sort multiplied, they made a noticeable inroad on theater attendance. "Public taste is vitiated and led out of its legitimate channel by those abominable places . . . ," mourned one observer in explaining the reason for a "sorry house" at the theater. Consequently the opera often had to raise its curtain at an inconveniently early hour in order to finish before ball time.[41]

Gambling too was a constant source of income in spite of occasional grumblings and moves to prohibit it in the theaters. Both John Davis and James Caldwell diligently maintained their licences for gambling. In addition, each theater had its dram shop where thirsty men could fortify themselves between the acts as well as before and after the show.[42]

In view of these gambling and drinking facilities, it was rather

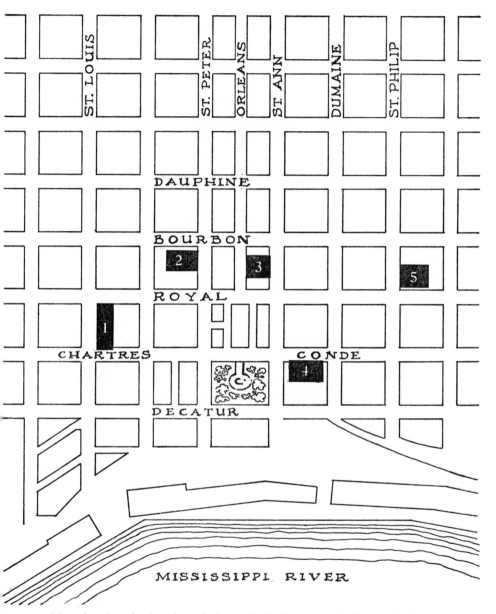

Map showing the location of the major ballrooms and theaters in New
Orleans. (1) St. Louis Hotel, (2) St. Peter Street Theater, (3) Orleans
Theater and Ballroom, (4) Conde Street Ballroom, (5) St. Philip Street
Theater, later the Washington Ballroom.

incongruent that one of the biggest financial supports to the opera came from the Council of the First Municipality. In 1836 that body voted to subscribe $200,000 to the Orleans Theater Company. The act was approved on the grounds that the theater was good for morals—it kept youth out of billiard rooms and cafes. A more rational argument for this subscription was the hope that it would allow a reduced price of admission, thus encouraging a taste for opera among the lower classes.[43]

Finally, the ordinary business activities of a port city provided a measure of financial help. From its inception the Orleans Theater building contained rental quarters for shops and other businesses; and in 1837, the state legislature authorized both the Orleans Theater Company and the St. Charles Theater Company to engage in the marine and fire insurance business.[44]

In spite of everything, the financial situation of the opera was constantly tight enough to cause recurrent hardships among the personnel. In 1840 one group of disillusioned performers publicized their grievances in a Parisian theatrical journal with the object of discouraging others from joining the French opera in New Orleans. It cost them, they contended, much more to live in New Orleans than they had been led to believe. They found that, excepting standard costumes, they were compelled to provide their own. One singer who was forced to take tenor roles when tenors were ill or lacking had to supply these extra costumes himself. Women artists had to pay the expense of hairdressers in addition to the cost of gowns. The social whirl in New Orleans was more demanding than they had anticipated, requiring a burdensome expenditure for proper clothing. Yellow fever made illness and even death an ever-present threat. To make matters worse, they were paid in paper money which could not be converted without loss. And being so far from home, they were at the mercy of an arrogant management which had worn a false face of deference and respect in France. Once in New Orleans, they had discovered that their eighteen-month engagement stretched out to twenty because of the summer without pay. They had even been refused their passage money home and had found themselves the victims of intrigue when they tried to collect in the courts. The result was that they had lived miserably while in America, and many of their comrades who had remained would never see home again unless a miracle happened.[45]

They claimed that their experience was typical, and they were not too far wrong. Whether it was the enforced auction of a singer's costumes, scores, and scripts; an announcement by a group of actors that they had received no salary for a long time; an offer to sell a performer's wardrobe "at a very moderate price for cash"; a benefit to help an esteemed soprano who, after twenty-two years of service, lacked passage money to join her daughter in France; or simply the unpretentious notice that Euphanie, the bilingual slave of one of the company, would sell cakes in front of the theater—it is plain that the lot of many connected with the theater was not always easy.[46]

There were indeed reasons enough to shun an engagement in New Orleans; but there were better reasons to accept—the New Orleans opera experienced little difficulty in recruiting musicians. Then, as always, members of this profession were forced to go where there was work. More than this, the city and the situation offered much to aspiring artists. Singers who might have to wait years for a chance in France found in New Orleans an opportunity to learn repertoire and gain experience in singing leads with a company that excelled most of those in France outside Paris. Musicians who composed in New Orleans could expect to see their works produced—an expectation almost nonexistent in France. Within the first twenty-one seasons of the Orleans Theater no fewer than eleven operas by resident composers were presented—some of them as many as three or four times—to say nothing of a host of overtures, cantatas, concertos, and symphonies.[47]

The possibility of hearing one's own composition performed was hard to resist. This was illustrated when one composer, Estevan Cristiani, who came to the city to give some concerts, leaped at the opportunity and composed on the spot an opera which he conducted personally from the piano at the Orleans Theater in 1823. And that the city appreciated and encouraged its composers was demonstrated by the reception it gave to *Cosimo*, the first opera composed by Eugene Prevost, the young orchestra leader at the Orleans in 1839. *Cosimo* was performed three times that season, and Prevost's second opera, *Le Bon Garcon,* was also produced.[48]

Another attraction for European artists was the opportunity to procure employment for more than one member of the family. Husband-and-wife teams were frequently hired whether both sang or one of the pair played in the orchestra. A very good singer such as Mme. Bamberger may well have been drawn to New Orleans by the fact that her husband was hired as cellist in the orchestra. No fewer than four married couples were employed in the fall of 1823. Sometimes the family combination might be father and son playing their respective instruments in the orchestra. Even if the husband or wife of an engaged artist was not also hired by the theater, there were other musical opportunities in New Orleans that were not available to the same degree back home. Thus the husband of one singer taught guitar and voice in addition to selling music and tuning pianos, while the wife of another theater artist gave voice lessons.[49]

The hiring of couples was as advantageous to the city as to those engaged. When Ernest Guiraud's father joined the orchestra of the Orleans Theater in 1832, he brought with him his wife who soon gave a piano recital. One leading New Orleans critic proclaimed that "never before this charming young virtuoso has one heard here a piano so perfect . . . ," and went on to predict that she would "draw a crowd of students." [50]

For that matter, nearly all the singers and instrumentalists who came over with the opera during these early decades of its existence found ample opportunity to teach. Not a few of them discovered teaching and related pursuits to be lucrative enough to induce them, at the expiration of their contracts, to remain as a permanent part of the city's musical life. Gregorio Curto, for one, sang only two seasons after joining the opera in 1830, before he withdrew to become a church organist and choir master, a prolific composer of church and other music, and a voice teacher who taught, among others, the famed Minnie Hauk.[51]

Finally, aside from material reward or musical opportunity, there was balm for the soul in being virtually lionized by the people of New Orleans. No sooner did the ship dock with its artist passengers than a crowd gathered to welcome and cheer them and to assist them royally to their hotel. Indeed, one of the complaints of the dissident letter writers quoted earlier was the need for clothing to accept all the invitations they received. And even these discontented ones conceded, "The public is very good to the artists: there is not one . . . [returning to France] . . . who does not carry tokens of its benevolence and esteem. . . ." There was in truth much to entice hopeful talent to New Orleans.[52]

Recruiting, however, was not the only problem connected with personnel. For one thing, their date of arrival was always uncertain, sometimes causing the theater to delay its opening with a consequent loss of good playing dates. Although it was known that the new recruits had left Le Havre on September 2, 1836, almost three months passed with their whereabouts unknown. November entered its last week with the management knowing only that the season was slipping by and that the expected ship had not come. In order to lose no more time, the theater tried to open on November 24 with the personnel on hand, but the attempt was blocked when one artist refused to perform on the grounds that his contract began only when the ship arrived.[53]

For another thing, while the policy of importing personnel from France was generally approved, resentment sprang up among those who thought that local talent was slighted. When a young singer, a long-time resident and pupil of Ferdinando Paer himself, sang at a concert, a reviewer called her voice "one of the most beautiful and brilliant to be heard even in Europe," and demanded to know why she never sang in the opera. His conclusion was that the girl was "nearly creole," and "we do not render her all the credit she merits; you know by experience that we prefer on our soil only the exotic plants, over those which are indigenous or naturalized." Another critic agreed with the first, claiming that New Orleans had never heard a better singer.[54]

In some cases, the visiting artists themselves incurred resentment by their cavalier disregard of local sensitivities. In the presentation of Auber's *Le Concert a la Cour* one performer, playing the role of an artist about to give a concert, was careless about his footgear. The boots he wore were described as nearly cavalry in type, and it was further noted that his heavy leather trouser straps seemed never to have been shined. "It is true," wrote one outraged viewer, that "the scene is in Germany, and . . . these gentlemen are not as fussy as us, who, although living on the banks of the Mississippi, are not completely savages, but we have a little more the sentiments of propriety." New Orleans, he said, was entitled to more regard.[55]

A reverse sort of resentment occurred when visiting artists achieved much local popularity and then for one reason or another were not rehired. "In France they might force the director to re-engage," remarked one complainant, "but this is a free country." The same writer charged that the administration "for which the inhabitants have done so much" was releasing its best stars "against the public wish."[56]

The problem of recruiting was further vexed by the hiring abroad of untried singers. There was always the chance that one of these might not measure up, and when this happened nothing could be done about it for at least a season. In February, 1833, the *Argus* lamented that every opera given that season had suffered because one of the lead singers had proved a disappointment. On the other hand it was gratifying to discover an unknown who delighted with a "manly and sonorous voice," earning the prediction that "he will be one of the distinguished members of the troupe."[57]

But even if the performers arrived on time, incurred no resentment, and proved to have no ineffective singers among them, other difficulties were inherent in the practice of hiring personnel so far from home. The company could usually afford to engage only one of each type of performer, and whenever any became ill or otherwise indisposed, the scheduled opera ordinarily had to be postponed. Last minute replacements of one opera with another were common occurrences made doubly difficult by the necessity for finding a substitute opera that didn't require the services of the missing performer. In one case several operas, presumably rehearsed and ready to play, had to be postponed because of the prolonged illness and eventual death of one artist. In another instance, the repeated postponement of *The Barber of Seville* caused a portion of the public to grumble illogically and to blame the management. Fortunately the singer on this occasion recovered. But M. Josse, the principal comic dancer in the first real corps de ballet at the Orleans Theater, died shortly after his arrival in New Orleans, thus handicapping the ballet for the entire season of 1822–23.[58]

In any event, tradition and financial necessity dictated that the show must go on if at all possible. Let a tenor be afflicted with a bad cold: if he were on his feet, he sang—even though the falsetto upon which he was dependent was rendered practically nonexistent by his condition. Let another fall and injure himself during the premiere of an important and expensively produced opera: an actress from the dramatic troupe would be impressed with but two days preparation for the next performance. When the illness of a singer delayed an opera overmuch, another who was essentially an actor found himself singing no less a role than Almaviva in Mozart's *Marriage of Figaro* because, said the management, it did not want "to deprive the public too long of this work." [59]

Even with all in good health the limited size of the company meant that actors were often compelled to sing secondary roles in the operatic presentations and vice versa. For sensitive theatergoers this was doubly distressful: it was unpleasant to witness the incongruity of a favorite dramatic performer singing some inconsequential part or working in the chorus. "One sees with pain a priestess of Melpomene shake the bells of Momus, or sing in the chorus of an opera," wrote one, referring to the acknowledged queen of tragedy, Mme. Clozel. The displeasure increased in proportion to the importance of the role; and comments ranged from "she was not able to sing very perfectly the delicious music of this opera" to a caustic "the charming duet between Elise and Victorine was barked by Mme. Bolze and wheezed by Mlle. Placide"—although the writer here kindly added that it was not their fault since they were not primarily singers.[60]

Others, however, while admitting that not everyone in a particular cast was first-rate or especially suited for his role, argued sensibly that the public should not be deprived of "the pleasure of hearing the compositions of an Auber, a Bellini, a Rossini, a Mozart and a hundred other masters, because they cannot get Malibrans and Rubinis." The more liberal of the attitudes here expressed do much to explain the eventual success of opera in New Orleans.[61]

Whatever talents the company's personnel possessed were utilized in other ways too. Both dancers and singers painted scenery. Possibly the ultimate in doubling was reached in 1840 when one of the singers played second bass in the orchestra while he was not on stage.[62]

Though singing suffered somewhat from limited personnel and the great distance from France, choreography was affected far more. In the early years what dances there were had to be composed by the local dancing teachers who promised that their work would be at least analogous to the opera and that they would adhere strictly "to the rules adopted by the best teachers of choreography." One wonders how analogous the resulting dance pieces might have been; at least it was worth special mention when a new opera could be advertised as having in it new dances as well. If an opera were canceled, the dance promised for that particular presentation was not dropped but simply retained in the substitute opera.[63]

Not until the rebuilt Orleans Theater entered its fourth season in the fall of 1822 did John Davis bring from France a genuine corps de ballet. Even though one of the lead dancers died, the group managed to stage such ballets as *Annete et Lubin* and *La Fille Mal Gardee* by Dauberval. (*La Fille Mal Gardee,* one of history's first ballets, was revived in 1960 by England's Royal Ballet.) The operas of course were greatly enhanced by the improved dancing—so much so that, as one put it, "the theatrical dance was a pleasure scarcely known in New Orleans and like all new pleasures had first to be tasted to be liked. [It has] . . . made a most agreeable diversion in our theatre. Therpsicore [*sic*] comes thus to our town." [64]

Terpsichore did not take up permanent residence, however. A regular corps de ballet was simply too expensive. The kind of dual service in both opera and drama that was expected of so many of the singers and actors could not be extended to the ballet. A singer might not make a good actor, nor an actor a good singer; still the substitution was at least possible, indeed necessary, to the existence of the company. It got by. But for a singer or an actor to double as a ballet dancer was a different matter. Croaks might be endured in an opera or ham in a drama for the sake of the whole. Besides, most of the company more often than not were fairly efficient in their secondary capacity. But to stumble around in a ballet was fatal. Accordingly, a first-class dance troupe had to be complete in itself and large enough to provide for possible disabilities among its members. A troupe of this kind was beyond the means of the privately supported Orleans Theater.

To be sure, the experiment with ballet was repeated now and then during the next twenty years, notably in 1829. But more often a solution was sought with fewer and inferior dances, or else the choreography of an opera was "eliminated or reduced to little significance." [65]

Unsatisfactory dancing was not accepted without protest, however. Guillaume Montmain, a critic and loyal supporter of the theater, warned that the policy of deleting dances from operas would draw neither honor nor profit to the Orleans Theater. He admitted that Auber's *La Muette de Portici* had succeeded in spite of the absence of a ballet but claimed that it was an exception. Not all operas had such grand music. Another critic remarked of Auber's opera, *Gustave III,* that "the dancers did the best they could with what they have—it is astonishing that they do as well as they do." Therefore he pleaded that since "the company has had enough good business this year (1837–38), why not take a little of the profits to procure us a little troup[e] of dancers?" He then wisely pointed out that "with such a troup[e] many of the old operas would be rejuvenated; as for example *Le Pre aux Clercs, La Muette,* and even *Robert le Diable.*" [66]

Perhaps the company's willingness to forego the benefits of rejuvenation may be understood—aside from any financial consideration—from a little news item which appeared in January of 1840: "The horses and mules used in the ballet were not well trained; they were not used to the smell of the lamps and some of the riders got thrown. We have not heard whether any of the actors sustained serious injury." [67]

Often lacking, then, a ballet or any overpowering stars, an opera had to stand much more upon its essential musical worth in New Orleans than in Paris. Operas like Auber's *Le Philtre* which had been a huge success in Paris proved disappointing in New Orleans, opinion being that the Paris success was a tribute to the stars that appeared in it there. "It is not necessary to believe that because a piece is played 100 times in Paris it is good," was a critical lesson easily learned in the Crescent City. Consequently, attention focused on the music itself; scores were of prime importance and were the object of three concerns: obtaining them at all, producing enough of them, and adapting them.[68]

For the first quarter of the nineteenth century, just to obtain the score of some operas was an achievement. At least one opera in its initial presentation was performed completely without music. The company had the libretto but not the score, and it could wait no longer. When the directors of the theater made a special point of advertising a new opera with the claim that they had "received from France the complete score," the inference is that there were other productions not so well blessed. Or when they announced an opera as now having "the original music from Paris, recently arrived," the suspicion arises that this opera must have played before with partial or improvised music. Under such circumstances one may well understand the consternation of M. St. Esteve, the manager of the Orleans Theater in 1822, when he offered a twenty-five dollar reward for the only score he had of a Dalayrac opera unaccountably lost in, of all places, the ladies room at the Orleans Ballroom.[69]

After 1825 the problem of obtaining scores eased off, although ten years later one of the promises made for the Camp Street Theater's production of *Robert le Diable* was that the director, Reynoldson, had "the whole of the original music, lent him by M. Pierce Butler of Philadelphia." [70]

Producing enough operas was a more persistent difficulty. Variety was desirable since the audience was limited and its choice of amusements restricted. Among the benefits hoped for in the launching of the Orleans Theater in 1819 was that "it would obtain many charming operas known as yet only by the success they had achieved in France." Accordingly the arrival of a new group of operas was always a newsworthy event, made even more important if they had "nearly all played in Paris in the last two years." But old or recent in Paris, they were new in New Orleans, and an opera, like prohibition whiskey, was choicest if it was just off the boat.[71]

Notwithstanding the need for variety, there was a limit to the number of operas the Orleans company could afford to keep in production. Moreover the effort involved in staging a new one had, by the 1830's, grown to proportions that prohibited undertaking more than one or two fresh productions in a season. Auber's *Gustave III*, first performed in the spring of 1838, had been announced for nearly a year ahead and promised "shortly" for three months. Even so, it caused the company to lose a night's revenue by necessitating a closed theater for yet another rehearsal.[72]

Despite such restraints the company managed to expand its offerings fairly often. Not often enough, however, to prevent a constant stream of complaints being directed at the repertoire throughout the 1830's. In 1833 it was "an old base of operas . . . everybody knows by heart"; and in 1835 offerings were disparaged as "things played and replayed . . . many times before." The musical journal *Le Moqueur* lamented in 1837 that critics were hard put to find anything more to say about familiar operas. The critics found their voices again the next year. The repertoire marches, said one, "from *Robert le Diable* to *l'Ambassadrice,* and from *l'Ambassadrice* to *Robert;* the other pieces are too well known to count." Another complained that "the repertoire the most used and least varied appears to be the order of the day," and warned, "the discontent will soon burst." [73]

One possible means of increasing the number of operas was to drop the dramatic efforts of the company, and early in 1838, yielding for a brief time to the pleas of several shareholders, the directors staged operas only. Now the theater found itself in the position of relying solely upon the music-loving portion of its audience. But aside from this troubling circumstance, there was inherent in the situation another obstacle that soon presented itself. The problem was well formulated in the question of a disturbed patron. Would "time permit them to mount enough operas to give the public what it needs?" he asked. "And if they could—if they could mount ten operas in six months, would they be constantly assured of a sufficient number, and not consume in one year that which must suffice for two?" The answer to both parts of the query was no. With an audience which must be essentially the same all season long, there was no way to avoid an irksome sameness of repertoire. If that audience wished to have an opera company, it must be prepared to support the same offerings time and again.[74]

The major difficulty which had to be met concerning scores during these years was the necessity of adapting them to the musical resources on hand. At no time during the period was the orchestra large enough and varied enough to permit playing a score without some rearrangement, but the need was most acute before 1810. To perform an opera at that time required major surgery on the instrumental portion as well as some modification of the vocal parts. That this was accomplished is a measure of the fervor and ingenuity of those musical pioneers who brought opera to New Orleans.

Some indication of the orchestral limitations that had to be surmounted may be seen in a pledge by the St. Philip Street company in 1807. It declared itself "determined, above all, to procure a good orchestra." When completed, this "good orchestra" could boast four musicians. Nor was the St. Peter Street Theater any better off in this regard.[75]

Fortunately there were at least three men—Louis H. Desforges, Philip Laroque, and Philip Valois—capable of rearranging the score for a small orchestra. Vocalists too were in short supply, at least before 1810. In *La Soiree Orageuse,* as a case in point, Valois' problem was to change quartets to trios and quintets to quartets. When all else failed, a weak singer was covered by the simple expedient of having the others sing louder. Desforges, Laroque, and Valois toiled valiantly up to the 1820's, and were indispensable in making opera possible in New Orleans.[76]

By 1811 the situation had eased somewhat. At a certain concert that year, there were four clarinets, two flutes, two horns, bassoon, and bass. Since violinists were always in considerably greater supply than other instrumentalists, an orchestra of eighteen to twenty musicians could be and most probably was assembled for operas. In 1819 the policy of importing musicians from France began; and throughout the next few years the orchestra at the Orleans Theater grew enough in size and quality to be enthusiastically acclaimed on its 1827 tour as the largest and best ever heard in the North.[77]

From that time on, competent musicians were plentiful in New Orleans. Noah Ludlow needed only ten days to send for and to obtain a new orchestra and leader when, on his tour to Natchez in 1831, the musicians he had brought with him went on strike. Ludlow's success in securing musicians was all the more remarkable in that his request for them reached New Orleans in February, the time of carnival and the city's busiest month in music. In 1834 Ludlow's famous theatrical partner, Sol Smith, preparing for a southern tour, recruited an orchestra in New Orleans in what he called "a very short time." When in the latter half of the decade the promoter needed a "first-rate orchestra" for a new amusement garden and theater to be opened in Mobile, he simply advertised in a New Orleans newspaper for musicians and vocalists.[78]

Thus when the St. Charles Theater opened in 1835 its orchestra consisted of twenty-nine instrumentalists besides the leader, and the group was enlarged steadily during the next three years. The New American Theater which opened on Poydras Street in November of 1840 also was able to muster a large orchestra of twenty-six musicians. The Orleans Theater orchestra remained of course larger and admittedly better than its rivals. Late in 1839 this finest of New Orleans' orchestras was still being compelled to render certain oboe parts on clarinets; but the welcome addition of an oboe as well as a bassoon for the next season marked orchestral maturity as the New Orleans opera entered its greatest period.[79]

The presence of a second major orchestra in the St. Charles Theater may have helped to promote opera, regardless of whether any were being produced there. For although the rest of the bill might be tragedy, comedy, or vaudeville, the St. Charles orchestra liked to play the overtures to operas. In one typical schedule in February, 1837, the group played five overtures in three days: on Monday, *Masaniello* and *Fra Diavolo;* on Tuesday *La Dame Blanche* and *Fra Diavolo;* and on Wednesday *Der Freischutz.* Such constant sampling could have induced some listeners to attend the actual operas.

However, the St. Charles catered primarily to Americans, and more often than not the overture elicited "much stirring, rustling, talking, uneasiness, etc." An unhappy Frenchman who came to the St. Charles expressly to hear the overture to *Semiramide* burst out that he had never seen people like these Americans. "He come to de theatre, and wen de grand overture is play supurb, magnifique, he no make de applause—he no say noting. Dam, he make de row—he chaw away on apple and chesnut, and everyting, like pig . . . he keep everyone from de enjoyment. . . . Wen dat gal come on de stage, and begin for sing 'one petite baby catch some sleep,' aha! dat is de music for him—den he clap his hand and make de grand encore all for nothing. I no make disturb anybody den—what for dey make disturb me now?" [80]

"Dey make disturb" because in truth they were not too happy with opera overtures no matter how well played. They enjoyed the fine orchestra of the St. Charles immensely but preferred a different type of music. "Many of the overtures . . . excellent in themselves, give no pleasure to the mass, when a good simple air would be relished . . . ," complained one spokesman early in 1838; while another demanded to "hear our national airs from the orchestra of the St. Charles." [81]

James Caldwell should have anticipated these demands for simple and patriotic music. A few years before in his first theater on Camp Street, the orchestra diligently prepared the overture from *La Dame Blanche* as a special treat for the Fourth of July. The musicians hadn't played long before the impatient audience began to roar for "Yankee Doodle." The conductor was Louis Hus Desforges, a veteran musician who had been associated with opera in New Orleans virtually from its start. M. Desforges was also a veteran of the Battle of New Orleans and as a result had been nearly deaf for fifteen years. Now therefore he was happily unaware of the uproar behind him, hearing only what he took to be a gentle murmur of approval. While he put his heart into this work with supreme vigor, the audience began to tear up chairs and benches. The old conductor came to a halt only when the distraught Caldwell reached the podium and shouted in his ear to stop! The audience wanted "Yankee Doodle"! Turning with hurt dignity to the unruly Americans, Desforges dressed them down: "You want Yankee Dude? Well, you no have Yankee Dude! Because Why? Because not necessair." Whereupon he finished his beloved overture without further interruption from the awed Americans.[82]

By 1838 the demands in the St. Charles for "Yankee Doodle" could not be stemmed. Caldwell felt obliged to offer a liberal prize for the best full orchestral arrangements of "Hail Columbia," "Washington's March," and "Yankee Doodle." When the award-winning arrangements were first played on April 15, 1838, the reaction was mixed. Some wrote in praise saying that there never had been before "a suitable arrangement of the National Airs, for a full orchestra." Now these would be played in the St. Charles in a manner not to be equalled anywhere else. Others remained unsatisfied, either accusing Caldwell of having sat on the scores far too long or of having displayed impatience with the whole business.

We had national airs . . . and no accompaniments, flourishes, or additions can ever alter the effect of our plain simple strain of Yankee Doodle. . . . If Mr. Caldwell was properly ashamed of having national airs without accompaniment in his fine theatre he must recollect that millions of native born citizens were not ashamed to hear them. None but the foreign foe ever expressed shame at the sound of Yankee Doodle, or Hail Columbia, tho' both were played upon a Jew's Harp! We never objected to the accompaniment, but to the clumsy excuse given for not playing our national airs—they were too plain and Mr. Caldwell was ashamed of them! . . . Why not be ashamed of our Declaration of Independence? Why not introduce some French, Spanish, or Italian quotations in it? . . . Why not decorate everything that is plain and simple with some foreign insignia? . . . our fathers marched barefoot to the tune of Yankee Doodle played on a simple fife. And yet we are told it could not be performed at the St. Charles in that style because Caldwell was ashamed of it! It would not do for his temple! Holy St. Paul! [83]

Caldwell couldn't win.

Although the foregoing tirade was motivated in part by the American nativism then waxing in New Orleans, it was also reflective of the musical taste of many Americans. Not only did they crack nuts and chomp apples during serious music, but they were prone to articulate their preference for sentimental over "scientific" singers; for the natural over the "artificial." Of a certain singer, one person complained that "after his journey to Italy his style . . . became completely vitiated by artifice as well as art. But when he chooses to give sweetly and simply a song of his native Scotland . . . there are few who excel him." [84]

The American antipathy for studied art (too often equated with foreign art) made Caldwell temper his offerings with "Yankee Doodle" and "Hail Columbia" and tended to discourage opera at the St. Charles. This same antipathy, however, worked with equal force in a reverse direction by helping to root grand opera even more firmly in New Orleans. For the more the American objected to music that was something beyond a "good simple air,"—especially when he called it "foreign,"—the more the Frenchman determined to preserve his opera.

Mere noise was the least hazard to be run in the American theaters. Pickpockets practiced their art with equal dexterity at both the Camp Street and the St. Charles. Where the former had "its hen-roost for ladies of a certain class and its dram shop for drunkards and smokers, to excite loungers and others to licentiousness and disorders," the St. Charles had "quarrels and fights, oaths, bitter and emphatic" to "diversify the scene." Brawls occurred nightly, according to the *Bee,* both "single combats, and general melees." The most memorable of these was the one in 1837 when the audience at the St. Charles broke chairs, ripped up seats, and even succeeded in damaging the impressive chandelier high overhead.[85]

The French took smug satisfaction in the behavioral lapses of the Americans. But they too had their troubles. Before there were any American theaters the city council had seen fit to pass ordinances entailing a twenty-five dollar fine for men who kept their hats on throughout the show; smoked cigars in the boxes; or talked and rapped their canes. Other notes of discord hint that all was not serene at the French theater: a manager promised to exert every effort to maintain order; a victim offered a one hundred dollar reward for money stolen during a performance; and a gentleman grumbled about those "who thought it smart to hiss." [86]

After the American theater made its appearance and the French opera achieved dignity, serious disturbances among the Gallics were rare—but not impossible. During a playing of Kreutzer's *Paul and Virginia* in 1826, a handbill thrown on the stage excited the pit to demand that it be read at once. The mayor himself had to take the stage to explain that a police order specifically forbade this and to express his regrets at not being able to satisfy the public; whereupon an orator harangued from the pit, protesting this law. Finally the mayor calmed the audience enough for the opera to continue. But on the whole, decorum at the Orleans became an additional reason for French pride in their theater.[87]

Such were the growing pains of the opera in New Orleans during its forty-odd years of youth. The danger period was successfully survived—the youth grew into splendid manhood. One need not take the word of the local press nor of partisans. During the twenty years preceding the Civil War visitors from many places confirmed the excellence of New Orleans' opera. A sophisticated New Yorker came to find: "None of your mushroom establishments which exist one day and are defunct the next . . . ; none of your half-and-halfs, whose orchestra is . . . temporary; . . . but an opera . . . worth your while; always good management; always good singing; always good instrumentation in the orchestra; always an agreeable fashionable and critical audience." [88]

Much-traveled Englishmen concurred. Charles Lanman was astounded to discover during his *Adventures in the Wilds of the United States* that the opera could "be enjoyed to such perfection . . . a pleasure he had found nowhere else." Sir Charles Lyell rated the orchestra the "best in America," and James Silk Buckingham informed his countrymen that operas were "given here in great perfection." Amelia Murray went farther when she wrote to her friends in England: "I have been little gratified by the operas elsewhere in the States. At New York, Grisi and Mario were wretchedly supported; and the dresses and choruses were so miserable that I was hardly inclined to do more than just look in at the house here; but I was most agreeably surprised. The Italian opera in London was never better." The sweetest praise—because it was French—came from Jean Jacques Ampere who heard Meyerbeer's *Le Prophete* in New Orleans only a year after its introduction in Paris. He agreed

that the opera in New Orleans was better than in New York, and
then bestowed the supreme accolade—it reminded him of Paris! [89]

And so the New Orleans French opera became a venerated institution. Boxes were hard to get, and even children were anxious to
go. The newcomer to antebellum New Orleans, or the winter visitor
who sought to establish himself socially, found that he must rent a
loge and be seen in it. Nor was it enough to attend only the lighter
presentations. To be fully accepted, he must be conspicuous above
all on those nights when the opera was heaviest.[90]

In 1836 the New Orleans *Bee* concluded: "Spectacles and operas
appear to amuse our citizens more than any other form of public
amusement—except balls." Thus, insofar as musical entertainment
is concerned, two widely disparate musical activities occupied first
place in New Orleans. Some conclusions seem here to be in order.
The first is that the connection between dancing and opera in New
Orleans was much closer than one would suspect was possible between these two opposite ends of the musical spectrum. It seems evident that the opera could not have existed without the presence of
an extraordinary passion for dancing. Other factors, such as the
French population's determined effort to preserve whatever it could
of things French, were necessary to support opera; but no means
would have proved sufficient without the direct and indirect aid
of ballrooms. It took a functional, earthy, social pastime to help
make possible the more esoteric one.[91]

The close alliance between social dancing and opera was more
than merely financially beneficial. The presence in ballroom orchestras of fine instrumentalists from the opera was bound to improve
the quality of dance music and to accustom the ear of the dancer to
better music. How much that may have had to do with bringing
some of these listeners to opera is indeterminable; but the simple,
persistent, personal contacts between dancers and opera instrumentalists must have induced a number of the former to attend the
opera at times. In short, the alliance between opera and dancing
served to make early New Orleans opera much more a real part of
the community than has been true of most of our latter-day opera.

In the same vein, the fact that the opera in New Orleans had to function as entertainment for as wide an audience as possible brought it closer to the average citizen. While the intermixing of opera with all sorts of other stage activities had its humorous aspects, it was, on the whole, a sound practice. People usually have to be induced to appreciate refined art, and if their homes and education have been inadequate in this regard, other means are essential. In a sense the opera in New Orleans did just what many critics argue that our television and other entertainment media should do today: people were offered the artistically good along with the popular.

It is true that the repertoire before the 1830's was primarily French and was what we now call light opera—but that was the opera of the time. As opera itself changed and developed, the opera in New Orleans kept pace. Thus when Caldwell imported Italian companies in 1836 and 1837 the way had been prepared by the French company. As we have seen, Rossini's *Barber of Seville* was performed in its entirety at the Orleans Theater as early as 1823. That the libretto was in French does not make it any less the same opera. Other Rossini operas also played in the Orleans prior to 1836, including *Le Comte Ory* in 1830 and *L'Italienne a Alger* in 1832. Similarly Bellini's *La Sonnambula* was premiered in the Orleans in 1832. Mozart's *Les Noces de Figaro* and Auber's *La Muette de Portici* were both performed in 1831. Operas by Halevy, Meyerbeer, and many others were heard in New Orleans before 1836. Indeed Caldwell brought in the Italians only because of the previous success of opera at the Orleans. He wanted equal prestige for his theater. In general, Italian operas were performed at the Orleans, both before and after Caldwell's experiment, as soon as they became available, albeit they were sung in French.[92]

If any criticism can be validly leveled at the French opera in New Orleans, it is that it failed to develop any lasting new compositions —especially any American operas. The charge is true and the reasons are evident. There were, to be sure, a number of works composed in New Orleans, including operas, but they were really works in the French tradition and by Frenchmen. The strong, almost frantic, effort to keep the opera a cultural tie to the old homeland

and the policy of importing talent were deterrents to the development of any truly indigenous activity. It is significant that the two best composers to come out of this environment, Ernest Guiraud and Louis Moreau Gottschalk, both received their advanced training in France. And only Gottschalk showed any American influences.

Conceivably it might have been different. In a penetrating search for the foundations of an American art, John Kouwenhoven postulates that in earlier, vital periods, what he labels the vernacular tradition and the classical tradition in art were closely allied. By "vernacular" he means the functional art of a people, and by the "classical" is meant the art of tradition and training. When the vernacular and the classical were not too distinct, each drew from the other to the benefit of both. But significant advances originated in the vernacular and were then given form in the classical. The classical by itself, cut off from its roots in the vernacular, tends to harden. Thus Kouwenhoven thinks that beginnings were made in a truly American art in many practical, functional areas; but because by the late eighteenth century the vernacular was too separated from the classical, these beginnings could never develop properly to infuse new life into formal art.[93]

It is intriguing to apply this theory to music in New Orleans. Here for a substantial time, the vernacular (dance music) and the classical (opera) were close in many ways. Had they remained thus, who knows what might have ensued? To some extent opera in New Orleans was always close to the community, but as the opera gained prominence it did draw away from the baser dance activities. Especially was this true from perhaps 1890 on, when the character of dance music was changing. Ironically, in 1919, when the French Opera House burned down, marking the end of resident opera in the city, New Orleans Dixieland dance music was carried abroad for the first time.

"Dey drums and fifes de whole bressed day."

Chapter Ten

THE BANDS

*I*n 1853 Frederick Law Olmstead toured the South gathering material for his book, *A Journey in the Back Country*. In Alabama he met a slave who gave a surprising reason for the general dread of being sold down the river in New Orleans: "Niggers doesn't have no Sunday dar, massa. Niggers has to work and white folks has muster; dey drums and fifes de whole bressed day; dat yer'll sound strange on a Sunday to a Northern man, eh?" It certainly sounded strange to Bishop Henry Whipple when he visited New Orleans in 1844. Sunday, he sadly noted in his diary, is "a day when the music is dedicated to the God of war & not to the God of peace." [1]

The bishop's lament wasn't entirely true—the churches did present the usual amount of religious music; the trouble was that it couldn't compete in volume with the martial sounds in the streets. James Creecy attended famous St. Louis Cathedral only to find that "while the organ in the venerable edifice is pealing anthems to Him on high . . . (the) rolling of drums, the fife's shrill whistle . . . are heard above all!" Directly in front of the cathedral was a favorite parade ground, the Place d'Armes. [2]

If the organ was overwhelmed by the sounds from the street, the human voice was even more so. An Episcopalian minister found himself forced to stop in the middle of his sermon and dismiss the congregation. Another complained that throughout his service "drums and clarions are heard on all sides . . ." He, however, being Scotch Presbyterian, doggedly completed his sermon.[3]

Sunday in New Orleans was indeed a day for comment. James Buckingham wrote that on Sunday the whole city became a vast field of war, while it seemed to James Davidson "that the Sabbath in New Orleans exists only in its Almanacs." Another visitor, Henry Didimus, protested at being jolted awake early on a Sunday morning in 1835 by the crash of fife and drum enthusiastically playing "Yankee Doodle" right under his window. Even hardened residents of New Orleans sometimes complained of bands "going about the city early on Sunday mornings, squeaking and rattle-te-banging away . . . and waking everybody." [4]

But such objections were rare; much more often the practice was defended. To those visitors who insisted that Sunday should be wholly dedicated to the saving of souls, the New Orleans *Picayune* pointed out that here Sunday was a day of rejoicing and it was good that "drums, fifes and music break in upon the solemnity of the day." Furthermore there was "nothing so spirit-stirring as a parade." [5]

With this the average New Orleanian agreed. When Henry Didimus left St. Louis Cathedral after worship, he saw again the band that had awakened him earlier in the morning. But it was now "preceded, followed and hemmed in on every side by a motley collection of all colours, sexes, and conditions." Bond and free, he noted, were "equally happy, and danced, sang, shouted." As the *Picayune* put it in the summer of 1837, "Last Sunday morning was delightful . . . people walking, soldiers marching, bands playing." [6]

It began early and grew fast, this romance between New Orleans and parades. Governor Miro, in 1787, thought it proper to entertain thirty-six Choctaw and Chickasaw chiefs with a parade. From then on opportunities for a parade were readily found. After the Americans took possession of Louisiana, the anniversary of the transfer, Washington's birthday, and Independence Day added new occasions. In 1806 Governor Claiborne wrote Henry Dearborn that the Fourth of July had been celebrated with a parade, a night at the theater, and a ball—a trilogy that foreshadowed the future development of music in the city.[7]

By the end of 1814, there were enough bands to fill the streets with martial airs as New Orleans prepared to do battle with the British. And of course each clash of arms in that campaign would provide further anniversaries on which to parade, especially December 23 and January 8. It was during a parade on the latter date in 1821 that James Audubon was relieved of his purse by a pickpocket.[8]

Mardi Gras, elections, weddings, and funerals all called for parades. March 4 annually saw several bands out to honor the firemen. The laying of a cornerstone, the dedication of a statue, or the blessing of a flag was reason enough for a parade. Thus, for example, the start of construction on the water works in 1834 brought forth a band followed by fifty laborers pushing their carts. Another batch of excuses was afforded by the early presence of so many different national groups. They all had national and holy days, and New Orleans was only too happy to parade for them all.[9]

But when one came right down to it, good weather on a Sunday was the only excuse needed to turn out the bands of the militia companies. The Spanish authorities had encouraged militia, officered and manned by the French, as a means of enlisting their support; and these companies took enthusiastic part in the war against the British during the American Revolution. Napoleon's victories and the Battle of New Orleans intensified the martial spirit in the city. Thus, on a random Sunday in 1833, one can find notices for at least ten different companies to parade.[10]

Most of the militia companies had their own bands. When a new volunteer company organized in 1831, as soon as the members chose a name and attached themselves to the Legion of Louisiana, they turned to the important business of selecting "a handsome uniform" for the musicians. At one time or another, the newspapers mention the bands of the Carabiniers, Cannoniers, New Orleans

Invincibles, Yagers, Washington Guards, an unnamed Spanish company, and an all Italian company calling itself the Mt. Vernon Musketeers. The Yagers were an all German company, and there were also Irish and Swiss companies plus at least a dozen other French and American companies. By 1838 the militia was estimated at around three thousand uniformed men.[11]

Those newspaper foes, the *Picayune* and the *Bee,* might argue about much, but they agreed that the band of the German Yagers was "the finest in our city." Next to the Yagers the *Bee* liked the Italian band of the Mt. Vernon Musketeers. This superiority of Germans and Italians was attributed to their "exquisite musical taste" which "generally ensures a proper organization to their bands." [12]

No hour of the day was immune from a parade. One visitor tells of his surprise at seeing a band "sweet and harmonious" at 7 A.M. On Washington's birthday in 1838, the *Picayune* reported that in every part of the city "drums were beating, bands . . . were playing" before noon. On the preceding Fourth of July "the night was enlivened by several bands . . . parading different parts of the city." At ten o'clock one summer night, a Spanish militia company paraded with its band, wheeling "a luscious looking cake of large dimensions . . . on a kind of hand barrow." Probably the men were marching to a wedding. And following an election in 1834, the victors paraded under the windows of the defeated candidates and of their supporting newspapers. Playing the "Dead March," the "Rogues March," and other tunes of that order, the paraders entertained the vanquished from midnight until nearly dawn.[13]

Inevitably the bands clashed. After praising the "magnificent display" of numerous uniformed companies and their bands, marching on December 23 in memory of the initial engagement with the British, one newspaper was moved to ask whether there shouldn't be some plans for those times "when a plurality of bands assemble?" Another objector complained of bands on adjacent river steamers "both playing different tunes at the same time." Whether or not such band battles were intentional at first, they became decidedly so as time went on. On the eve of the Civil War, the *Picayune* described two brass bands deliberately waging a "windy war . . . to the huge delight of a continuous line of listening admirers." [14]

And that's what it was most of the time—a huge delight. One reads of a parade: "Boys, negroes, fruit women and whatnot followed the procession—shouting and bawling, and apparently delighted." But it could also be a matter for serious concern. In 1832 the State Legislature designated the first days of July for state elections. After doing some calculation, the city discovered that in those years when Sunday was involved, July 4 would fall on election day, meaning no parades. Shocked New Orleanians immediately pressured the legislature to change this unthinkable law. And finally the sound of brass in New Orleans was a matter for pride. As the *Picayune* boasted in 1838, "our numerous martial bands . . . are perhaps unrivaled on this side of the Atlantic." [15]

In a city so taken with bands and parades, what more fitting means could there be to honor the dead? When the architect Benjamin Henry Latrobe came to New Orleans in 1819, he was struck by the funeral parades which he said were "peculiar to New Orleans alone among all the American cities." He described two such funerals, both of them Negro burials. In one he estimated that there were at least two hundred people in the procession, "all the women and many of the men . . . dressed in pure white." At the grave he noticed some boys nearby cutting up and tossing skulls and bones which had been dug up; "the noise and laughter was general by the time the service was over." [16]

Latrobe thought such funerals may have grown out of the Catholic custom of the procession of the Host, which he said no longer paraded the streets. In 1802, Dr. John Sibley had witnessed this earlier type of procession. Five or six friars and four or five boys, all habited, "walked as fast as they could," chanting at intervals. But only six years later, in 1808, when a wealthy Creole planter and militia officer, Colonel Macarty, was buried, the custom had already changed. Colonel Macarty's body was preceded by twenty militia officers, mostly Creoles, and followed by a band, the clergy, flag bearers, the governor of the territory, legislators, militia officers, army officers, the mayor, and the council—in that order.[17]

Any occasion—a funeral, a holiday, a visiting dignitary—inspired New Orleans' numerous brass bands to parade through the city's streets.

By the 1830's the newspapers carried frequent notices for funeral parades. Military men, veterans of the Revolution or of the War of 1812, or simply members of any of the numerous militia companies, were usually buried with a parade. Masons were customarily requested to march for one of their deceased, often being joined by some of the military. A typical notice, this one for Brother Dominique Bouligny in 1833, advised that "the officers and members of the several lodges and masonic bodies of this city are invited to attend his funeral at 4 P.M." Similarly, fire companies, benevolent societies, mechanics societies, and kindred organizations all marched to bury their dead. Where but in New Orleans would Masons be summoned to march in a funeral parade for a Catholic priest, Pere Antoine, on the grounds that he had never refused to accompany the remains of their departed brethren.[18]

Nor was it always necessary that the deceased be present in the parade. When the news of Lafayette's death in 1834 reached New Orleans, the Mechanics Society, the Fire Engine companies, and a number of the military promptly turned out for a funeral parade on July 26. Not to be outdone, the Masonic lodges promised a second and bigger parade for Lafayette soon. They were following a custom already firmly established. Napoleon had been so honored; and the parade for Thomas Jefferson and John Adams in 1826 surpassed anything yet seen in New Orleans, even though it took place in the overpowering heat of mid-August, six weeks after the deaths of the two heroes.[19]

These were however great parades honoring great men. The usual kind was more like one on an All Souls' Day when the Cazadores De Orleans were ordered together with complete arms and uniform "to honor in a funeral parade all their comrades" who had passed on.[20]

Only when yellow fever or cholera struck did there seem an excess of the "mournful notes of the death march customarily played by full brass bands en route to the grave." Most of all, these sounds disturbed the sick who were not likely to be cheered by this constant reminder of their mortality. On the other hand, the return march following the burial was different. Here was a band, this was New Orleans, and so it was only natural that they strike up a "gay and lightsome air as they returned from the grave." Mournful music to go, cheering music to return; it is as good a way as any to honor the dead.[21]

Brass bands were perhaps at their best in parades, but New Orleans liked them on other occasions too. In January of 1807, dancing master Jean Francisqui was able to offer a special added attraction for one of the grand balls he conducted. He borrowed a military band from General James Wilkinson to play for the waltzes. Waltzing this way proved so popular that Francisqui borrowed the band again a week later. From then on the presence of a band for waltzing was frequent and welcome. To take one example, the band of the Carabiniers played at five balls within a single month in 1814. Later on when the Vauxhall Gardens opened for the summer in 1835, it offered two bands, one for promenades and a special cotillion band for dancers. The popularity of bands for dancing was clearly evident in 1840 when the Neptune Band advertised its availability for quadrilles, adding almost as an afterthought that it could also be a military or brass band if required. (Thus brass band instrumentalists had a long tradition in New Orleans of playing dance music as well as street parades—an important factor later on, in the birth of jazz.) [22]

Elsewhere too bands were in demand. Circuses, of course, must promise a "powerful," "efficient," or "splendid" band. But they were not alone in this. Wax museums, political rallies, a "Grand Peristrephic Panorama," and a Gallery of the Fine Arts had a common need to attract the customers with a band. Balloons were sent aloft to the sound of fireworks and brass bands. Even those revolting spectacles of that day wherein bulls, dogs, tigers, bears, and other animals were put in a pit to fight and die, were accompanied by band music. Bands played at banquets, for German glee singing, and for charity fund raising. At one concert for orphan boys in 1841 no fewer than forty brass instrumentalists blew their best.[23]

It is not surprising then that when Lafayette paid his memorable visit to New Orleans in 1825, the city made him welcome the best way it knew: it sent a band to meet him in Montgomery, Alabama.

The musicians boarded the steamer "Anderson" there and proceeded to regale Lafayette with band music for the three day trip down river to Mobile. What the general thought of this is not known.[24]

Interest in brass, never low, reached new heights in the 1830's, partly because the expanding theater orchestras were bringing more and better performers to New Orleans, and partly because of technical advances in the construction of brass instruments. The newspapers told, in 1834, of how the two best known trumpeters of the day, John T. Norton and Alessandro Gambati, engaged in a much balleyhooed battle of music at Niblo's Gardens in New York. The contest was not only between men but between mechanical features as well, since Norton used a slide trumpet while Gambati used one of the new valve trumpets. How thrilling then to read shortly that both of these contestants were on their way to New Orleans to be part of the orchestra at the new St. Charles Theater.[25]

As it happened, Gambati did his playing in the older American theater on Camp Street, but he and Norton were in town together even if in different orchestras. At once the St. Charles featured "the unequalled Norton" playing on stage his own "celebrated Concerto" as well as more familiar fare like "The Star Spangled Banner," "The British Grenadier," "Yankee Doodle," and "Auld Lang Syne." At the older theater Gambati who "excels our anticipations," also became a regular attraction, his solos on the valve trumpet sharing the stage even with Shakespear's *Othello*.[26]

It was inevitable that public comparisons of Gambati and Norton be made, especially since Gambati was nothing loath to play "the same piece of music which he played at the trial of skill between Mr. Norton and himself at New York." The verdict was polite but definite. As the *Bee* expressed it, "Norton appears to have less facility of performance and brilliancy of execution than Gambati; but this may be attributed to the difference of their trumpets." And that was indeed Gambati's edge—Norton's slide trumpet had to give way before the new valve trumpet.[27]

Before the season was over, Norton left New Orleans. But he

strongly denied that he had been driven away, and offered to put up $1,000 against $500 that he could best Gambati. This offer however was posted in a New York publication after Norton was no longer in New Orleans. Gambati, on the other hand, remained in the city three years, playing in the theaters, in parades, for dances, and in frequent concerts. His trumpet solos, said the *Bee,* are "touted by us." [28]

Another who found a warm appreciation in New Orleans was James Kendall, a clarinet player. He came with Norton to play in the St. Charles orchestra, and within a few months the *True American* could say: "He is known to all—the militia of the city have marched under the soul-stirring notes of his clarionett." Besides, this paper went on, "Kendall is a native American, and self taught." By 1839 he was referred to as "the celebrated leader of the Brass Band," and when he later left New Orleans to go to West Point as band director, a New York magazine, *The Spirit of the Times,* called him the best clarinet player in the Union.[29]

Above all, though, it was Felippe Cioffi's trombone that completely captivated New Orleans. The city had been treated to its first solos "on that difficult instrument the Tromboon" in the spring of 1832 when the trombonist of the Camp Street Theater attempted some variations on stage. For whatever reasons, that was enough until two years later when the trombonist of the Orleans orchestra tried the same in that theater. Here too it was a once only affair.[30]

If these efforts created any doubts about the feasibility of trombone solos, they were utterly dispelled when Cioffi played his first solo on the stage of the St. Charles Theater in 1835. As the editor of the *Bee* wrote: "Though we are not oversolicitous to hear such an instrument performed alone, we were very much pleased with the skill and taste evinced by Cioffi." Not only did the audience agree and demand an encore, but the other musicians joined in the demand, a sight which the *Bee* said was unprecedented.[31]

Thereafter the "inimitable" and "unrivalled" Cioffi was a permanent feature at the St. Charles, regardless of the rest of the bill. As his popularity grew, he played in the other theaters as well as in summer promenade concerts, in the St. Charles and the St. Louis

Hotels, in innumerable concerts, in the Vauxhall and Carrollton Gardens, and even in the St. Louis Cathedral. In truth, as Cioffi himself advertized, he was "ready to furnish music . . . for any occasion, on short notice." To New Orleans he was "incomparably the best trombone player in America, and we have been told in the world." [32]

Cioffi often teamed up with Gambati and occasionally with other wind instrumentalists. A peak of some sort was reached when Cioffi and Gambati played the duet from Bellini's *Norma* at a concert. It was perhaps brassier than Bellini intended, but as a visiting newspaper reporter informed his readers: "We have heard them once and shall never forget their heavenly music." Nor would New Orleans. Cioffi and Gambati, along with James Kendall, did much to make the trombone, trumpet, and clarinet pre-eminent in that city.[33]

The demand for brass solos uncovered other fine performers such as H. E. Lehmann. Originally a French horn player in the Orleans orchestra, Lehmann played that instrument in a concert with Gambati early in 1836. Before the year was out, he switched to the new valve trumpet and found himself in demand at concerts and elsewhere, frequently playing his own compositions. Lehmann also teamed with Cioffi often and at times with Gambati for trumpet duets. D. Bailly, trumpeter in the Orleans orchestra, and Mr. Conduit, who took Norton's place in the St. Charles orchestra, were likewise much in demand.[34]

It was brass everywhere. If one went to the St. Charles to see the French ballerina Mlle. Celeste dance the "Revolt of the Harem," he heard Cioffi accompany her "in a grand trombone solo by Weber." On other nights one would hear there "the deep melody of Cioffi's trombone, the witching sweetness of M. Conduit's trumpet." At the Orleans the favorite prima donna, Julie Calve, would share the stage with Lehmann playing his own variations on an air from *Der Freischutz*, or with Bailly soloing on his trumpet between the acts of Auber's *L'Ambassadrice*. At the farewell concert in the St. Charles Hotel for the ten-year-old Creole genius, pianist Louis Moreau Gottschalk, Lehmann and Gottschalk played a trio by Mayseder for piano, trumpet, and violin. In the summer one might go to the Vauxhall Gardens for "ice creams and songs, soda water and Cioffi's trombone." It was heaven on earth.[35]

So it went. Parades and funerals, concerts and balls, opera and summer gardens—all to the sounds of brass. So much so that by the summer of 1838 the *Picayune* diagnosed "a real mania in this city for horn and trumpet playing." You could hardly turn a corner, the paper reported, without running into someone trying to blow. There might even be some in agreement with the man who said he never thought he would run from a horn, but now he earnestly hoped to hear the *last* trumpet.[36]

But most had no desire to hear Gabriel as long as there was good brass below. There simply couldn't be too much. A German brass band came to town in January, 1838. By fall the band was simply absorbed into the St. Charles orchestra. A little later a British band also found New Orleans a good place to earn money, playing for all occasions from a parade to a ball. Mr. Harper, "the great American magician" insured an audience by presenting the magic of the Boston Band along with his own. The newly opened American Theater on Poydras Street won customers by having a double military band in the pit. And in the music stores were large stocks of band music, with arrangements for up to four bands playing together.[37]

It seems only natural, then, that when the city wanted to tender a heartfelt welcome to the world famous dancer Fanny Elssler in 1841, it serenaded her with brass bands—first outside the entrance to her hotel, then in the lobby, and finally under her bedroom window. One hopes she liked brass. Certainly New Orleans had no doubt that everyone did.[38]

"All the fashion and beauty of New Orleans attended those concerts."

Chapter Eleven

THE CONCERTS

Although the ballrooms, theaters, and military bands provided bread and butter employment for the New Orleans musicians, these were all functional activities which could never fully satisfy their desire to show off their own abilities. Only concerts could do this, and it was inevitable that a city so full of musicians would have an impressive number of concerts. The writer has counted well over two hundred in the forty-five years from December of 1805 through the spring of 1841. Not included in this number were a great many concerts offered in the theaters, mainly during the last decade of the period, as part of the regular fare. Still others were conducted in summer gardens and resorts. In the spring of 1812 a summer pleasure garden at Bayou St. John promised that on every Sunday and on festival days "various symphonies" would be played by a "numerous and well selected orchestra." And there must have been even more. For example, in 1815 reference can be found to only one concert, but most of the newspapers are missing for that year.[1]

For the first twenty-five years, through the spring of 1830, these concerts averaged more than six per year, usually crowded into the winter season. During the next five years there were only three, but this was a time when most of the concerts moved into the theaters. And from 1836 through the spring of 1841 there were sixty-one offerings in concert halls—usually ballrooms—in addition to many in the theaters.

All too often the announcement of a concert or a soiree mentions the time, place, and sponsorship of the event, but omits anything more in the way of a program. However, the writer has found a total of 147 programs, all but 11 of them for concerts occurring between December 17, 1805, and June 3, 1830. Here too one would like further information, for as often as not the programs are incomplete, merely listing "a symphony" or "an overture" for the orchestra; "a concerto" or "an air and variations" for the soloists. Indeed, the first program to list every composer is that of March 31, 1824, and this by no means set a precedent. Even so, these programs are a mine of information, and it is from them that the following analysis is taken. The reader must simply keep in mind that we are here recounting only a part of the story.[2]

Concerts added several important elements to the musical life of the city. They were, in a sense, the bond that held the other areas of music together, for it was on these occasions that the musicians of the different theaters could play with each other as well as with musicians not connected with the theater. Amateur musicians too got a chance to play with professionals, thus increasing their confidence and enhancing their interest. These concerts also provided opportunities for the playing of symphonies, concertos, quartets, and all the other kinds of music not ordinarily played in the theater; and it was at these times that local composers were able to present their own efforts and to gain inspiration and encouragement.

Of course the immediate purpose of a concert was to make money for the musicians of New Orleans. Each concert was put together and sponsored by one or sometimes two musicians, in most cases for their own benefit. Usually the sponsor took a prominent part in his concert, performing two or more numbers and presenting his own compositions if he also composed. In 1814 there was a bassoonist named Passage who doubled as a fencing master. He took advantage of his concert to display both his talents—first playing a bassoon concerto, then duelling in an exhibition with another fencing master.[3]

Not all concerts were given for the personal profit of the sponsor. Some were organized for charitable purposes, the proceeds going to orphans, "respectable widows," "poor families," or to lost causes such as the New Orleans Temperance Society. A refugee, usually from Haiti, or simply a needy person passing through town might also be the beneficiary of a concert. In 1827, for example, there was Captain Ramati, a veteran of Bonaparte's army who "had lost his all for liberty," and who, it was said, "had no other resource except his cultivated music" which consisted of playing the guitar and singing. The captain was on his way to offer his services to Mexico, but it is uncertain whether, twelve years after Waterloo, this was in his military or his musical capacity.[4]

Similarly, if a local musician suffered misfortune, an extra concert was in order. Louis Hus Desforges, violinist, composer, and perhaps most eminent local musician prior to 1820, sought aid on more than one occasion through concerts. The first took place early in 1807 when his house almost burned down. The second came in 1816 after he had been "dangerously wounded at the lines" a year before at the battle of New Orleans and rendered "unable to exercise his profession as formerly." In 1827 Desforges was again beneficiary of a concert, having "lost his all" in yet another fire. So also did M. Coeur de Roi obtain assistance in his "truly disastrous situation" caused by a fall from the balcony of the first Orleans Theater.[5]

One other function of the concerts was to introduce teachers and newcomers. Upon arriving in New Orleans, a teacher found that the surest way of becoming known and securing pupils was to enlist the aid of established musicians and give a concert. After his debut, a teacher used concerts to further his income and to give his better students a chance to gain experience in playing with professionals. In the same way newcomers to the theater orchestras introduced themselves to the city and sought to supplement their salaries.[6]

How much could be earned this way is never stated. The admission was usually one dollar for adults and fifty cents for children. The free colored were also solicited, being admitted usually for fifty cents, but on occasion for seventy-five cents. It was a bargain—at least for the white adults—since the admission price included the ball which customarily followed each concert. The colored could only watch. Because of the dancing the concerts started most often at 7:00 P.M. and never later than 7:30 P.M.

Whether all the proceeds went to the sponsor or were divided to some extent among the other participants is not clear, but the musicians of the city seemed always willing to participate, whether to help one of their colleagues or to launch a newcomer. In any case, such help was always reciprocated. Thus the participants seem to be drawn from the same pool of musicians season after season. Only when one compares programs that are separated by a number of years do the changes in personnel become marked.

A typical concert would have ten or twelve numbers on the program, including a short intermission. Each half of the program would begin with an orchestral selection, usually an overture or a symphony. Frequently the orchestra also played elsewhere on the program. The other selections were solos, duets, quartets, and various combinations of voice and instruments, some with orchestral accompaniment.

The very first program extant, that of December 17, 1805, lists ten selections, four of them by a "full orchestra." Just how full this early orchestra might have been can only be guessed, but two of the offerings were the overtures to Cherubini's *Demaphon* and to Gretry's *Panurge*. The other two were "The President's March," arranged by the local musician Desforges, and a pastorale composed by Philip Laroque, another prominent New Orleans composer. Filling out the program were a clarinet concerto, a piano concerto, and four vocal offerings.[7]

Inasmuch as Desforges and Laroque were both violinists, we see that at least two violins, a clarinet, and a piano were available for the orchestra. By analyzing all of the programs, we should be able to form a good picture of just what instruments were on hand in New Orleans; when they were brought to the city; and what the capabilities were of the men who played them. This is significant not only for viewing orchestral development in New Orleans, but for comparison with other American cities.

CLARINET: Going back to the program mentioned above, we see that one of the two solo instruments was the clarinet. Five weeks later, on January 14, 1806, two clarinets appeared in a symphony concertante; and two years after that, four clarinets played a quartet. By the close of 1810 the clarinet had been used twenty-two times, thirteen of these for concertos. In the next twenty years (1811–30), the clarinet appeared eighty-nine more times. There were thirty-two concertos plus a variety of other offerings using up to four clarinets, alone or in combination with other instruments.

PIANO: The other solo instrument in that first concert was the piano. Before the end of 1810 the piano had been featured thirty-eight times, exclusive of its use as accompaniment for instrumentalists and vocalists. Ten concertos and fourteen sonatas were performed during these five years. In the following two decades the piano appeared sixty-five times. Among these offerings were fifteen concertos, at least two of them with orchestra; five sonatas and five polonaises. At one time three pianos were played together; and at another time Emile Johns, a local pianist and music dealer, improvised pieces "composed for the moment." [8]

VIOLIN: Inasmuch as a "full orchestra" took part in the initial concert, and we know that Desforges and Laroque were violinists, it seems probable that there were at least a few violins present. We do not, however, get any specific mention of violin performances until January 19, 1807, when Desforges played a concerto by Giovanni Jarnowic. From that time through 1810—just four years—fifteen concertos and two symphony concertantes helped make up a total of twenty-two violin selections. The next twenty years added another eighty-four violin offerings which included thirty-one concertos and eleven concertantes. One of the latter was for three violins; two were for violin, viola, and clarinet. Giovanni Viotti, Joseph Fodor, Maestrino, Ignaz Joseph Pleyel, and Jacques Pierre Rode were among the more popular composers.

HARP: The harp has a puzzling concert history in New Orleans. Appearing first with piano and voice on February 20, 1807, the harp was played twenty-three times in ten concerts during the next ten years. The harp was used mainly in duets, for accompaniment, or for light airs and variations; but even so, five sonatas and one concerto were played. The last of these appearances occurred on February 25, 1817, and thereafter the harp is not listed again for almost twenty years, although harps were frequently advertised for sale and harp instruction was offered. Perhaps it was simply too large to carry conveniently in those days. In January of 1836, a Madame Zimmer played excerpts from *La Dame Blanche,* and in the next three years the harpist of the Orleans Theater orchestra appeared once a year in light duets.

CELLO: A cello concert was played on Januay 25, 1808, and a year later there was a symphony concertante for cello and violin. Before the close of 1810 the cello appeared twice again, but after that it was not heard from until 1824 when it was played in combination with a clarinet, violin, and two violas. Then no more is heard of it until 1836 when a caprice by Bernard Romberg was played by Alfred Boucher of the St. Charles Theater. Boucher soloed fairly often on the stage, but the cello appeared outside in only three more concerts.

VIOLA: On March 9, 1810, a viola and cello sonata marked the concert debut of the viola. In the next two decades this instrument was heard fourteen times, all but two of them in combination with other instruments. One of the two solos was a concerto; the other, variations on a theme. Among the combinations were two concertantes for viola, clarinet, and violin and a concertante for viola and violin. In February, 1824, two violas formed part of a quintet.

BASS: That largest of the stringed instruments, the bass, appeared first on Washington's birthday in 1808; and toward the end of that year, two basses participated in an ensemble of six instruments. By the end of 1830 the bass had been heard in concerts twenty-two times, all but once as a part of combinations. The exception was a potpourri composed by Bernard Romberg and played in February, 1829, by a Charles Dantonnet, recently arrived from Paris where he had studied in the Paris Conservatory.[9]

FRENCH HORN: This was the next wind instrument after the clarinet to appear in concerts. On January 28, 1808, one M. Labat accompanied a singer on the French horn, probably to show off the horn rather than the singer. In November of that year, two French horns took part in the same ensemble that included the two basses mentioned above; and a pair of horns appeared again in December. From then until February, 1829, the French horn was played in concerts thirteen more times, usually in combinations; but a horn and piano nocturne and a symphonic concerto for two horns appeared in 1821, and a symphony concertante for horn and bassoon by Jacob Wiederkehr was played twice in May, 1827.

FLUTE: Mozart's *Magic Flute* overture was on the program for January 14, 1806, and one hopes that there was a flute on that occasion. It is not, however, until December 17, 1810, that the flute is specifically mentioned, at which time a symphony concertante for two flutes was offered. One week later a flute concerto was performed by M. Coeur de Roi, a newcomer who probably had played one of the two flutes the week before. He had come from Cuba the year before to teach clarinet, French horn, bassoon, and flute in New Orleans.[10]

In the ensuing twenty years the flute is listed thirty-one times, including eight concertos and three symphony concertantes for two flutes. In March, 1839, four flutes played together a piece called "The Orphan's Prayer" at a concert for the benefit of orphans.

BASSOON: On March 9, 1811, the bassoon was first heard as part of an ensemble. Thereafter it appeared twice in ensembles before the first concerto for bassoon was performed on December 28, 1813. The bassoonist on this occasion was M. Passage, mentioned earlier because of his interesting performance at a concert wherein he played a concerto and fought an exhibition duel. Between 1811 and February, 1829, the bassoon appeared in concerts seventeen times, including four concertos and two performances of a symphony concertante by Wiederkehr for bassoon and horn.

OBOE: This difficult woodwind is first mentioned in a quartet with bassoon, horn, clarinet, and flute, on March 9, 1813. Then it was not heard again until January 29, 1821, when it was part of an octet. The next month a program offers a symphonic concerto to be played by "oboes," clarinets, French horn, and trumpet—an ensemble which, incidentally, marks the first appearance of a trumpet in anything other than the orchestra or band. Thereafter the oboe is not listed again until January, 1836. There were two more oboe solos that year and one in 1839, all by the same oboist.

Another way of observing the available instrumentation in New Orleans is to catalog concert offerings that involved four or more instruments, exclusive of the orchestral or band selections:

January 28, 1808	4 CLARINETS
November 4, 1808	2 CLARINETS, 2 FRENCH HORNS, 2 BASS VIOLS.
December 26, 1808	2 VIOLINS, CLARINET, 2 FRENCH HORNS, BASS.
February 5, 1810	VIOLIN, CLARINET, FRENCH HORN, BASS.
March 9, 1811	4 CLARINETS, 2 FLUTES, 2 FRENCH HORNS, BASSOON, BASS.
March 13, 1811	HARP, 2 FRENCH HORNS, 2 CLARINETS, 2 FLUTES, BASSOON.
March 9, 1813	CLARINET, OBOE, FLUTE, FRENCH HORN, BASSOON.
February 27, 1819	CLARINET, VIOLIN, VIOLA, BASS.
December 11, 1819	GUITAR, VIOLIN, VIOLA, BASS.
January 31, 1820	2 CLARINETS, 2 FRENCH HORNS, 2 BASSOONS.
January 29, 1821	3 CLARINETS, 2 BASSOONS, FLUTE, OBOE, FRENCH HORN.
February 2, 1821	"CLARINETS," "OBOES," FRENCH HORN, TRUMPET.
February 2, 1821	CLARINET, VIOLIN, VIOLA, BASS— (Haydn).
January 2, 1822	CLARINET, VIOLIN, VIOLA, BASS— (Haydn).
February 9, 1824	CLARINET, VIOLIN, 2 VIOLAS, CELLO.
February 9, 1824	CLARINET, FLUTE, FRENCH HORN, BASSOON.
June 3, 1830	2 VIOLINS, VIOLA, BASS.
March 9, 1839	4 FLUTES.

Taking the above all together, it is easy to see that from some time before 1810 a good number and variety of instruments were available for concerts and opera in New Orleans. The "full orchestra" promised in December, 1805, may not have been large by today's standards, but it was very creditable for the time and place. Thereafter growth was steady; and from 1819 when John Davis opened his Orleans Theater, the orchestra's growth accelerated until at a concert in the St. Louis Hotel on December 24, 1838, there were sixty musicians. This seems considerably ahead of the rest of the country. As one authority on America in the 1830's has written: "All New York could not produce enough cellos for the William Tell overture or sufficient talent for an acceptable string quartet. Seldom could as many as fifteen or twenty men be collected even for a symphony and then some of them sat blankly impotent during parts that they could not play." Such was certainly not the case in New Orleans.[11]

In considering the kind of music played in these concerts, we must remember that very often no composer is named. Furthermore, except for Rossini, we shall not concern ourselves with composers whose concert listings are primarily drawn from their operas since they are discussed in the chapters on opera. A few of these latter, however, are included where their compositions are specifically for the concert hall.

One hundred and thirty-four overtures had been presented by the close of 1830, twenty-five of them before 1810. In the same time span, thirty symphonies and twelve symphony concertantes were offered. How many of the numerous concertos were accompanied by orchestra is not clear, but inasmuch as an orchestra was present at most of the concerts, it is reasonable to think that many of the concertos must have been accompanied by the orchestra. Finally, the orchestra performed seventy-seven other compositions such as pastorales, marches, rondos, etc.

Seven of the symphonies were played before the close of 1810. The first of these was a Mozart symphony, played on January 14, 1806. Three by Paul Wranitzky and three by Haydn made up the other six, the first Haydn symphony having been played on February 18, 1809. It is worth noting also that a symphony concertante for violin and cello played during this early period was composed by a local musician, Louis Desforges.

Mozart, for some reason, appears not to have been popular in New Orleans. The symphony mentioned above was the only one to be heard unless there were Mozart symphonies among those for which no composer is given. The overtures to *The Magic Flute*, to

Figaro, and to one other were played before the end of 1810, but for the next thirty years only six Mozart airs are included in these concerts, plus the overture to *Don Giovanni* and a repeat of *The Magic Flute.*

Haydn fared better. Besides the three symphonies already mentioned, an air and a duet from *The Creation* were given. In the next decade (1811–20), there were no fewer than six Haydn symphonies, one of them the *Queen's Symphony,* played first on March 10, 1814, though the Allegro and something they called the "Grand Overture" of this composition had been played earlier. A rondo and an oratorio duet were also performed within the decade. After that came a quartet in 1821 and another in 1822; a symphony in 1821 and the *Farewell Symphony* in 1824; and finally, a rondo from a symphony in 1826.

Rossini's great opera, *The Barber of Seville,* was introduced to New Orleans on March 4, 1823. Prior to that Rossini had been heard only once when some of his songs were sung at a concert in March of 1821. After the introduction of the *Barber,* however, Rossini's concert popularity equalled and even surpassed his opera popularity in New Orleans. By 1839, his songs, arias, duets, and other extracts from his operas had formed parts of concert programs at least twenty-five times. The overtures to seven of his operas and two unnamed overtures were played sixteen times. A "Grand symphony" and a string quartet rounded out the instrumental offerings except for some overtures played on guitar.

The only other major composers to be heard in concert were Gluck and Beethoven. A scene from Gluck's *Armide* was played in 1808, and a duet and scene from the same composition were given in 1813. A piano concerto by Beethoven in 1819 was the single work by this master that is specifically listed.

Composers whose stature today is somewhat less than that of the major composers were apparently more popular with the musicians who gave the concerts. In this their tastes paralleled those of their European contemporaries. (See Appendix for a list of the more important of these composers, together with the kind of composition and the number of playings. In each time period the composers are listed in the order of their first appearance.)

A most impressive aspect of the concerts in New Orleans was the opportunity they gave resident musicians to present their own compositions. The opera theater was severely limited in this respect for obvious reasons, but concerts were not, and most of them included one or more local offerings. From December, 1805, through the spring of 1841, no fewer than twenty-three local composers presented compositions which, in all, were played over one hundred times.

It should be noted, however, that the greatest incidence of local works came in the earlier years. As the orchestras grew more competent, the proportion of local compositions on the programs decreased. Thus the first five-year period (December, 1805–10) saw thirty-one playings of compositions by six local musicians; the next decade (1811–20) had forty playings of local compositions; the decade after that had twenty-two such works; and the final eleven years (1830–41) had only eight. Therefore the average in the first period was six per year; in the second, four per year; in the third, a little over two per year; and thereafter, under one per year.

The local composers offered works ranging from instrumental solos or variations through concertos to overtures, marches, pastorales, and symphony concertantes for the full orchestra. Here too we notice that the more ambitious compositions were most frequently played before 1825. After that they are principally instrumental solos composed by the performer. Both the frequency of playings, then, and the scope of the works presented indicate that the period 1805–25 was by far the best for local composers.

During that time a number of the local compositions showed some of the political and social winds swirling through New Orleans. In a concert on March 15, 1808, the orchestra played General Moreau's favorite march as arranged by Philip Laroque. Moreau was then living in New Jersey, having been exiled for heading a republican and royalist plot against Napoleon in 1804. Also on the program was "Hail Columbia" in an arrangement by Desforges. This is the first American patriotic music offered in the concerts; and coming only a little over four years after the Louisiana Purchase, it is a gauge of the spread of American nationalism. But Desforges also offered here another of his compositions called "A Creole

Waltz," dedicated to Major General Jacques Villere, commander of the local militia. This composer liked to keep things in balance. A short while later an ariette entitled "Washington, or the Glory of American Heroes" was sung in French.[12]

The most ambitious patriotic composition, however, was naturally inspired by the great victory over the British at New Orleans itself. Something grand might have been expected from Desforges who was easily the most prolific local composer. But he had deserted his violin for a more lethal weapon during the fighting and "unfortunately had suffered a wound which left him nearly deaf and partially incapacitated for a while." At a concert given for his benefit in January, 1816, the most he was able to produce were some variations dedicated to General Andrew Jackson. "Washington's March" and "General Jackson's March" were also on the program.[13]

It was left then to Philip Laroque, who had already composed three operas for the local company, to undertake the grand musical celebration of victory. On January 31, 1816, Laroque introduced his "Battle of the Eighth of January, 1815," composed for full orchestra "according to the historical facts." The overture, beginning with a pastoral scene at daybreak quickly shattered by the bursts of guns and rockets, reached a climax with the death of General Pakenham and his funeral dirge. Then came music for the wounded, a flourish of wind instruments for victory, a grand triumphant march, and the final rondo.[14]

Laroque's depiction of the battle in music, having been "so well received," was repeated in a couple of weeks and dedicated to General Jackson. The overture helped commemorate the victory for the next two anniversaries of the battle—after which it disappeared from sight and hearing.

Desforges meanwhile was recovering from his wound except for a degree of deafness, and in a concert on December 30, 1816, celebrating Louisiana's transfer to America, Desforges had something for almost everybody. For the Americans there was a chasse dedicated to General Eleazor Ripley and his exploits in the late war; for Creole pride there was a march dedicated to Governor Villere; and for French memories of recent glory, there was a march dedicated to

one of Napoleon's faithful generals, Lefebvre-Desnouettes, then residing in America after the defeat at Waterloo.[15]

A couple of months later, Desforges returned to an earlier interest. In 1813 he had composed a "Masonic March" and arranged
"The Masonic Tie." Now he expressed the sentiments of many of
his fellow Creoles when he hailed the progress of Masonry in New
Orleans with a composition called "The Free Mason's Joy." On the
same program, another local musician offered a further celebration
of the victory over the British with a grand march for Commodore
Daniel Patterson whose naval efforts had not been noted in Laroque's battle overture. But this was the last composition inspired
by that battle; before very much longer, another local composer was
offering a "Hymn to Peace." [16]

How well attended the concerts were cannot be known, but their
persistence and frequency argue that they must have been fairly
profitable for the musicians giving them. In February, 1824, Messrs.
Cheret and Johns did not hesitate to give two concerts on Monday
and Wednesday of the same week. They acknowledged that their
second concert "may seem too soon to some," but so heavy were the
demands on suitable places and musicians that "they have no other
days." And some years later, a newspaper reported that concerts
were attended by "all the fashion and beauty of New Orleans."
After all why not when there was always the ball that followed? [17]

"Beating time all the while"

Chapter Twelve

NEGRO MUSIC

*T*here is a tale, often told, about the origins of jazz. It goes like this: before the Civil War Negro music was crude and primitive, played on homemade instruments and directly linked to the African jungle. Then when the war ceased, returning Confederate band musicians discarded their instruments right and left, literally flooding the pawn shops and thereby making regular instruments "readily available to the Negro at low cost." Now the New Orleans Negro could put his primitive inspiration into civilized instruments and what came out would in time develop into jazz. The theory probably has an element of truth in it, but it is far too simple.[1]

To begin with, let us give the primitive theory its due. There is no doubt that the Negroes of New Orleans long assembled in various open places whenever they could to relax by dancing. As early as 1786 the law forbade slaves to dance in the public squares on Sundays and holy days until the close of evening service. Early in 1799 a visitor to the city took a stroll after his Sunday dinner. On the edge of town he saw "vast numbers of negro slaves, men, women, and children, assembled together on the levee, . . . dancing in large rings." On the following Sunday he again saw, this time inside the city, "upwards of one hundred negroes of both sexes" dancing and singing on the levee. In 1804 John Watson reported seeing Negroes "in great masses on the levee on Sundays," making themselves "glad" with song and dance. On another Sunday afternoon four years later the "sight of twenty different dancing groups" of Negroes prompted Christian Schultz to describe it: "They have their own national music, consisting for the most part of a long kind of narrow drum of various sizes, from two to eight feet in length, three or four of which make a band. The principal dancers or leaders are dressed in a variety of wild and savage fashions, always ornamented with a number of the tails of the smaller wild beasts." To see this on a Sunday and to hear the sound of drums from another quarter announcing a theatrical performance about to begin, moved one of Schultz's New England friends to cry out, "Oh where are our select men of Salem?" [2]

Schultz and his scandalized friend saw these dancing parties in the rear of the city and most probably witnessed the dancing in Congo Square, the favorite site for these Sunday hoe-downs. In the rear of the old city at Rampart and Orleans streets and originally known as Circus Square, it is today Beauregard Square. In 1817 a law restricted Negro dancing to Sundays before sundown and in places to be designated by the mayor. He approved one site only, Congo Square, where the dancing could be held under police supervision. [3]

Several witnesses recorded their impressions of the dancing in Congo Square, but the best by far is that of the architect, Henry Latrobe. One Sunday in 1819 Latrobe accidentally came upon the sight of five to six hundred dancers:

They were formed into circular groups in the midst of four of which . . . (but there were more of them), were two women dancing. They held each a coarse handkerchief extended by the corners in their hands, & set to each other in a miserably dull & slow figure, hardly moving their feet or bodies. The music consisted of two drums and a stringed instrument. An old man sat astride of a cylindrical drum about a foot in diameter, & beat it with incredible quickness with the edge of his hand & fingers. The other drum was an open staved thing held between the knees & beaten in the same manner. They made an incredible noise. The most curious instrument, however, was a stringed instrument which no doubt was imported from Africa. On top of the finger board was the rude figure of a man in sitting posture, & two pegs behind him to which the strings were fastened. The body was a calabash. It was played upon by a very little old man, apparently 80 or 90 years old.

The women squalled out a burthen to the playing at intervals, consisting of two notes, as the negroes, working in our cities, respond to the song of their leader. Most of the circles contained the same sort of dancers. One was larger, in which a ring of a dozen women walked, by way of dancing, round the music in the center. But the instruments were of different construction. One, which from the color of the wood seemed new, consisted of a block cut into something of the form of a cricket but with a long & deep mortice down the center. This thing made a considerable noise, being beaten lustily on the side by a short stick. In the same orchestra was a square drum, looking like a stool, which made an abominably loud noise; also a calabash with a round hole in it, the hole studded with brass nails, which was beaten by a woman with two short sticks.

A man sung an uncouth song to the dancing which I suppose was in some African language, for it was not French, & the women screamed a detestable burthen on a single note.

Latrobe found no disorder among the dancers and was told that they never had produced any mischief.[4]

One other early dancing custom of the Negro deserves mention. This was a procession in the streets on holidays. The Reverend Timothy Flint saw such a parade sometime before 1825:

Everything is license and revelry. Some hundreds of negroes, male and female, follow the king of the wake. . . . For a crown he has a series of oblong, gilt-paper boxes on his head, tapering upwards, like a pyramid. From the ends of these boxes hang two huge tassels, like those on epaulets. He wags his head and makes grimaces. By his thousand mountebank tricks, and contortions of countenance and form, he produces an irresistible effect upon the multitude. All the characters that follow him, of leading estimation, have their own peculiar dress, and their own contortions. They dance, and their streamers fly, and the bells they have hung about them twinkle.[5]

This then is about as primitive as Negro music in New Orleans ever got, save for an occasional and secret voodoo dance. Several things in the descriptions are worth comment. Although in 1808 the dancers are depicted as dressed in "wild and savage" fashion, adorned with tails of small beasts, a little over ten years later such a careful observer as Latrobe saw none of this. In fact he describes the dance as rather slow and dull. And a holiday street parade wherein the king wears a paper crown and the followers wear streamers with tinkling bells is common in Europe.

To be sure the instruments and manner of playing them described by Latrobe do suggest Africa, or at least the West Indies, but this is not the whole story. As early as 1799 fifes and fiddles were used, and in time banjos, triangles, jews harps, and tambourines were added. Moreover, observers tell of seeing jigs, fandangos, and Virginia breakdowns in the square, and they speak of hearing melodies like "Old Virginia Never Tire," "Hey Jim Along Josey," and "Get Along Home You Yellow Gals." George W. Cable described the so called Congo dance itself as a kind of fandango. However much of the primitive there was in the Congo Square dances, it seems apparent that they were borrowing rapidly from the culture around them.[6]

By the early 1820's the dancing of Negroes on Sundays had begun to meet objections on the grounds of respectability, and eventually they were forbidden. When Norman's *City Directory* was published in 1845, it referred to the square as the "place where the negroes, in olden times were accustomed to meet," and went on to state that only the older inhabitants recall seeing these dance festivals. In June of that year, however, the city restored the "ancient privilege" of dancing in the square, probably because it was a convenient safety valve for the city slaves, while at the same time it provided a pleasant Sunday spectacle for visiting whites.[7]

But was such dancing the only, or even major, musical activity of the New Orleans Negroes? Far from it. As was mentioned in the discussion of Negro dancing and the origins of the theater, more or less formal balls were held for free Negroes; and very early in the city's history these affairs resembled the ones for white people. Such dances were numerous and profitable enough to underwrite the white theater for a while and to persist and grow through the years. Let us remember, too, that although these balls were supposedly limited to free colored, slaves and even whites managed to attend many of them—so much so that in one raid, fifty of the seventy-five colored men arrested were slaves.[8]

Moreover, despite laws prohibiting them, there were always plenty of cabarets and kindred places where "mobs . . . of our slaves nightly assemble at their orgies." In one Sunday raid on a store-tavern, sixteen slaves were arrested out of about fifty Negroes who were there dancing and gambling. In another, thirty-four slaves were arrested and their owners fined.[9]

But neither raids nor the frequent fines levied on tavern keepers put any noticeable dent in this business. "Not a street, nor a corner can be passed without encountering [them]," said the *Bee*. One disturbed neighbor wrote a bitter complaint to the papers about a room on Suzette Street where slaves held a ball "almost every Saturday night . . . and kept up until daylight on Sunday morning. The noise and disturbance is very disagreeable to the neighbors, although it may be profitable to the proprietors." That was just it—to run a tavern, or store, or simply a room large enough so that Negroes could relax and dance was certainly profitable. The *Bee* estimated that "thousands" flocked to them, and it was common to see parties of Negroes, free and slave, singing songs like "Coal Black Rose" on their way to balls and taverns.[10]

What kind of music did they play in these places? There is very little to guide us here. No doubt in the small cabarets and stores it must have been impromptu, making use of whatever talent was there. In one small room, three slaves were seized and charged with playing the violin and dancing with white persons. Which crime was considered the greater is not stated. In another report of a raid in which eleven slaves were taken, banjos are mentioned.[11]

In the larger, scheduled affairs, the music was more likely to have been planned. One Sunday at 2:30 A.M. the police broke into a house "where a negro ball was in full tide" and arrested over thirty slaves. Luckily a reporter was along who described the scene: "In one part of the room a cotillion was going on, and in a corner a fellow was giving a regular old Virginia 'breakdown' . . . A genteel looking darky, with Devonshire brown mustachios was acting as master of ceremonies, and the music consisted of a clarionet, three fiddles, two tambourines, and a bass drum." This orchestra, he said, played the same dances, gallopades, cotillions, etc. that one heard at white balls. And in the refreshment room an elderly man was strumming "Jim Along Josey" on the banjo.[12]

Negro musicians also supplied much of the music at the quadroon balls. Indeed the colored male musician was the one exception to the prohibition against colored males being present at these balls. And he also played for many white balls as well, from private parties to subscription dances. One of the first orchestras to be described at a New Orleans ball in 1802 consisted of six Negroes, mainly fiddlers. In 1826 the Duke of Saxe-Weimar attended a white society ball at the Orleans Ballroom itself and found the music— conventional waltzes and cotillions—being played by Negroes who sounded "pretty good" to his European ear. And in 1834 the proprietor of a commercial ballroom took extra space to advertise that for a special ball in memory of the December 23 battle against the British, he had engaged white musicians. The inference is that ordinarily the musicians were Negroes.[13]

Family parties might employ as small an orchestra as one Negro musician—perhaps Massa Quamba who charged three dollars a night for his violin playing. Massa Quamba felt secure enough to give free expression to his displeasure one rare winter night when snow fell in New Orleans. What bothered him was not the snow, but that the young ladies had deserted his violin to make snowballs. Another man in demand was William Martin, who started playing the banjo and then learned piano and violin. By 1839 he was earning enough to dress well, even to sport a large breast pin—an attire which offended the *Picayune*.[14]

Elsewhere we read of slaves supplying an orchestra of two violins, a flute, triangle, and tambourine for a plantation party just outside the city; or fiddle, fife, and flute for a New Year's serenade; or "Virginia breakdown fiddle music" for one of their own Christmas parties.[15]

It is not surprising then to find references to musical ability in the advertisements of slaves who had escaped or who were up for sale. A random dozen of these notices from 1810–20 show that most played violin, but the tambourine, fife, and drums are also mentioned. To read of a slave escaping with only his clothing and a violin, or attempting to carry with him both a violin and tambourine, reveals much. Gabriel, who ran away in 1814, was described as "fond of playing upon the fiddle," while Abraham's master broadcast that he "played well on the violin." A mulatto, offered for sale in 1811, was said to play "superbly on the tambourine and a little on the fife, beats the drum better than any other in this city, very intelligent, sober and faithful." And in 1833 the Western Hotel on Tchoupitoulas Street posted a fifty dollar reward for Joe, who played the violin "very well." It seems possible that one of Joe's duties was to supply music in the hotel where he was owned.[16]

Virtually all avenues of contact with European music were open to Negroes. At the white balls a section of the hall was usually reserved for the free colored. They couldn't dance, but they could watch and listen. Slaves too must have gotten in often, judging from frequent appeals and warnings to owners not to insist on taking their slaves in with them—"not one slave will be admitted." The Orleans Ballroom declared such a prohibition in January, 1819 and fifteen years later was still insisting on it. At one point the managers tried having their own ballroom slaves wear an identifying arm band.[17]

The same situation obtained in the opera. One of the early drawbacks in the theater on St. Philip Street was that it had no balcony for colored. Because of this the company remained in the older theater on St. Peter Street until the deficiency could be remedied. When it was, the free colored sat in the second loges, while slaves could sit in the amphitheater for fifty cents. When the Orleans Theater opened, that house offered the third row of boxes for free colored but made no provision for slaves. Consequently we soon find the Orleans making the usual insistence that no slaves would be admitted. By 1822 they had given up trying to exclude slaves and had reserved the third balcony for them while moving the free colored down (in other words up) to the second balcony. Evidently, though, there were slaves who thought they might like the view from the second balcony better, for we now find the management insisting that slaves would not "under any pretence, be admitted, except in

Little wonder then that someone got the idea of opening a theater for the free colored. On April 3, 1838, appears the first advertisement for the Marigny Theater. Located on the corner of Champs Elysees and Bons Enfants, it featured French vaudevilles and comedies. In less than a month we find the familiar insistence that slaves would not be admitted. And, again, it was not only slaves that sought entrance but whites as well. By July, however, the theater was up for sale, though a new administration gave it further life, at least to the middle of September—after which it disappears.[26]

A little over a year passed before another theater for the free colored was proposed. As the announcement delicately put it, "A theater open to all classes has long been lacking in New Orleans." To fill this need the *Theatre de la Renaissance* would open on January 19, 1840, featuring comedies, dramas, opera-comiques, vaudevilles, and tragedies. There would also be a ballroom, the whole located at the corner of Champs Elysees and Grands Hommes, two blocks closer in from the former theater. The theater didn't actually open until a week later on Sunday, January 26, and thereafter ran on Sundays and one or two weeknights for the rest of the season. The "peculiar" insistence showed up after one month's operation: "The administration reminds that . . . this theater was established for persons of color. These will be admitted exclusively." In other words, slaves and whites please stay away.[27]

Was the music at either of these theaters provided by Negroes? There is no direct evidence, but there is one tantalizing clue which suggests that for the latter theater, at least, the answer is yes. In February it is announced that the theater orchestra, directed by "M. Constantin" will play several overtures. Then in April an announcement reads that the orchestra "de la Societe Philharmonique" directed by M. Constantin will play several overtures. Now a free Negro violin teacher named Constantin Deburque was in fact at times the director of the orchestra of the Negro Philharmonic Society. Were they not the same? The first name only was often used in theatrical billings. There was, to be sure, another Philharmonic Society composed of whites in New Orleans at this time, but it seems unlikely that they would be playing in this theater. Taking it all in all, the writer is convinced that the orchestra at the Renais-

sance Theater was made up of members of the **Negro Philharmonic**
Society, and that the director of that society's orchestra was the director of the theater orchestra.[28]

One thing is certain: the Negro in New Orleans had ample opportunity to hear and to participate in the music around him. Indeed he could not escape it. In the dance field it is possible that he
played more than whites, as the trade of musician was not encouraged for the native born white male, even though the imported musician was respected.[29]

And always the Negro could make music somehow. On the public
squares all that was needed to get a dance going was a good lead
singer. Soon there would gather a group to improvise a counter line
to his lead, while keeping time with their hands and feet. Along the
levees and in the streets, they could be heard singing for the sheer
joy of it. One lad who whistled "Settin' on a Rail" and other popular songs was declared to be almost the equal of the great Cioffi and
his trombone. "The little scamp has not only an ear but a most capital mouth for music . . . difficult passages and variations." Another fellow who was "patting Juba on top of a molasses barrel" got
to breaking down so hard towards the end of his dance that the
head broke in; . . . he went down in the molasses." [30]

In church such hearty improvised music heightened devotion.
Frederick Olmstead tells of a Negro service in New Orleans: "The
congregation sang; I think everyone joined, even the children, and
the collective sound was wonderful. The voices of one or two
women rose above the rest, and one of these soon began to introduce variations. . . . Many of the singers kept time with their feet,
balancing themselves on each alternately and swinging their bodies
accordingly." Before long the preacher "raised his own voice above
all, clapped his hands, and commenced to dance . . . first with his
back, and then his face to the audience." So danced the Hebrews in
their worship long before.[31]

Melody and rhythm also helped to lighten the burden and monotony of daily tasks. Oarsmen in the river boats, longshoremen on
the levee, boathands on the steamers sang their way into the books
and diaries of travelers. The simple act of brushing off a customer

in a barber shop became a rhythmic art in the hands of the barber
boy. "With what facility he moves his supple wrist and makes the
down-driving broom play over your back the most complicated
tunes . . . beating time all the while with his foot, with a precision
that would do honor to the leader of the orchestra of the Orleans
Theater. . . . How often does the double and triple and common
time put you in mind of the castanets of the Castillian maid, and
rub-a-dub-dub of the drummer at tattoo or reveille!" [32]

"Green-sass" men with vegetables, "cymbal" men with crullers,
Negro maids carrying rice cakes on their heads, and all sorts of
vendors peddled their wares with song and rhythm. A knowledgable
listener could detect satire directed at local public figures in some of
the songs.[33]

Most of these street musicians must remain anonymous, but of
one of them we can say more. Early in February, 1840, a young
Englishman named Francis C. Sheridan landed in Galveston,
Texas, on his way to Houston. He was on a diplomatic mission to
the Republic of Texas. But he claimed that he instantly forgot all
about Texas when his ears picked up the strains of "Old Rosin the
Bow" sung by a Negro dock hand who accompanied himself with
his iron cotton bale hooks.[34]

The song was extremely popular in America at the time, and
Sheridan had already heard it enough times to fill several pages in
his journal extolling its superiority over the favorite English songs
of the day. Indeed, he had even learned to sing it himself. "It really
was marvellous," he said, "to hear the number of persons whistling
or singing this song at all times and in all places." But he added, "If
anyone should be so enraptured with the song as to desire to hear it
in perfection he must travel to New Orleans & enquire for Signor
Cornmeali." [35]

Who was "Signor Cornmeali"? Sheridan himself supplied some
description: "This worthy is an old Nigger who derives his name
from the article he sells—which is Corn Meal. He rides about New
Orleans in an old cart drawn by an older horse, & pulling up in
front of the Exchanges—generally a little before dinner time when
the rooms begin to fill, he commences his performances." [36]

Better known as Old Corn Meal, this extraordinary Negro vendor

Music, ranging from primitive dances on the levee to refined orchestral performance, allowed the Negro to lighten the burden and monotony of his daily tasks.

and singer had achieved enough fame and popularity in New Orleans by the spring of 1837 to be invited to appear on the stage of the famed St. Charles Theater. Nor was Corn Meal to be merely a curiosity treading the boards for a brief moment. Rather, with his horse and cart, he was to be featured in a new "melodrama" called "Life in New Orleans." [37]

Corn Meal's introduction as a theatrical performer was set for May 13, 1837, on a Saturday night. In the announcement and even in editorial comments about the show, he was variously referred to as "the celebrated sable satellite"; "old Corn Meal"; "the well known vendor"; or simply "the celebrated amateur." Likewise, Corn Meal's own original song was called the "well known extravaganza"; "his celebrated song"; or "the popular song of Fresh Corn Meal." It was promised that as he drove around the stage in his "real dug-out" he would also sing others of his favorite melodies. All of which makes clear that the colorful character and his rig, his vending song and his renditions of popular tunes, had long been admired.[38]

The show "met with such a warm reception" that a repeat performance was scheduled for the following Tuesday. In this second appearance the public was assured that "the celebrated Corn Meal will come out with a new effusion of his comic Extravaganzas." There might well have been further showings, but unfortunately Corn Meal's horse, perhaps frightened, fell on the stage and was killed.[39]

This first appearance of a Negro on the American stage in New Orleans, indeed perhaps the first in the United States, brought some objections and furnished material for one of the dialect skits then beginning to appear in the New Orleans *Picayune*. In the course of a dialogue between Cato Griffe and Sam Jonsing, who were discussing the depression and the resultant difficulty in obtaining corn, Cato says: "But look here, Sam Jonsing, your 'marks about corn makes me remember Old Corn Meal heself. Don't you tink 'twas too 'gradin altogether, for a 'spectable old nig, like Corn Meal is, to make a public spectacle of heself upon de stage? Don't you think it was highly unwrong?" Sam replied: "Ob course. It's bad enough for a nigger to go singing about de streets, making a rang-a-tang ob himself—why, its worse dan a kangeroo. If he goes on in dis way, he'll t'row disgrace on de entire populashun ob colored Americans. . . ." Another would-be humorist joked about the accident to Corn Meal's horse, claiming it died of stage fright.[40]

But the pendulum swung the other way when a minister made a mock defense of Corn Meal's appearance on the stage of the St. Charles by saying that "he is probably as respectable . . . as most of those who live by the profession!" This remark, said the *Picayune,* was neither Christian nor charitable and deserved "the severest censure of all honest men." From then on the newspapers, especially the *Picayune,* showed only admiration for the old street singer. Just a few days later, in reporting the success of Cooke's Company of Equestrians in Boston, the *Picayune* declared: "We would make an even bet that Old Corn Meal, horse and cart, with a small sprinkling of animals such as a racoon and a kangaroo, for instance, would cut this company of Cooke's entirely out." [41]

At the end of a long summer, "amidst the solitude and dreariness of our city," this paper expressed its thanks for the "highly musical notes of that old and staunch resident, Fresh Corn Meal." It was a newsworthy item when "Camp street was vocal with the voice . . . of old Corn Meal again yesterday." At times the paper was carried away: "We acknowledge the favor of a ditty from 'Old Corn Meal,' . . . [whose] voice broke upon the stillness . . . like the strains of a chanticleer at early dawn . . . waking the maiden from her virgin dreams of love and youth. Oh!" [42]

If he was not seen for a time, the *Picayune* used some of the limited space of its mere four pages to inquire after him: "Where is old Corn Meal? Has he retired from the trade or has he taken laudanum? We miss the music of his Ethiopian melodies . . . his slouched hat and black burley body . . . his rickety go-cart and shaggy pony. . . . The old boy is a character, and we would not like to see him retire." And the paper was quick to acknowledge his serenade when he reappeared.[43]

Again, when fever was rampant in New Orleans, the *Picayune* worried about his absence. "Where is fancy bread, or in other words . . . Old Corn Meal," it asked, and added the hope that he hadn't taken the fever. Another time when it missed what it called in a friendly pun "his meal-odious voice," the *Picayune* wanted to know if his horse had died or was ill, or if his wagon had broken down. "These are important interrogations," the paper insisted. On one occasion when his cart had indeed broken down, the *Picayune* expressed its regrets to the "old ballad singer," and reported to the public when repairs were made. Likewise when Corn Meal's horse was indeed sick, the public was informed.[44]

Such comments and concerns were not the only evidence of Corn Meal's popularity. Early in 1838 the *Picayune* went to the trouble of making a special cut of the old singer, along with his horse and cart. After announcing that it was negotiating with Corn Meal "to transport the ordinary slow mail," the paper used the cut to head one of its two columns of exchange news, the one containing older items. This news, it said, was brought in by Corn Meal and his go-cart. And in the Mardi Gras parades of 1839 many masquers dressed themselves to represent the picturesque character.[45]

In the summer of 1840, over three years after his first stage appearance, Corn Meal again sang on the stage, this time at the old Camp Street Theater and without his horse and cart. He wasn't risking another horse. Billed as the "eccentricities of the original Corn Meal." his act was promised for one night only, Wednesday, June 10, but as on the earlier occasion, the show had to be repeated for "positively the last time" on the following Saturday. Corn Meal's presence in a theater was completely accepted this time; the protests that appeared before were heard no more. In fact, on his second night, the Negro artist shared the stage with a white black-face entertainer, Mick Saunders, who did the characters of "Ginger Blue" and "Pompey Quash." [46]

What made Corn Meal so well liked in a city as full of music and musicians as New Orleans? For one thing, he sang currently popular tunes. Besides his own vending song, "Fresh Corn Meal," the old street performer sang such numbers as "My Long Tail Blue," "Sich a Gettin Up Stairs," and "Nigger Jim Brown." He even rendered the "Star Spangled Banner," giving his own variations of our difficult national anthem. Also he must occasionally have offered something a little spicy. Once the *Picayune* commented that "the production of the Corn Meal Bard is pretty fair, considering the subject; but it will not suit our columns." [47]

His greatest hit, however, was undoubtedly "Old Rosin the Bow," the song that so impressed the English diplomat, Sheridan. Everybody in New Orleans who could sang "Old Rosin," even nice young ladies whose mothers sometimes disapproved, considering it "too robust." And it was published in the city by Benjamin Casey in 1839, arranged for the piano by one of the local musicians. But, as Sheridan advised all, if you would really hear it you must ask for Signor Cornmeali. [48]

"He sings in a manner as perfectly novel as it is inimitable," Sheridan wrote in his journal, "beginning in a deep bass & at every other 3 or 4 words of his song, jumping into a falsetto of power. . . . It has precisely the same effect as one of our street duets where the Man & Boy alternately sing a line." But, Sheridan added, Corn Meal's songs were much livelier than those heard in English streets, and besides, the New Orleans singer rendered the duet all by himself. [49]

This ability to change his voice, along with a remarkable range, was Corn Meal's great stock in trade. "We never heard," said the *Picayune*, "a vocalist who could make his voice 'wheel about and turn about' so quick from tenor to bass and from bass to falsetto. He has a great compass of voice. . . ." His admirers were hard put to find an adjective to describe that voice. The best they could come up with was "epicene"; it was easier simply to speak of his "Voices" rather than of his voice. [50]

Corn Meal's constant effort to extend his repertoire with fresh melodies came in for favorable comment, and his consistency drew praise. "Let what will come—yellow fever, cholera, or whatnot— Signor Cornmealiola is always at his best." But above all, Corn Meal won recognition because he was unique. As one admirer put it: "It is not the barrel-looking body, the happy phiz, the aguish go-cart, nor the pig-like squeak of his falsetto that commends Old Corn Meal to our esteem; he has won our regard because he is an original." Another spoke of "his own peculiar & most singular manner," and went so far as to call him "a genius, after his own fashion." [51]

It was realized that under other circumstances Corn Meal would be worth more than the tips he got from street audiences. One paper urged "scheming" Yankees to engage "this greatest of musicians," and promised "a fortune to any man who would start on a professional tour with him." "Could he emigrate to London," asserted another, "he would make a fortune and consign the memory of Jim Crow to the tomb of all the Capulets." The paper was here referring to the song and dance "Jump Jim Crow" with which Thomas D. Rice had recently scored a huge success abroad. And rumors of Corn Meal's possible retirement from his trade to devote all his time to singing were not dismissed lightly.[52]

On a Friday night, May 20, 1842, New Orleans' old folk-singer died. That the passing of a Negro street peddler in that day was noted with respect in the city's leading journals is proof enough of the mark he had made. The most staid and conservative of New Orleans' newspapers, the *Bee,* said it would give his Christian and surnames if it but knew them, and called for "a commendable eulogy on his virtues and peculiar qualities." For its part, the *Bee* had this to say: "Poor old Corn Meal . . . is gone. Never again shall we listen to his double toned voice—never again shall his corn meal melodies, now grumbled in a bass—now squeaked in a treble, vibrate on the ear. He was as public-spirited a character as any we ever met with, and was as thoroughly known as a popular politician—and as good humored as a man who has got rid of his municipal notes at par. [They had just tumbled.]" Quite an obituary for anyone.[53]

But did his passing mean so definitely that never again would Corn Meal's style be heard? Some who have written of the American minstrel show have argued that the minstrel Negro character was drawn from the town Negro rather than from the plantation slave, and that before the Civil War the portrayal was more accurate than it later became. In his history of the minstrel show, *Tambo and Bones,* Carl Wittke states that one of the very first minstrels, the circus clown George Nichols, learned much of his material from two New Orleans singers, Picayune Butler and Corn Meal.[54]

The source of Wittke's statement is an article by T. Allston Brown on "The Origins of Minstrelsy" in an old book called *Fun in Black.* Since this book was published in 1874, it is entirely probable that Brown had much first-hand information. Brown himself says that "Nichols first sang 'Jim Crow' as a clown, afterwards as a Negro. He first conceived the idea from . . . a banjo player, known from New Orleans to Cincinnati as Picayune Butler," who sang and accompanied himself "on his four-stringed banjo. . . . But," continued Brown, "an old darkie of New Orleans known as 'Old Corn Meal' furnished Nichols with many airs, which he turned to account." [55]

It is a pity that Picayune Butler sang his songs before newspapers concerned themselves with local color. His story will probably never be told. He did exist, however. Just before Christmas in 1830, an actor who used blackface in the Camp Street Theater in New Orleans was judged a bore. "We trust he will not . . . again . . . play Juba," hoped his critic. "If he does, we would recommend him to borrow old Butler's banjow [*sic*], as an admirable accompaniment." This is undoubtedly a reference to Picayune Butler, one which indicates he had been quite well known for some years prior to 1830. Later that same season, George Nichols often sang "Jim Crow" in New Orleans, first in Bailey's and then in Brown's circus. So it is wholly probable that Nichols did hear Picayune Butler strum and sing.[56]

It was in the 1830's that Corn Meal became so prominent. While it is true that we first specifically hear of him in 1837, when he went on the stage, that fact and the way he was billed show that he had been popular for some time already. Brown mentions that Corn Meal often sang in front of Bishop's Hotel, a place famous in its day. This hotel opened in April, 1832, and changed names six years later. Since George Nichols returned to New Orleans for several seasons after 1830, he could hardly have missed hearing old Corn Meal sell his wares.[57]

But what about the great Thomas D. "Daddy" Rice himself, America's first internationally famous blackface entertainer, whose character of Jim Crow and whose subsequent "Ethiopian Operas" were the immediate forerunners of American minstrelsy? Aside from anything he may have borrowed from Nichols and hence indirectly from Corn Meal, Rice too must have gone directly to the source. Daddy Rice first came to New Orleans in 1835, when Corn Meal's popularity was soaring, and again in 1836 and in 1838 when Corn Meal was at his height. Surely it is significant that in his second season in New Orleans Daddy Rice prepared a skit entitled "Corn Meal." [58]

It is of course impossible to assess neatly the lasting influence of performers like Corn Meal who lived before the inventions of film and sound recording. But the foregoing story does permit at least some strong suggestions. For one thing, Corn Meal helped focus attention on the Negro as a valid and valuable source of American entertainment. Corn Meal brought his own art to the white theater and hotels of New Orleans, where he impressed both residents of the city and travelers like Sheridan. In the great fusion of various national musical traditions then taking place in New Orleans, Corn Meal did his part to inject Negro interpretations and originations. For another thing, besides Mick Saunders, George Nichols, and Daddy Rice, other blackface entertainers came through New Orleans in those years appearing either on the stage or in the circus. They too must have heard Corn Meal and probably borrowed from him. Corn Meal, Picayune Butler, and no telling how many others left their mark on American minstrelsy.

Is it not here, then, in street minstrels such as Corn Meal; in the dance halls and churches; in brass bands and opera; in fiddlers and dancers and banjoists; in the whole overpowering atmosphere of music in New Orleans that the Negro began to shape the music that would eventually be Jazz? Certainly all these strands were a part of his life, and if to the weaving of them he brought something of his own, it was as an American rather than as an African. Or so it seems to this writer.

Appendix

Shown below (listed by composer) are compositions, other than opera, played in concerts in New Orleans. Of course, composers whose operas were popular were played often in these concerts. But since they are discussed in the text, this appendix will, for the most part, exclude them.

1806–10

Soler	1 symphony concertante—two clarinets.
Vogel	5 overtures—orchestra; 1 overture—harp.
Clementi	3 sonatas—piano.
Jarnowic	1 concerto—violin.
Steibelt	1 sonata—piano; 7 other compositions—piano; 1 variations—harp.
Viotti	1 concerto—piano; 1 symphony concertante—two violins; 1 concerto—violin.
Wranitsky	3 symphonies, 1 grand rondo, and 1 chasse—orchestra.
Cramer	2 concertos—piano; 1 sonata—piano; 2 grand marches—harp and orchestra.
Anfossi	1 overture—orchestra; 1 bouffon and recitative—voice.
Fodor	1 concerto—violin.
Devienne	1 symphony concertante—two clarinets; 1 concerto—flute.
Pleyel	2 trios and 1 sonata—piano, violin, and bass; 1 concerto—violin.

Dussek	1 concerto and 1 sonata—piano; 1 variations of a concerto by Hermann—piano.
Maestrino	2 concertos—violin.
Scheyermann	1 sonata—piano.
Bomtempo	1 concerto—piano.
Berton	1 polonaise—two pianos.
Cimarosa	1 duet and 1 solo—voice; 1 composition—voice and clarinet.
Campanello	2 trios—vocal.
Nadermann	1 variations—harp.
Dalvimare	1 sonata—harp.
Duport	1 variations—cello; 1 variations of a sonata by Schetky—cello and viola.
Paisiello	1 duet—voice.
Guglielmi	1 air and recitative—voice.
Sacchini	1 duet—voice; 3 ariettes—voice and orchestra.

1811–20

Steibelt	1 polonaise and 2 sonatas—piano; 4 other compositions—piano; 1 composition—lyre and piano; 1 composition—harp; 1 composition—orchestra.
Dussek	4 concertos—piano.
Cramer	1 variations of a sonata by Dussek—piano; 1 sonata and two concertos—piano; 1 march—orchestra; 1 concerto—clarinet.
Viotti	1 polonaise—voice and piano; 6 concertos—violin; 3 symphony concertantes—two violins; 1 "symphony concerto"—orchestra.
Dalayrac	3 ariettes (bravoure)—voice and orchestra.
Lachnith	1 concerto—piano; 1 rondo—piano and orchestra.
Duvernoy	1 concerto—clarinet; 1 nocturne—piano and French horn (with Nadermann).
Dalvimare	1 concerto—harp; 1 duet—two harps.
Paisiello	1 composition—harp, two horns, two clarinets, two flutes, bassoon; 1 duet—voice; 1 concerto—clarinet.
Paer	1 overture—orchestra.
Guglielmi	1 trio—voice.
Lefebvre	3 concertos—clarinet.
Cardon	2 sonatas—harp.
Tomeoni	1 ariette—voice.
Rode	7 concertos—violin; 1 variations—violin.
Sacchini	1 duet—voice.

Gyrowetz	3 symphonies—orchestra.
Franzl	1 symphony concertante—two flutes and orchestra; 2 variations—violin.
Kreutzer	1 overture—orchestra; 1 concerto—violin.
Soler	1 concerto—clarinet.
Pleyel	1 concertante—two violins and bass; 1 concerto—violin.
Jarnowic	1 concerto—violin.
Krommer	1 symphony concertante—two clarinets.
Devienne	1 symphony concertante—two flutes; 2 concertos—flute; 1 symphony concertante—two clarinets.
Vogel	2 overtures—orchestra.
Bomtempo	1 sonata—piano.
Solier	1 concerto—clarinet.
Berger	1 ariette—voice.
Gelinek	2 compositions—piano.
Catrufo	1 overture—orchestra; 2 ariettes—voice; 1 duet—voice.
Ries	1 variations on a theme by Mozart—piano.
Martin y Solar	1 overture—piano (*La Cosa Rara*).
Kalkbrenner	1 fantasy—piano.
Crusell	1 concerto—clarinet.
Kuffner	1 quartet—clarinet, violin, viola, bass.
Bochsa	1 variations—clarinet and orchestra.
Nadermann	1 nocturne—piano and French horn (with Duvernoy).

1821–30

Ries	2 compositions—piano.
Franzl	1 variations—violin.
Kalkbrenner	4 compositions—piano; 1 concerto—piano.
Rode	2 concertos—violin; 2 compositions—piano.
Woefel	2 rondos—piano.
Herz	1 variations—piano.
Gelinek	2 rondelays—piano.
Gebel	1 concerto—piano.
Martini	3 rondelays—voice.
Braham	6 compositions—voice.
Viotti	5 concertos—violin; 1 polonaise—violin; 1 allegretto—orchestra.
Fodor	1 potpourri—violin.
Lefebvre	1 concerto—clarinet; 1 rondelay—clarinet.
Gaveaux	1 symphony—orchestra.
Cramer	1 variations—piano; 1 concerto—piano.
Paisiello	1 composition—voice.

Bishop	1 song—voice.
Dussek	1 variations—piano; 1 concerto—piano; 1 overture—two pianos.
Habeneck	2 compositions—violin.
Steibelt	1 concerto—piano and orchestra.
Farinelli	2 duets—voice.
Mayseder	1 polonaise—piano.
Kuffner	1 quintet—clarinet, violin, two violas, cello; 1 overture—orchestra.
Bochsa	1 nocturne—piano and clarinet; 1 overture—orchestra.
Boieldieu	1 variations—clarinet.
Vogel	1 overture—orchestra.
Paer	3 compositions—voice; 1 duet—voice.
Generali	2 duets—voice; 1 composition—voice.
Mayer	1 aria—voice.
Moscheles	1 composition—piano.
Hummel	1 rondo—piano.
Kreutzer	2 concertos—violin; 1 symphony concertante—two violins.
Pleyel	1 concerto—violin.
Wiederkehr	2 symphony concertantes—horn and bassoon.
Pacini	1 composition—voice and guitar.
Muller	1 duet—clarinet and bassoon.
Gail	1 trio—voice.
Lafont	1 concerto—violin.
Tulou	2 concertos—flute.
Drouet	2 variations—flute; 1 composition—two flutes.
Romberg	1 potpourri—bass viol.
Weber	1 quartet—two violins, viola, bass.

1831–41

Berr	1 composition—clarinet.
Romberg	1 caprice—cello.
Herz	2 variations—piano.
Kalkbrenner	1 fantasy—piano.
Thalberg	1 composition—piano.
Mayseder	1 trio—piano, cornet, and violin; 1 variations—violin.

Notes

To conserve space a single footnote is used for each paragraph. Those who may require a more detailed documentation are referred to Henry A. Kmen, "Singing and Dancing: A Social History of Music in New Orleans," (Ph.D. dissertation, Tulane University, 1961; also available on University Microfilms, Ann Arbor, Michigan). This dissertation contains three tables: Table I lists all of the ball-rooms with their location and date of opening; Table II lists all concerts that were followed by a ball, with the name of the sponsor; and Table III gives a complete list of all opera performances from 1796 to 1841. The composer of each opera, the date of performance, and the theater in which the opera was given, are included; and all premieres are clearly indicated. There is also a considerable amount of explanatory comment in Table III. These tables will be cited throughout this book. Anyone desiring a copy of Table III may obtain one by writing to the author at Tulane University and paying the cost of photo-copying.

CHAPTER ONE

1 Dunbar Rowland (ed.), *Official Letter Books of W. C. C. Claiborne, 1801–1816* (Jackson, 1917), I, 354–55.

2 Garnie William McGinty, *A History of Louisiana* (New York, 1949), 59.

³ Berquin-Duvallon, *Vue de la Colonie Espagnole du Mississippi ou des Provinces de Louisiane et Floride Occidentale, en l'Annee 1802* (Paris, 1803), 283–84; Amos Stoddard, *Sketches, Historical and Descriptive of Louisiana* (Philadelphia, 1812), 321.

⁴ Joseph Hold Ingraham, *The South-West, by a Yankee* (2 vols.; New York, 1835), I, 109; Baron de Montlezun, *Voyage Fait dan les Annees 1816 et 1817, de New-Yorck a la Nouvelle-Orleans* (Paris, 1818), I, 245, 253, 306; Louis Fitzgerald Tasistro, *Random Shots and Southern Breezes* (New York, 1842), II, 51. See also James E. Alexander, *Transatlantic Sketches, Comprising Visits to the Most Interesting Scenes in North and South America and the West Indies* (London, 1833), II, 17; Paul Alliot, "Historical and Political Reflections on Louisiana," in James A. Robertson (ed.), *Louisiana under Spain, France and the United States, 1785–1807* (Cleveland, 1911), I, 75; Thomas Ashe, *Travels in America, Performed in 1806* (London, 1808), III, 267; Karl Bernhard, *Travels through North America during the Years 1825 and 1826* (Philadelphia, 1828), II, 55, 56, 69, 70, 72; Henry M. Brackenridge, *Views of Louisiana together with a Journal of a Voyage up the Missouri River, in 1811* (Pittsburgh, 1814), 137; James Silk Buckingham, *The Slave States of America* (London, 1842), I, 342; Timothy Flint, *Recollections of the Last Ten Years . . . in the Valley of the Mississippi* (Boston, 1826), 336; Henry Dart (ed.), "William Johnson's Journal," *Louisiana Historical Quarterly,* V (January, 1922), 38; (hereinafter cited as Dart (ed.), "Johnson's Journal."; James Logan, *Notes of a Journey through Canada, the United States of America, and the West Indies* (Edinburgh, 1838), 180; M. Isidore Lowenstern, *Les Etats-Unis et la Havane, Souvenirs d'un Voyageur* (Paris, 1842), 271, 304–305; Francois Marie Perrin du Lac, *Voyage dans les Deux Louisianes, et chez les Nations Sauvages du Missouri, par les Etats-Unis, l'Ohio et les Provinces qui le Bordent, en 1801, 1802 et 1803* (Paris, 1805), 394–95; Charles Sealsfield, *The Americans as They Are* (London, 1828), 185; James Stuart, *Three Years in North America* (3rd ed.; Edinburgh, 1833), II, 205; John F. Watson, "Notitia of Incidents at New Orleans in 1804 and 1805," *American Pioneer,* II (May, 1843), 231–35.

⁵ Pierre-Clement de Laussat, *Memoires sur Ma Vie* (Paris, 1831), 146; Matilda Charlotte Houstoun, *Texas and the Gulf of Mexico* (London, 1844), I, 162; New Orleans *Argus,* January 27, 1827; *Courrier de la Louisiane,* February 23, 1829, hereinafter cited as *Courier.*

⁶ Grace H. Yerbury, "Concert Music in Early New Orleans," *Louisiana Historical Quarterly,* XL (April, 1957), 97; Henry A. Kmen, "Singing and Dancing: A Social History of Music in New Orleans," (Ph.D. dissertation, Tulane University, 1961), Table III, hereinafter cited as Kmen, "Singing and Dancing"; *L'Ami des Lois,* January 24, 1822; *Courier,* March 4, 1808; February 3, 1811; February 13, 15, 1822; March 5, 1832; April 5, 9, 1838; Louisiana *Gazette,* February 26, 1805; *Moniteur de la Louisiane,* February

26, 1811; *Daily Picayune,* April 8, 1838. The newspapers will hereafter be cited as *Ami, Courier, Gazette, Moniteur,* and *Picayune.* All newspapers used in this study were published in New Orleans.

7 Montlezun, *Voyage,* I, 307, 308, 340; Watson, "Notitia," 234; John Smith Kendall, "The Humors of the Duello," *Louisiana Historical Quarterly,* XXIII (April, 1940), 445.

8 Laussat, *Memoires,* 136–37.

9 *Union,* February 23, 1805; *Argus,* April 14, 1825; Ingraham, *The South-West,* I, 118.

10 *Gazette,* December 21, 1804; February 26, 1805; *Moniteur,* February 11, 1809; *Courier,* February 5, 1812; *Ami,* January 27, 1817.

11 Kmen, "Singing and Dancing," Table I; J. G. de Baroncelli, *Le Theatre-Francais a la Nouvelle Orleans* (New Orleans, 1906), 22; Buckingham, *Slave States,* I, 337; *Picayune,* December 27, 1837.

12 *Moniteur,* January 22, 1806; January 7, 1807; *Gazette,* February 21, 1815; *Argus,* January 4, 1826; February 19, 1827; *L'Abeille de la Nouvelle Orleans,* April 6, 1840, hereinafter cited as *Bee.*

13 *Gazette,* December 21, 1804; *Moniteur,* November 23, 1805; December 17, 1806; *Argus,* January 5, 1827; January 10, 1828; *Bee,* January 4, 7, 1837; *Courier,* April 7, 8, 1826; Sealsfield, *Americans,* 186; Montlezun, *Voyage,* I, 308.

14 Tasistro, *Random Shots,* II, 51. See also Houstoun, *Texas,* II, 16; Sealsfield, *Americans,* 185. See *Argus,* January 4, 1826; *Courier,* January 4, 1840, for typical ball announcements during Carnival.

15 Bernhard, *Travels,* II, 69–70; *Argus,* February 3, 1826; *Bee,* February 18, 1833.

16 J. C. Flugel, "Pages from a Journal of a Voyage down the Mississippi to New Orleans in 1817," *Louisiana Historical Quarterly,* VII (July, 1924), 427; Bernhard, *Travels,* II, 72; *Bee,* February 17, 20, 1837; *Courier,* March 18, 1814; March 5, 1824; *Louisiana Advertiser,* March 19, 1835; *Moniteur,* March 15, 1806; March 18, 1807.

17 *Courier,* March 21, 1838; *Ami,* February 29, 1816; February 25, 1817; February 10, 1818; February 13, 1823; *Bee,* March 1, 1833; April 6, 1840; *Louisiana Advertiser,* March 25, 1829; *Argus,* February 3, 10, 1826; March 2, 1827; February 22, 1833; Bernhard, *Travels,* II, 70; *Picayune,* March 13, 1838.

18 Watson, "Notitia," 231–34; *Bee,* June 2, 1837; *Courier,* June 5, August 1, 1838; *Picayune,* June 14, July 1, October 12, 1838; *True American,* August 21, 1838. See also Elise Lathrop, *Early American Inns and Taverns* (New York, 1926), 234; and Eliza Ripley, *Social Life in Old New Orleans* (New York, 1912), 143.

19 *Courier,* June 22, 1826; May 6, 1835; June 5, 1838; *Louisiana Advertiser,* June 15, 1832.

20 *Picayune,* October 13, 1837.

[21] For a description of frontier characteristics of New Orleans, see Alfred Toledano Wellborn, "The Relations between New Orleans and Latin America, 1810–1824," *Louisiana Historical Quarterly,* XXII (July, 1939), 711. See William R. Hogan, "Amusements in the Republic of Texas," *Journal of Southern History,* III (November, 1937), 406–10, for an entertaining account of the passion for dancing in the southwest frontier country. There was surprisingly little religious objection to dancing on that frontier.

[22] Rowland, *Letter Books,* I, 328. See also Flint, *Recollections,* 334–35; and Robert Baird, *View of the Valley of the Mississippi* (Philadelphia, 1834), 281, for comments on the language barriers in 1823 and 1830 respectively. On dancing in spite of these barriers see, for example, a letter from Claiborne to Madison, December 31, 1804, in Rowland, *Letter Books,* III, 35. See also pp. 26–30 below.

[23] Flint, *Recollections,* 274, 307. See also Buckingham, *Slave States,* I, 347–48; Dart (ed.), "Johnson's Journal," 38; G. P. Whittington (ed.), "The Journal of Dr. John Sibley," *Louisiana Historical Quarterly,* X (October, 1927), 384; Stuart, *Three Years,* II, 205; Watson, "Notitia," 236. On the Protestants, see the Reverend William Bingley, *Travels in North America* (London, 1821), 166; John F. Schermerhorn and Samuel J. Mills, *A Correct View of That Part of the United States Which Lies West of the Allegany Mountains with Regard to Religion and Morals* (Hartford, 1814), 34; Henry Benjamin Whipple, *Bishop Whipple's Southern Diary, 1843–1844.* ed. Lester B. Shippee (Minneapolis, 1937), 99; *Bee,* December 10, 1831; *True American,* September 24, 1836.

[24] *Bee,* December 10, 1831.

[25] *Bee,* November 22, 1837; Buckingham, *Slave States,* I, 347–48.

[26] *True American,* September 24, 1836; John Smith Kendall, *History of New Orleans* (Chicago, 1922), I, 78.

[27] Grace King, *Creole Families of New Orleans* (New York, 1921), 355; Kate Mason Rowland and (Mrs.) Morris L. Croxall (eds.), *The Journal of Julia Le Grand* (Richmond, 1911), 355; Charles Augustus Murray, *Travels in North America during the Years 1834, 1835, and 1836* (London, 1839), II, 187; Vincent Nolte, *Fifty Years in Both Hemispheres: Or, Reminiscences of a Merchant's Life* (London, 1854. Reprinted New York, 1934), 86; Ripley, *Social Life,* 5, 48, 178, 204; Jean Jacques Ampere, *Promenade en Amerique* (Paris, 1855), II, 153; William Wood, *Autobiography of William Wood* (New York, 1895), II, 191.

[28] Alexander, *Transatlantic Sketches,* II, 38–39.

[29] Laussat, *Memoires,* 128–30.

[30] *Ibid.,* 135–36.

[31] *Ibid.,* 136–37.

[32] Ripley, *Social Life,* 116–19.

[33] *Ami,* January 10, 1817; *Courier,* November 23, 1810; January 30,

December 9, 1811; December 18, 1812; December 5, 1838; *Gazette,* February 12, 1805; November 18, 1806; January 6, 1807; *Louisiana Whig,* January 22, 1835; *Moniteur,* November 19, 1806; *Bee,* February 27, 1840.

34 *Ami,* January 10, 1817; *Courier,* November 23, 1810; November 24, 1815.

35 *Picayune,* October 3, 5, 1838; *Louisiana Whig,* January 22, 1835.

36 *Bee,* December 24, 1830.

37 *Bee,* February 1, 1833. Italics mine.

38 *Bee,* February 15, 1831; *Argus,* April 14, 1825; January 10, 1828; February 20, 1833; *Courier,* March 23, 1825; Bernhard, *Travels,* II, 72; Francis P. Burns, "Lafayette Visits New Orleans," *Louisiana Historical Quarterly,* XXIX (April, 1946), 319; A. Levasseur, *Lafayette en Amerique en 1824 et 1825* (Paris, 1829), II, 217; Henry Renshaw, "Lafayette's Visit to New Orleans," *Louisiana Historical Quarterly,* I (September, 1917), 5–8; Maurice de Simonin, "Centennial Anniversary of Visit of Lafayette," *Louisiana Historical Quarterly,* IX (April, 1926), 202.

39 Francis P. Burns, "Henry Clay Visits New Orleans," *Louisiana Historical Quarterly,* XXVII (July, 1944), 746.

40 *Picayune,* December 27, 1838.

41 Documents of the Cabildo, Book 4079, Document 254 (Louisiana State Museum Library, New Orleans).

42 *Courier,* April 1, 1811; Gayarre, *History of Louisiana,* III, 191–92; *Gazette,* November 18, 1806; *Moniteur,* November 19, 1806. These announcements speak of dances during the previous season as well as those of the current one.

43 Documents of the Cabildo, Book 4079, Document 254; Acts of Pedro Pedesclaux, January–August, 1796, Act of May 20, 1796, Folio 242–44 (Notarial Archives, Civil Courts Building, New Orleans). See also Caroline Maude Burson, *The Stewardship of Don Esteban Miro, 1782–1789* (New Orleans, 1940), 257.

44 Letter from Joseph de Pontalba to Esteban Miro, October 6, 1792, cited in Rene J. Le Gardeur, Jr., *The First New Orleans Theater, 1792–1803* (New Orleans, 1963), 6; Documents of the Cabildo, Book 4079, Document 254; Berquin-Duvallon, *Vue,* 31–32; Watson, "Notitia," 232. The *prefet,* Pierre Laussat, thought Berquin-Duvallon unnecessarily sarcastic. Laussat, *Memoires,* 161–62. See also Minter Wood, "Life in New Orleans in the Spanish Period," *Louisiana Historical Quarterly,* XXII (July, 1939), 689–90.

45 Berquin-Duvallon, *Vue,* 39; Will H. Coleman, *Historical Sketch Book and Guide to New Orleans and Environs* (New York, 1885), 18; Dart (ed.), "Johnson's Journal," 38.

46 Berquin-Duvallon, *Vue,* 32.

47 *Courier,* February 7, 11, 25, 1814.

48 Documents of the Cabildo, Book 4088, Documents 338, 415.

[49] *Moniteur,* December 27, 1810.

[50] Henry Bradshaw Fearon, *Sketches of America: A Narrative of a Journey of Five Thousand Miles through the Eastern and Western States of America* (3rd ed.; London, 1819), 274; Benjamin Henry Boneval Latrobe, *Impressions Respecting New Orleans,* ed. Samuel Wilson, Jr. (New York, 1951), 34; Bernhard, *Travels,* II, 55–56; Henry Rightor (ed.), *Standard History of New Orleans, Louisiana* (Chicago, 1900), 458.

[51] Bernhard, *Travels,* II, 69–70; *Ami,* March 8, 23, 1824; *Argus,* February 3, 1826; *Bee,* February 18, 1833; *Courier,* January 11, 1838; *Mercantile Advertiser,* February 26, 1831.

[52] Buckingham, *Slave States,* I, 335; Herbert Asbury, *The French Quarter* (New York, 1936), 140; Coleman, *Sketch Book,* 74, 78; Sir Charles Lyell, *A Second Visit to the United States of North America* (London, 1849), II, 112; Cecile Willinck (ed.), "An Old Lady's Gossip," *Louisiana Historical Quarterly,* VI (July, 1923), 386.

[53] Brackenridge, *Views,* 137; Laussat, *Memoires,* 137; *True American,* August 21, 1838; Berquin-Duvallon, *Vue,* 284; Baroncelli, *Le Theatre-Francais,* 23; Sealsfield, *Americans,* 174.

[54] Murray, *Travels in North America,* II, 188; Sealsfield, *Americans,* 173.

[55] See p. 5 above; *Courier,* March 21, April 5, 9, 10, 11, 12, 1838; *Picayune,* April 8, 1838.

[56] Watson, "Notitia," 234; Ashe, *Travels in America,* III, 275.

[57] *Gazette,* February 7, 8, 1825; *Picayune,* October 27, 1837; Tasistro, *Random Shots,* II, 20; *Bee,* January 17, 1831; Alexander, *Transatlantic Sketches,* II, 17; Logan, *Journey,* 180; Sealsfield, *Americans,* 158.

[58] Watson, "Notitia," 235; *Ami,* June 7, 1822; *Courier,* April 8, 1824; June 22, 1826; Tasistro, *Random Shots,* II, 21.

[59] *Gazette,* March 29, 1805; *Ami,* June 7, 1822; *Bee,* December 23, 1834.

[60] *Courier,* April 7, 8, 1826.

[61] *Courier,* April 11, 1826; April 23, 1840.

[62] *Argus,* March 13, 1828; *Courier,* March 29, 1838.

[63] *Bee,* May 13, June 2, 1837; *Picayune,* October 12, 1838; *Courier,* April 8, 1840.

[64] *Ami,* May 10, 1822; March 17, 1824; *Courier,* April 8, 1824.

[65] Bernhard, *Travels,* II, 63; Berquin-Duvallon, *Vue,* 38; Ingraham, *The South-West,* I, 109, 119–20; *Courier,* January 7, November 13, 29, 1811; January 23, 1813; January 14, 1814; *Moniteur,* December 14, 1805; December 6, 10, 1806; December 26, 1807; February 4, 1809; January 20, 1814.

[66] Ingraham, *The South-West,* I, 124; *Courier,* January 7, February 13, 27, November 13, 29, 1811; January 23, 1813; January 14, 1814; *Moniteur,* December 12, 1805; December 6, 10, 1806; February 4, 1809; Bernhard, *Travels,* II, 63.

[67] Bernhard, *Travels,* II, 63; Brackenridge, *Views,* 137.

⁶⁸ *Moniteur,* January 18, 1806.

⁶⁹ *Moniteur,* February 4, 1809; *Courier,* November 13, 1811; February 19, 1813.

⁷⁰ *Moniteur,* December 14, 1805; Rowland, *Letter Books,* I, 351–52, 354–55; Edward Laroque Tinker, *Creole City* (New York, 1953), 35; Documents of the Cabildo, Book 4088, Document 338.

⁷¹ Wood, "Life in New Orleans," 690–91.

⁷² Asbury, *The French Quarter,* 118–20; Berquin-Duvallon, *Vue,* 35–37; Coleman, *Sketch Book,* 16–17; Wood, "Life in New Orleans," 654.

⁷³ Laussat, *Memoires,* 147–48; Rowland, *Letter Books,* I, 331.

⁷⁴ Laussat, *Memoires,* 150–52; *Le Telegraphe et le Commercial Advertizer,* February 1, 1804; Rowland, *Letter Books,* I, 352; *Gazette,* January 25, 1805.

⁷⁵ Watson, "Notitia," 235; Nathaniel Cox to Gabriel Lewis, September 17, 1807, in "Letters from Nathaniel Cox to Gabriel Lewis, 1802–1817." (Typescript in Howard-Tilton Library, Tulane University.)

⁷⁶ *Courier,* October 9, 1811; Latrobe, *Impressions,* 36.

⁷⁷ Bernard Marigny, "Reflections on the Campaign of General Andrew Jackson," trans. Grace King, *Louisiana Historical Quarterly,* VI (January, 1923), 78; Tinker, *Creole City,* 33–34.

⁷⁸ Rowland, *Letter Books,* II, 278.

⁷⁹ Sealsfield, *Americans,* 186; Ingraham, *The South-West,* I, 121.

⁸⁰ *Louisiana Advertiser,* March 19, 1835.

⁸¹ *Courier,* February 25, 1840; *Picayune,* February 25, 1840.

⁸² Documents of the Cabildo, Book 4088, Document 338; Berquin-Duvallon, *Travels in Louisiana and the Floridas in the year 1802,* trans. John Davis (New York, 1885), 53–54; *Gazette,* March 17, 1821.

⁸³ Wood, "Life in New Orleans," 689; *Ami,* February 14, 1820; *Argus,* December 23, 1826; *Bee,* February 19, 1833; April 6, 1840; *Courier,* January 30, 1811; *Louisiana Advertiser,* February 20, 1829.

⁸⁴ *Gazette,* March 1, 1805; *Courier,* March 1, 1811; January 31, 1816; *Louisiana Advertiser,* February 10, 1826; Buckingham, *Slave States,* I, 352–53.

⁸⁵ *Telegraphe,* February 1, 1804; Tasistro, *Random Shots,* II, 20.

⁸⁶ Lowenstern, *Souvenirs,* 304; *Picayune,* January 22, 23, 1840.

⁸⁷ Tasistro, *Random Shots,* II, 20; Matilda Charlotte Houstoun, *Hesperos: Or Travels in the West* (London, 1850), II, 57. See also Bernhard, *Travels,* II, 70.

⁸⁸ Bernhard, *Travels,* II, 61; *Gazette,* February 17, 1829; George Vandenhoff, *Leaves from an Actor's Notebook* (New York, 1860), 207; *Picayune,* May 26, 1840.

⁸⁹ John Augustin, "The Oaks," in Thomas M'Caleb (ed.), *The Louisiana Book,* (New Orleans, 1894), 74–75; John Smith Kendall, "According to the Code," *Louisiana Historical Quarterly,* XXIII January, 1940), 151; Logan,

Journey, 180; Berquin-Duvallon, *Travels in Louisiana,* 27–28; Houstoun, *Hesperos,* II, 59. See also a similar incident in Harnett T. Kane, *Queen New Orleans* (New York, 1949), 147–48.

90 *Courier,* February 7, 1812.

91 *Ami,* February 14, 1820; *Argus,* December 23, 1826; *Bee,* February 19, 1833; December 3, 1834; December 7, 1835; December 1, 19, 1836; April 6, 1840; *Courier,* March 5, 1824; April 1, 1839; *Picayune,* March 13, 1838; *Telegraphe,* February 1, 1804; Albert E. Fossier, *New Orleans, the Glamour Period, 1800–1840* (New Orleans, 1957), 459–60; *Mercantile Advertiser,* February 19, 1834; Houstoun, *Hesperos,* II, 57–58; Lowenstern, *Souvenirs,* 305.

92 *Ami,* February 14, 1820; *Bee,* February 19, December 10, 1833; *Louisiana Advertiser,* February 20, 1829; Logan, *Journey,* 180.

93 *Bee,* March 14, 16, 1831; January 1, 1833; December 3, 1834; December 7, 1835; *Argus,* March 13, 1828.

94 *Bee,* February 1, 1834; March 14, 1835; *Courier,* January 28, 1825.

95 *Moniteur,* February 4, 1806; Acts of Pedro Pedesclaux, January–August, 1796. Act of May 20, 1796, Folios 242–44; Kendall, *History of New Orleans,* I, 68.

96 *Argus,* January 4, 1828; *Bee,* December 10, 1831.

97 *Bee,* December 10, 1831.

98 Fossier, *New Orleans,* 460–61; *Picayune,* October 27, 1837. Early in the year the city had been divided into three separate municipalities. Thus this prohibition applied only to the First Municipality. However, most of the principal ballrooms were in that jurisdiction.

99 Fossier, *New Orleans,* 461; Edwin L. Jewell, *Jewell's Digest of the City Ordinances* (New Orleans, 1882), 2; Kendall, *History of New Orleans,* I, 111–12; *Argus,* January 4, 1828; *Courier,* May 8, 1811; January 17, 1831; *Louisiana Advertiser,* January 31, 1831; *Moniteur,* February 4, 1806; May 2, 1807; Acts of Pedro Pedesclaux, January–August, 1796. Act of May 20, 1796, Folios 242–44; Baroncelli, *Le Theatre-Francais,* 23; Coleman, *Sketch Book,* 16.

100 *Bee,* February 18, 1834.

101 Ripley, *Social Life,* 119; *Ami,* January 22, March 8, 1824; *Argus,* November 11, 1826; *Bee,* November 29, 1834; January 23, 1837; January 25, March 4, 1840; *Courier,* November 12, 1825; December 11, 1826; December 17, 1829; January 16, 1830; January 20, 1834; *Picayune,* February 23, 1840; February 17, 1841.

102 *Ami,* January 4, 27, 1817; *Courier,* January 18, 1809; January 6, 15, February 12, 1812; February 9, 1824; March 21, 1838; Fossier, *New Orleans,* 461; *Picayune,* September 14, 1841.

103 See pp. 68–69 below; Berquin-Duvallon, *Vue,* 32; Dart (ed.), "Johnson's Journal," 38.

104 *Ami,* January 27, 1817; *Courier,* November 9, 1812; *Moniteur,*

April 11, 1807; November 17, 19, 1812; Montlezun, *Voyage,* I, 307.

105 *Moniteur,* January 28, February 4, 1807; February 5, 9, 14, 1811; *Ami,* February 8, 15, 17, 1814; *Courier,* May 6, 1835.

106 *Louisiana Advertiser,* February 20, 1829; *Bee,* December 12, 1836; November 8, 9, 1837; *Courier,* April 7, 8, 1826; June 5, 6, 1838; December 19, 1839; November 20, 1840; *Picayune,* June 19, 1838. In 1839 the orchestra of the German theater played for balls. (*Courier,* December 31, 1839.)

107 *Picayune,* December 14, 1839, February 6, 1840; *Bee,* November 8, 1837; January 20, 1840; *Courier,* November 27, 1838; November 20, 1840.

108 *Bee,* November 8, 9, 1837.

109 *Louisiana Advertiser,* February 20, 1829; *Courier,* November 20, 1840.

110 *Bee,* January 20, 1840; Henry Didimus, *New Orleans as I Found It* (New York, 1845), 25; *Picayune,* February 6, 1840.

111 *Bee,* December 14, 1833; December 7, 1835; November 27, 1838; November 23, 1840.

112 *Bee,* December 12, 1836; January 4, 1837; *Ami,* February 14, 1820.

113 *Bee,* December 14, 1833; December 7, 1835; December 12, 1836; November 23, 1840; *Courier,* October 23, 1815; November 27, 1838; *Louisiana Advertiser,* February 20, 1829.

114 *Picayune,* January 18, 1839.

115 *Ibid.* Bernhard, *Travels,* II, 58; Houstoun, *Hesperos,* II, 57; Murray, *Travels in North America,* II, 187.

116 *Picayune,* October 13, 1837.

CHAPTER TWO

1 For example, see Asbury, *French Quarter,* 131.

2 *Ibid.,* 132.

3 Documents of the Cabildo, Book 4088, Document 338.

4 *Courier,* August 6, 1810; May 21, 1813; April 17, December 9, 30, 1833; *Gazette,* June 11, 1805; May 8, 1808; April 16, 1837; *Louisiana Advertiser,* March 31, 1832; *Mercantile Advertiser,* April 26, June 30, 1831; *True American,* May 12, 1836; Fossier, *New Orleans,* 373–75.

5 Documents of the Cabildo, Book 4088, Document 338.

6 *Ibid.*

7 *Ibid.,* Documents 341, 380.

8 *Ibid.,* Document 341.

9 *Ibid.,* Document 367.

10 *Ibid.,* Document 380.

11 Berquin-Duvallon, *Vue,* 185–86.

12 Documents of the Cabildo, Book 4088, Document 367.

13 *Moniteur,* November 20, 1805; Ashe, *Travels in America,* III, 275; *Moniteur,* November 23, 27, December 28, 1805.

14 *Moniteur,* April 12, 1806; August 22, 1807.

15 *Courier,* December 9, 23, 1808.

16 *Moniteur,* December 23, 1808.

17 *Bee,* November 23, 1840; *Picayune,* November 28, 30, 1841; *Courier,* April 11, 1826; April 24, 1827; Bernhard, *Travels,* II, 64, 70; Stanley Clisby Arthur, *Old New Orleans* (Rev. ed., New Orleans, 1959), 76; Eleanor Bentley, "Walt Whitman's Visit to New Orleans" (M.A. thesis, Tulane University, 1943), 212; Henry C. Castellanos, *New Orleans as It Was* (New Orleans, 1895), 161; Frederick Law Olmstead, *A Journey in the Seaboard Slave States* (New York, 1904), II, 245; William L. Robinson, *The Diary of a Samaritan* (New York, 1860), 159.

18 *Argus,* December 18, 1826; *Louisiana Advertiser,* March 2, 1831; Max Freund (trans. and ed.), *Gustav Dresel's Houston Journal: Adventures in North America and Texas, 1837–1841* (Austin, 1954), 115; Houstoun, *Hesperos,* II, 74–75; Christian Schultz, *Travels on an Inland Voyage . . . in the Years 1807 and 1808* (New York, 1810), II, 195; Bernhard, *Travels,* II, 62–64, 70–71.

19 Bernhard, *Travels,* II, 58; Irene Blanche Pujol, "Robin's Voyages dans l'Interieur de la Louisiane, Translated and Annotated," (M.A. thesis, Louisiana State University, 1935; typescript in Howard-Tilton Library), 55; *Gazette,* September 22, 1810.

20 See pp. 21–23, 30–32 above; Joseph G. Tregle, Jr., "Early New Orleans Society: A Reappraisal," *Journal of Southern History,* XVIII (February, 1952), 35; *Mercantile Advertiser,* January 18, 1825; G. W. Pierson (ed.), "Alexis de Tocqueville in New Orleans: January 1–3, 1832," *Franco-American Review,* I (June, 1936), 36; Herbert A. Kellar (ed.), "A Journey through the South in 1836: Diary of James D. Davidson," *Journal of Southern History,* I (August, 1935), 361.

21 Tregle, "Early New Orleans Society," 35–36; Fossier, *New Orleans,* 363; *Picayune,* December 25, 1855; Bentley, "Whitman's Visit to New Orleans," 212; Castellanos, *New Orleans as It Was,* 111; Donald E. Everett, "Free Persons of Color in New Orleans, 1803–1865" (Ph.D. dissertation, Tulane University, 1952), 264; Robinson, *Diary of a Samaritan,* 159.

22 Joe Cowell, *Thirty Years Passed among the Players in England and America* (New York, 1844), 103; Albert J. Pickett, *Eight Days in New Orleans in February, 1847* (Montgomery, 1847), 38; Tasistro, *Random Shots,* II, 20.

23 *Argus,* December 18, 1826.

24 Ashe, *Travels in America,* III, 271; Davidson, "A Journey through the South," 362; Stoddard, *Sketches,* 321; Vandenhoff, *Leaves,* 207; Edward Sullivan, *Rambles and Scrambles in North and South America* (London, 1852), 223.

25 Sullivan, *Rambles and Scrambles*, 223–24; Bernhard, *Travels*, II, 71; Coleman, *Sketch Book*, 17; Everett, "Free Persons of Color," 264–65; Annie Lee West Stahl, "The Free Negro in Ante-Bellum Louisiana," *Louisiana Historical Quarterly*, XXV (April, 1942), 310; Tasistro, *Random Shots*, II, 20; Tregle, "Early New Orleans Society," 35.

26 Bernhard, *Travels*, II, 62; Achille Murat, *A Moral and Political Sketch of the United States of North America* (London, 1833), 353–54; Stoddard, *Sketches*, 321–22; Watson, "Notitia," 236; Vandenhoff, *Leaves*, 207–208. See also Tasistro, *Random Shots*, II, 19.

27 *Argus*, December 18, 1826.

28 Fossier, *New Orleans*, 362; Tregle, "Early New Orleans Society," 35; *Bee*, November 21, 1835.

29 *Bee*, November 30, 1835.

30 *Picayune*, October 27, 1837.

31 Everett, "Free Persons of Color," 264.

32 Documents of the Cabildo, Book 4088, Document 367; *Argus*, January 4, 1828; *Courier*, April 11, 1826.

33 See p. 44 above.

34 Everett, "Free Persons of Color," 248; Fearon, *Sketches of America*, 277; *Picayune*, January 12, 1841.

35 Rowland, *Letter Books*, III, 357.

36 *Courier*, January 20, 1834.

37 *Bee*, November 8, 1837; *Picayune*, November 5, 1839; July 22, 1841; *True American*, November 6, 1839.

38 *True American*, January 1, 1839; *Picayune*, August 19, 1841.

39 *Picayune*, April 19, 1840.

40 George Washington Cable (ed.), "War Diary of a Union Woman in the South," in *Famous Adventures and Prison Escapes of the Civil War* (New York, 1893), 5.

CHAPTER THREE

1 *Bee*, November 18, 1837.

2 Arthur, *Old New Orleans*, 64; Fossier, *New Orleans*, 467; Kendall, *History of New Orleans*, II, 727; Andre Lafargue, "Opera in New Orleans in Days of Yore," *Louisiana Historical Quarterly*, XXIX (July, 1946), 662; Harry Brunswick Loeb, "The Opera in New Orleans," in *Publications of the Louisiana Historical Society*, IX (Proceedings and Reports, 1916), 30. For an extensive list of books and articles carrying this account see Rene J. Le Gardeur, Jr., "Les Premieres Annees du Theatre a la Nouvelle-Orleans," *Comptes Rendus de l'Athenee Louisianais* (New Orleans, 1954), 70–72.

3 Le Gardeur, Jr., "Les Premieres Annees du Theatre," 54–60; Marion

Hannah Winter, "Juba and American Minstrelsy," in Paul Magriel (ed.), *Chronicles of the American Dance* (New York, 1948), 40. Mr. Le Gardeur has traced the origins and subsequent repetitions of this account of the beginning of New Orleans' opera in the splendid monograph here cited. Mr. Le Gardeur's article is invaluable in deciphering the 1790's. Mr. Le Gardeur is a businessman in New Orleans who has had a lifelong scholarly interest in the origins of the theater in his city. He has recently summed up his researches in *The First New Orleans Theatre, 1792–1803* (New Orleans, 1963). This is an invaluable little book which gives the complete and conclusive story.

4 *Bee,* February 2, 1831; Le Gardeur, Jr., *The First New Orleans Theatre,* 40–43.

5 Le Gardeur, Jr., "Les Premieres Annees du Theatre," 39–54; Le Gardeur, Jr., *The First New Orleans Theatre,* 10–34; O. G. Sonneck, *Early Opera in America* (New York, 1915), 199–202.

6 Acts of Pedro Pedesclaux, July–December, 1811, Act of October 16, 1811, Folio 44; Le Gardeur, Jr., "Les Premieres Annees du Theatre," 62; Le Gardeur, Jr., *The First New Orleans Theatre,* 2–10.

7 Le Gardeur, Jr., *The First New Orleans Theatre,* 6–17.

8 *Ibid.,* 21; Kurt Pahlen, *Music of the World,* trans. James A. Galston (New York, 1949), 178. Those portions of the Pontalba letters that relate to the theatre are reprinted in Le Gardeur, Jr., "Les Premieres Annees du Theatre," 66–69.

9 Le Gardeur, Jr., "Les Premieres Annees du Theatre," 37–38.

10 *Ibid.,* 68.

11 See pp. 44–45 above.

12 Rene J. Le Gardeur, Jr., "En Marge d'une Affiche de Theatre de 1799," *Comptes Rendus de l'Athenee Louisianais* (New Orleans, 1955), 24–26; Le Gardeur, Jr., "Les Premieres Annees du Theatre," 36; Berquin-Duvallon, *Vue,* 29–30; Whittington (ed.), "The Journal of Dr. John Sibley," 478, 483; *Moniteur,* September 4, 1802.

13 *Moniteur,* November 5, 1803; Whittington (ed.), "The Journal of Dr. John Sibley," 485; "Proceedings of the City Council" (New Orleans Public Library), 20 Frimaire, An XII (December 12, 1803); *Union,* December 27, 1803.

14 "Proceedings of the City Council," September 27, November 28, 1804.

15 Rowland, *Letter Books,* III, 35; *Gazette,* January 25, 1805; Tinker, *Creole City,* 35–36.

16 Rowland, *Letter Books,* III, 84–85.

17 *Ibid.,* III, 344; Charles Gayarre, *History of Louisiana* (3rd ed.; New Orleans, 1885), IV, 147.

18 *Bee,* February 2, 1831; Le Gardeur, Jr., "Les Premieres Annees du Theatre," 55–56.

19 Letter to the City Council from Louis Tabary, received July 13,

1805 (Howard-Tilton Library, Tulane University); *Moniteur,* March 8, 1806.

[20] Kmen, "Singing and Dancing," Table III; *Time,* LXXVII (August 29, 1960), 34; Wallace Brockway and Herbert Weinstock, *Men of Music* (Rev. ed., New York, 1950), 243 fn.; Deems Taylor and Russell Kerr (eds.), *Music Lovers' Encyclopedia* (Rev. ed., New York, 1954), 183. Henry Edward Krehbiel, *A Book of Operas* (2nd ed.; New York, 1946), 4, mentions "an opera in 3 acts," with text by Colman, entitled "The Spanish Barber; or The Futile Precaution," which was played in Baltimore, Philadelphia, and New York in 1794. Although no composer's name was given, Krehbiel believes that this opera, such as it was, might have been Paisiello's. Others who cover the early years of opera in America seem to dismiss "The Spanish Barber" as just another of the light musical comedies or ballad operas then popular. O. G. Sonneck, *Early Opera in America,* 133–219, *passim,* lists seven playings of "The Spanish Barber," from 1794 to 1799. Paisiello is not mentioned with any of them although Sonneck does mention him once in another connection. Reese Davis James, *Cradle of Culture: The Philadelphia Stage, 1800–1810* (Philadelphia, 1957), 41, 45, found "The Spanish Barber" to have played in Philadelphia on October 26, 1801, but the only mention of music is that Mrs. Oldmixon's singing of "Ah Hapless is the Maiden" was well received. Wallace Brockway and Herbert Weinstock, *The Opera: A History of Its Creation and Performance, 1600–1941* (New York, 1941), 472, first mention Paisiello in America in a New Orleans performance of 1810. Herbert Graf, *The Opera and Its Future in America* (New York, 1941), 213–15, says that the New Orleans company "brought the opera comique . . . northward to the cities along the Atlantic seaboard. These works were soon followed by Italian opera buffa, like Paisiello's *Barber of Seville,* and Pergolesi's *Serva Padrona,* given in English." Graf also states that "until Garcia's time (1825–26), the American opera repertory had consisted only of folk opera." He is obviously not including New Orleans in America here. See also Donald Jay Grout, *A Short History of Opera* (New York, 1947), II, 500.

[21] Kendall, *History of New Orleans,* I, 85; Martin, *History of Louisiana,* II, 205; George E. Waring and George W. Cable, *History and Present Condition of New Orleans, Louisiana* (Washington, 1881), 30, 35–36; *Moniteur,* March 29, April 19, May 24, 1806. Pages inserted in the regular edition for May 24, 1806.

[22] *Moniteur,* May 24, 1806.

[23] *Ibid.,* June 4, July 2, October 11, 1806; "Proceedings of the City Council," October 9, 1806.

[24] *Moniteur,* March 11, 1806.

[25] *Ibid.,* April 4, 15, 18, May 2, 1807.

[26] *Ibid.,* April 29, May 16, 1807.

[27] *Ibid.,* August 22, 1807.

[28] *Ibid.,* June 13, 17, September 30, 1807.

[29] *Ibid.,* September 30, 1807; *Telegraphe,* October 13, 1807; *Courier,* October 23, 1807.

[30] *Courier,* November 4, 1807; January 15, 1808; *Moniteur,* November 4, 1807, January 15, 16, March 19, July 15, 1808.

[31] *Telegraphe,* October 13, 1807; *Courier,* November 4, 1807; *Moniteur,* November 4, 1807.

[32] *Courier,* January 15, 1808; *Moniteur,* January 16, 30, 1808.

[33] Kmen, "Singing and Dancing," Table III; Schultz, *Inland Voyage,* II, 196.

[34] Kmen, "Singing and Dancing," Table III; *Courier,* March 21, 1808.

[35] *Courier,* March 18, 1808; *Moniteur,* April 13, 1808.

[36] Schultz, *Inland Voyage,* II, 196; *Moniteur,* April 23, 1808.

[37] *Moniteur,* April 23, 1808.

[38] Kmen, "Singing and Dancing," Table III.

[39] *Moniteur,* May 7, 14, 21, 28, 1808.

[40] *Ibid.,* June 4, 11, 18, 25, July 2, 1808.

[41] *Ibid.,* July 16, 1808; *Courier,* July 15, 1808.

[42] *Courier,* August 17, 1808; *Moniteur,* August 24, 1808.

[43] *Moniteur,* August 24, 1808.

[44] *Ibid.,* August 27, 31, September 3, 1808; *Courier,* August 22, 1808.

[45] *Courier,* August 8, 1808; *Moniteur,* August 6, 27, 31, September 10, 1808.

[46] *Moniteur,* September 14, 17, October 8, 12, 1808; *Courier,* September 21, December 9, 23, 1808.

[47] *Moniteur,* May 31, June 10, 1809; Kmen, "Singing and Dancing," Table III.

[48] *Courier,* August 28, 1809.

[49] *Ibid.,* September 15, 22, 1809; *Moniteur,* September 23, 27, 30, 1809; Kmen, "Singing and Dancing," Table III.

[50] *Courier,* November 23, 28, December 3, 1810; *Moniteur,* December 1, 1810.

[51] Kmen, "Singing and Dancing," Table III; *Courier,* December 3, 1810; *Moniteur,* December 1, 5, 8, 1810.

[52] Kmen, "Singing and Dancing," Table III.

[53] *Courier,* December 10, 1810; March 4, 18, 1812; *Moniteur,* December 8, 12, 1810; Arthur, *Old New Orleans,* 64.

CHAPTER FOUR

[1] *Moniteur,* November 25, 1809.

[2] *Ibid.,* December 8, 18, 1810; *Courier,* December 7, 1810.

[3] *Moniteur,* December 12, 18, 20, 1810.

[4] *Ibid.,* April 25, 1811; *Courier,* April 24, 1811; John Smith Kendall, *The Golden Age of the New Orleans Theater* (Baton Rouge, 1952), 4.

[5] *Courier,* May 22, July 17, 20, 1811; February 10, 1812; *Moniteur,* August 27, 29, 31, 1811.

[6] *Courier,* September 25, 1811.

[7] *Ibid.,* December 13, 1811; *Moniteur,* December 14, 19, 26, 28, 1811; Kmen, "Singing and Dancing," Table III.

[8] *Courier,* February 10, May 8, 15, 21, 1812.

[9] *Ibid.,* June 19, 1812; *Moniteur,* June 20, July 23, 25, 1812; Kmen, "Singing and Dancing," Table III. The terms actors, singers, performers, and artists are used interchangeably in this study, for in the period under consideration there was no clear cut division among the performers. Actors functioned as singers and vice versa. In the same way, the terms theater and opera are used to mean the same thing; they are impossible to separate in early New Orleans. Actually, the great bulk of theatrical offerings of the French theater in New Orleans were musical. See Charles I. Silin, "The French Theatre in New Orleans," *American Society Legion of Honor Magazine,* XXVII (Summer, 1956), 127–32.

[10] *Courier,* August 12, September 14, 1812.

[11] *Ibid.,* August 26, 1812; August 28, November 18, 1822.

[12] *Ibid.,* November 18, 1812; March 31, 1813.

[13] *Moniteur,* July 3, 1813.

[14] *Ibid.,* January 29, 1814; *Courier,* January 28, 1814.

[15] *Moniteur,* June 15, 1813; *Gazette,* July 18, 22, 1815.

[16] *Courier,* October 18, 23, 1815; *Gazette,* October 24, 26, 1815. Possibly the Orleans opened a bit earlier than October 19, 1815—French newspapers for 1815 are missing prior to October 16. But if so, it cannot have been very much earlier. It seems probable that October 19 was very close to the starting date for the new theater, if not indeed the actual opening day.

[17] *Courier,* November 8, 17, 24, 1815.

[18] *Ibid.,* January 12, 22, 29, 1816; *Ami,* January 5, 10, 22, 1816.

[19] *Ami,* January 12, 1816.

[20] *Ibid.,* April 13, 1816.

[21] *Ibid.,* May 23, October 5, 11, 1816.

[22] Kmen, "Singing and Dancing," Table III.

[23] Krehbiel, *A Book of Operas,* 28–29; Pahlen, *Music of the World,* 179; Kmen, "Singing and Dancing," Table III.

[24] *Ami,* October 11, 1816; *Courier,* October 25, 1816.

[25] *Ami,* October 28, 1816; Kmen, "Singing and Dancing," Table III.

[26] *Bee,* June 15, 1839; *Courier,* March 25, 1811; June 14, 1839; *Picayune,* June 15, 1839.

[27] *Courier,* August 7, 1811; March 20, 1812; *Bee,* October 8, 1835; *Gazette,* January 29, 1821; Asbury, *French Quarter,* 216.

[28] *Courier,* June 14, 1839; *Bee,* June 15, 1839; *Picayune,* June 15, 1839; see p. 150 below.

[29] *Courier,* April 1, 1811; *Ami,* November 3, 1814; January 26, October 5, 1816.

[30] *Ami,* November 14, 1816; *Courier,* November 13, 15, 18, 22, 1816.

[31] *Ami,* November 14, 1816; *Courier,* November 13, 15, 18, 22, 1816.

[32] Asbury, *French Quarter,* 97; *Courier,* April 3, July 15, August 2, September 2, 6, 9, 1816.

[33] *Courier,* December 4, 1816; Asbury, *French Quarter,* 97; Castellanos, *New Orleans as It Was,* 157.

[34] *Ami,* February 22, 1817.

[35] *Ibid.,* February 25, 1817.

[36] *Ibid.,* May 2, November 21, 1817; *Courier,* May 9, 1817.

[37] *Ami,* November 4, 1817.

[38] *Ibid.,* October 10, 1817.

[39] *Ibid.,* November 3, 1817.

[40] *Courier,* December 12, 1817; Pahlen, *Music of the World,* 72, 124; Taylor and Kerr, *Music Lovers' Encyclopedia,* 330–31.

[41] *Ami,* January 10, September 17, 1818; Kendall, *Golden Age,* 6–9; Noah M. Ludlow, *Dramatic Life as I Found It* (St. Louis, 1880), 137–39.

[42] *Ami,* October 29, November 17, 1817.

[43] *Ibid.,* December 15, 1817.

[44] *Ibid.,* June 1, September 25, 1818; Kendall, *History of New Orleans,* I, 114.

[45] *Gazette,* November 11, 15, 1819.

[46] *Courier,* November 19, 1819.

[47] Coleman, *Sketch Book,* 134; Didimus, *New Orleans as I Found It,* 52; David Barrow Fischer, "The Story of New Orleans's Rise as a Music Center," *Musical America,* XIX (March 14, 1914), 3; Lafargue, "Opera in New Orleans," 665; Loeb, "The Opera in New Orleans," 32; Amelia M. Murray, *Letters from the United States, Cuba and Canada* (New York, 1856), 272; *Paxton's New Orleans Directory* (New Orleans, 1822), 17; *Bee,* March 24, 1837; *Courier,* November 19, 1819.

[48] *Courier,* November 24, 1819; *Gazette,* October 30, 1819.

[49] *Ami,* January 19, 1820.

[50] *Courier,* December 8, 13, 20, 24, 1819; January 3, February 11, 1820; *Ami,* January 21, February 8, 1820.

[51] Kmen, "Singing and Dancing," Table III.

CHAPTER FIVE

[1] For an account of Caldwell's early career and background, see Kendall, *Golden Age,* 14–20.

[2] *Ami,* January 6, February 11, 1820; *Gazette,* January 19, 1820; Harold F.

Bogner, "Sir Walter Scott in New Orleans, 1818–1832," *Louisiana Historical Quarterly,* XXI (April, 1938), 434–36; Kendall, *Golden Age,* 18; Nelle Smither, "A History of the English Theatre at New Orleans, 1806–1842," *Louisiana Historical Quarterly,* XXVIII (January, 1945), 106, 156, 173, 178; Dorothy Hebron, "Sir Walter Scott in New Orleans, 1833–1850" (M.A. thesis, Tulane University, 1940), 12, 32.

3 Kendall, *Golden Age,* 17–19; Kmen, "Singing and Dancing," Table III.

4 *Gazette,* March 6, 1820.

5 Kendall, *Golden Age,* 20.

6 *Ami,* July 25, November 11, 1820.

7 *Ibid.,* November 21, 1820; Kmen, "Singing and Dancing," Table II,

8 *Ami,* November 2, December 10, 1821.

9 *Courier,* February 8, 11, 1822.

10 Benjamin M. Norman, *Norman's New Orleans and Environs* (New Orleans, 1845), 71.

11 *Courier,* February 8, 13, 15, 22, March 11, April 10, May 1, 1822; *Ami,* January 24, March 16, 1822; Kmen, "Singing and Dancing," Table III. As a case in point *Aline, la Reine de Golconde,* a three-act opera by Berton, was played on Wednesday, March 13, 1822, at the St. Philip Theater, and again on Sunday, March 17, at the Orleans. *Aline* had been played at the Orleans on February 28, and the fact that it was played on a Wednesday night at the St. Philip, when the American players occupied the Orleans, leads one to suspect that although the St. Philip Theater was a separate enterprise, offering operas on many of the same nights as did the French company at the Orleans, the latter company might have used the St. Philip on some of the nights when their own theater was being used by the Americans. *Ami,* March 16, 1822; *Courier,* March 11, 1822; Kmen, "Singing and Dancing," Table III.

12 *Courier,* November 20, 1822; March 7, 1823; *Ami,* March 3, 1823; March 27, 1824; Brockway and Weinstock, *Men of Music,* 231; Graf, *Opera and Its Future,* 214–15; Krehbiel, *A Book of Operas,* 1.

13 *Ami,* May 31, June 7, 1823.

14 *Ibid.,* July 18, 1823.

15 *Ibid.,* July 26, 1823; *Courier,* July 25, 1823.

16 *Courier,* October 8, 1823.

17 *Ami,* October 10, 1823.

18 *Ibid.,* October 10, 1823.

19 *Ibid.,* October 15, November 25, 1823.

20 *Ibid.,* November 25, 1823; January 19, 20, 24, 1824; *Courier,* November 28, 1823.

21 *Gazette,* January 3, 1824; Fossier, *New Orleans,* 470–71; Kendall, *Golden Age,* 30–32.

22 Kendall, *Golden Age,* 31–32; *Ami,* April 14, 1823; *Louisiana Advertiser,* February 1, 1826.

23 *Ami,* March 23, 1824.

[24] *Ibid.*, March 23, 1824.

[25] *Ibid.*, March 23, 24, 29, April 6, 1824; *Argus,* April 30, 1824.

[26] *Ami,* April 6, 1824.

[27] *Argus,* April 30, 1824.

[28] *Ibid.*, June 2, 1824.

[29] Kmen, "Singing and Dancing," Table III.

[30] *Argus,* November 8, 1824.

[31] *Ibid.*, November 29, 1824; *Courier,* January 10, 1825.

[32] *Journal de la Ville,* December 6, 1824; *Courier,* January 7, 1826; Kmen, "Singing and Dancing," Table III.

[33] *Argus,* January 4, 10, July 7, 1826; Kmen, "Singing and Dancing," Table III.

[34] *Argus,* January 7, 1826.

[35] *Ibid.*, January 10, 1826.

[36] *Ibid.*, February 24, 1826.

[37] *Louisiana Advertiser,* February 1, 22, March 16, 18, 1826.

[38] Bernhard, *Travels,* II, 81; Sealsfield, *Americans,* 184; Kmen, "Singing and Dancing," Table III.

[39] *Argus,* May 13, June 1, 1826; *Courier,* May 22, 31, 1826.

[40] *Argus,* June 21, July 7, 1826.

[41] *Ibid.*, July 7, 1826.

[42] *Courier,* July 28, August 3, 15, 1826; *Argus,* August 16, 1826.

[43] *Argus,* October 31, November 30, 1826; *Courier,* November 30, December 1, 1826.

[44] *Argus,* December 9, 1826; January 13, 1827.

[45] *Ibid.*, December 12, 1826; *Courier,* November 3, 11, 20, 1830.

[46] *Courier,* February 7, 1827; *Argus,* February 3, 5, 8, 1827.

[47] *Courier,* February 12, 14, April 6, 27, May 18, June 11, 1827.

[48] Bogner, "Scott in New Orleans," 490–94; *Courier,* February 12, 1827.

[49] *Courier,* May 30, 1827; *Saturday Review,* XLIII (December 31, 1960), 37.

[50] Kmen, "Singing and Dancing," Table III.

[51] *Argus,* June 9, 1827; *Courier,* June 11, 1827.

CHAPTER SIX

[1] Sylvie Chevalley, "Le Theatre d'Orleans en Tournee dans les Villes du Nord, 1827–1833," *Comptes Rendus de l'Athenee Louisianais* (New Orleans, 1955), 29–34, hereinafter cited as Chevalley, "Northern Tours." This invaluable article gives a thoroughly researched and full account of the six northern tours of the New Orleans Opera. It contains a complete list of all performances and an abundance of critical comment. The writer has drawn heavily on this article throughout this chapter. See

Sylvie Chevalley, "La Premiere Saison Theatrale Francaise de New York," *French Review,* XXIV (May, 1951), 471–79. For the failure of *Der Freischutz* in Philadelphia see William B. Wood, *Personal Recollections of the Stage* (Philadelphia, 1855), 306–307.

2 *Courier,* May 30, 1827; *Argus,* June 9, 1827.

3 Robert E. Riegel, *Young America, 1830–1840* (Norman, 1949), 371. See also Brockway and Weinstock, *Men of Music,* 231; Brockway and Weinstock, *The Opera,* 472; David Ewen, *Music Comes to America* (New York, 1947), 48–50; Graf, *Opera and Its Future,* 214; John Tasker Howard, *Our American Music* (3rd ed.; New York, 1954), 239; W. L. Hubbard (ed.), *The American History and Encyclopedia of Music* (New York, 1908), VIII, 235; John Smith Kendall, "Patti in New Orleans," *Southwest Review,* XVI (July, 1931), 460; Krehbiel, *Book of Operas,* 2–3; Henry C. Lahee, *Grand Opera in America* (Boston, 1901), 28.

4 Chevalley, "Northern Tours," 35–37. The piston valve had only been invented twelve years before in 1815, and the rotary valve only two years before in 1825.

5 *Courier,* November 30, December 7, 18, 1827; *Argus,* March 25, 1828.

6 *Argus,* May 29, 1828; *Courier,* May 27, 1828; Chevalley, "Northern Tours," 39.

7 Chevalley, "Northern Tours," 39–43.

8 *Ibid.,* 39, 41, 44. For Jandot see *Argus,* January 30, 1828; *Courier,* January 25, February 2, 28, 1828.

9 Quoted in *Courier,* October 8, 1828.

10 Quoted in *Courier,* October 17, 1828.

11 *Ibid.,* October 17, 1828.

12 *Ibid.,* October 8, 1828; *Louisiana Advertiser,* October 4, 1828.

13 *Courier,* December 10, 11, 22, 1828.

14 *Argus,* September 2, 26, November 28, 1829; Chevalley, "Northern Tours," 47, 48, 53; *Courier,* December 5, 1829.

15 Chevalley, "Northern Tours," 48–52.

16 *Courier,* November 19, 30, December 5, 14, 1829; *Argus* November 28, 30, 1829.

17 *Courier,* February 18, 20, 23, March 3, April 3, 13, 19, 21, 27, 1830; *Argus,* March 13, 22, 1830; *Louisiana Advertiser,* April 15, 1830; See below, Chapter Nine. For more on Madame Feron see fn. 15, Chapter Nine below.

18 Chevalley, "Northern Tours," 53; Minnie Hauk, *Memories of a Singer* (London, 1925), 23, 24, 30.

19 Chevalley, "Northern Tours," 59; *Courier,* September 10, 15, November 3, 1830.

20 Chevalley, "Northern Tours," 54–56.

21 *Courier,* November 11, 1830; *Bee,* November 11, 1830.

22 *Courier,* November 12, 17, 20, December 4, 1830.

23 *Ibid.,* February 23, 1831.

24 *Louisiana Advertiser,* March 2, 1831; *Bee,* March 15, 1831; *Mercantile Advertiser,* April 22, 1831; *Courier,* May 5, 1831.

25 *Courier,* May 7, 9, 1831; *Bee,* May 12, 1831.

26 *Mercantile Advertiser,* May 14, 1831.

27 *Ibid.,* May 21, 1831.

28 Chevalley, "Northern Tours," 61–63; *Courier,* April 28, 1831; Kmen, "Singing and Dancing," Table III.

29 Chevalley, "Northern Tours," 63–64; *Bee,* November 21, 1831; *Mercantile Advertiser,* October 27, 1831.

30 *Bee,* December 6, 1831.

31 Chevalley, "Northern Tours," 64; *Courier,* May 26, 1832.

32 Fossier, *New Orleans,* 404–18.

33 *Courier,* November 24, 27, 28, 1832.

34 *Ibid.,* November 28, 29, 30, 1832.

35 *Ibid.,* December 15, 1832; January 24, March 9, 26, April 2, 1833; *Argus,* February 18, 1833.

36 *Courier,* February 23, April 2, May 11, 1833; *Argus,* April 4, 1833.

37 *Courier,* May 21, 1833.

38 Chevalley, "Northern Tours," 66–69.

39 *Courier,* August 10, 1833, citing the Boston *Gazette.* For Graupner see Howard, *Our American Music,* 129–33.

40 *Courier,* August 27, 1833, citing the New York *Standard;* Chevalley, "Northern Tours," 66–68.

41 Chevalley, "Northern Tours," 69; *Courier,* November 16, 1833.

42 Wood, *Personal Recollections,* 306–307; Hubbard, *American History and Encyclopedia of Music,* VIII, 239; *Argus,* August 24, 1827, citing the New York *American.*

43 A complete list of all operas played and the date for each performance may be found in Chevalley, "Northern Tours," 31–70. For New Orleans performances see Kmen, "Singing and Dancing," Table III.

44 Kmen, "Singing and Dancing," Table III.

45 Chevalley, "Northern Tours," 31–70; Kmen, "Singing and Dancing," Table III.

46 Kmen, "Singing and Dancing," Table III.

CHAPTER SEVEN

1 *Courier,* November 23, 28, December 28, 1833; January 6, March 1, June 21, 1834; *Bee,* January 6, 10, 1834; *Mercantile Advertiser,* January 6, 1834.

2 Kmen, "Singing and Dancing," Table III.

3 *Louisiana Advertiser,* January 15, 21, 1834; *Mercantile Advertiser,* January 17, 22, 1834.

4 *Louisiana Advertiser,* January 24, March 28, 1834; *Mercantile Advertiser,* February 10, 11, 1834; *Bee,* February 28, 1834.

5 *Mercantile Advertiser,* January 19, 1834.

6 *Ibid.,* January 27, 1834; *Louisiana Advertiser,* January 23, February 10, 1834; *Mercantile Daily News,* February 8, 1834; *Courier,* February 8, April 4, 1834; *Bee,* April 4, 1834.

7 *Courier,* February 8, 1834; *Bee,* February 10, 1834.

8 *Bee,* February 28, 1834; *Courier,* June 21, 1834.

9 *Bee,* October 30, November 10, 20, 22, 29, 1834; *Louisiana Advertiser,* December 2, 1834.

10 *Louisiana Advertiser,* December 23, 1834.

11 *Courier,* February 21, 1835.

12 *Ibid.,* February 21, 1835.

13 *Louisiana Advertiser,* December 30, 1834.

14 *Courier,* February 12, 1835; *Bee,* March 2, 5, 1835.

15 *Bee,* March 7, 14, 1835.

16 *Ibid.,* March 31, 1835; *Courier,* April 1, 1835.

17 *Bee,* April 1, 1835.

18 *Courier,* April 1, 1835.

19 Edward J. Dent, *Opera* (London, 1949), 71; *Courier,* April 2, 1835; *Bee,* April 2, 1835.

20 Kmen, "Singing and Dancing," Table III.

21 *Bee,* May 13, 1835.

22 *Courier,* May 14, 1835.

23 *Ibid.,* May 23, 1835.

24 Kmen, "Singing and Dancing," Table III.

25 Kendall, *Golden Age,* 63–64, 77–78, 97, 111–13, 136.

26 *Ibid.,* 112–13; *True American,* June 4, 1836; *Bee,* September 18, 1835.

27 *True American,* June 4, 1836; Kendall, *Golden Age,* 114–16.

28 *Bee,* September 18, November 5, 1836; Riegel, *Young America,* 368.

29 Kendall, *Golden Age,* 114–21; *Bee,* April 7, September 30, November 5, 30, 1835; *Courier,* November 5, 1835; *Spirit of the Times,* VIII (February 24, 1838), 9.

30 *Bee,* November 30, December 1, 4, 16, 1835; Kendall, *Golden Age,* 117, 120.

31 *Bee,* November 30, 1835.

32 *Ibid.,* December 4, 5, 1835; Riegel, *Young America,* 368.

33 *Bee,* December 1, 2, 3, 5, 10, 17, 1835; *Courier,* December 7, 8, 16, 17, 18, 28, 1835. For more on these and other instrumentalists see chapters on bands and concerts.

34 *Bee,* December 3, 5, 8, 10, 16, 17, 22, 1835; *Courier,* December 18, 1835.

35 *Bee,* December 16, 22, 1835.

[36] *Ibid.*, February 1, 27, March 4, 1836; *True American*, June 4, 1836; Kendall, *Golden Age*, 136.

[37] *Bee*, February 26, 1836.

[38] *Ibid.*, March 7, 8, 1836; Kmen, "Singing and Dancing," Table III.

[39] *Bee*, February 27, 1836; *True American*, May 11, 27, 30, June 4, 1836.

[40] Kmen, "Singing and Dancing," Table III.

[41] *Ibid.*, Table III; *Bee*, March 19, April 23, 1836.

[42] *Bee*, March 29, April 5, 1836.

[43] *Ibid.*, April 12, 22, May 31, 1836.

[44] *True American*, May 2, 30, 1836; *Bee,* May 31, 1836.

[45] *True American*, May 31, 1836; *Bee*, June 7, 1836.

[46] *Bee*, May 27, June 7, 1836; *True American*, May 26, 1836; Kmen, "Singing and Dancing," Table III. (Kendall mistakenly places Orlandi in the original company. *Golden Age*, 136–37.)

[47] *Bee*, May 30, June 7, 1836; *True American*, May 30, 31, July 28, August 16, 1836.

[48] *Bee*, March 7, 9, June 8, 1836.

[49] Kmen, "Singing and Dancing," Table III.

[50] *Ibid.*, Table III.

[51] *True American*, July 9, 1836; *Bee*, September 16, 1836.

[52] *Bee*, September 16, 1836.

CHAPTER EIGHT

[1] *True American*, August 16, 1836; Louisville *Advertiser*, August 12, 1836, reprinted in *True American*, September 6, 1836; *Bee*, November 21, December 23, 31, 1836.

[2] *Courier*, November 22, 1836; *Bee*, November 12, 21, 22, 1836.

[3] *Courier*, November 23, 1836; *Bee*, November 24, 1836.

[4] *Bee*, December 3, 1836.

[5] *Courier*, December 3, 1836; *Daily Picayune*, February 19, 1837; Kendall, *Golden Age*, 142–43; Kmen, "Singing and Dancing," Table III.

[6] *Bee*, January 12, 1837.

[7] *Picayune*, January 27, February 1, 1837.

[8] *Courier*, December 5, 9, 1836; *Bee*, December 9, 1836.

[9] *Courier*, December 10, 1836; *Bee*, December 21, 28, 1836.

[10] *Courier*, December 22, 1836.

[11] *Ibid.*, February 7, 8, 27, April 1, 1837; *Picayune*, February 5, 1837; *Bee*, April 3, 1837; Kendall, *Golden Age*, 143–44.

[12] *True American*, March 21, 1837; *Bee*, March 22, 23, 1837; *Courier*, March 30, 31, 1837; Kmen, "Singing and Dancing," Table III.

[13] *Bee*, June 2, July 7, September 16, December 13, 1836; March 24, April 3, 13, 1837; *Courier*, December 14, 1836; *Le Moqueur, Journal des*

Flaneurs, I (March 26, 1837), 1; *Le Moqueur,* I (April 16, 1837), 1; *Le Moqueur,* I (April 23, 1837), 3. *Le Moqueur* was a weekly four page journal devoted primarily to music, opera, and literature. It sought to take the place of *L'Echo,* which was suspended because someone absconded with the funds. *Le Moqueur* addressed itself to the old shareholders of *Franc-Parleur* and *L'Echo.* Volume I (March 22–September 10, 1837) was found in the Louisiana State Museum Library in New Orleans.

14 *Le Moqueur,* I (March 26, 1837), 1.

15 Ibid., I (April 7, 1837), 3.

16 *Courier,* June 14, 1839; *Picayune,* June 15, 1839.

17 *Courier,* June 14, 1839; *Bee,* June 15, 1839; *Picayune,* June 15, 1839.

18 Riegel, *Young America,* 372–76.

19 *Courier,* April 1, 1837; *Bee,* April 3, 1837.

20 *Courier,* April 4, 1837; *True American,* April 4, 1837; *Bee,* April 6, 1837.

21 *Picayune,* April 5, 1837; *Courier,* April 20, 1837.

22 *Picayune,* April 5, 1837; *Bee,* April 15, 1837; *Courier,* April 20, 1837.

23 *Picayune,* April 7, 1837; *True American,* April 7, 1837; *Bee,* April 7, 1837.

24 *Picayune,* April 7, 1837; *Bee,* April 7, 1837; *True American,* April 7, 8, 1837.

25 *Bee,* April 17, 1837; *Picayune,* April 18, 19, 1837.

26 *Le Moqueur,* I (April 16, 1837), 1, 3; *Le Moqueur,* I (April 23, 1837), 3.

27 *Courier,* April 20, 1837.

28 *Picayune,* April 8, May 19, 1837; *Bee,* April 15, 1837; *True American,* April 17, 1837; *Courier,* April 20, May 19, 1837. To make matters worse, the panic of 1837 had just caused the price of cotton to fall by half.

29 Kmen, "Singing and Dancing," Table III.

30 Kendall, *Golden Age,* 145; *Bee,* April 21, 1837; *True American,* April 21, 22, 1837.

31 Kendall, *Golden Age,* 144; *Bee,* June 3, July 6, 1837; *Courier,* June 6, 1837; *Picayune,* June 6, 1837.

32 *Picayune,* May 23, 1837.

33 *Ibid. Le Moqueur,* I (May 28, 1837), 4; *Courier,* May 22, 1837.

34 *Picayune,* May 23, 24, 1837.

35 *Ibid.,* May 30, 1837; *Bee,* June 10, 1837.

36 *Bee,* May 26, 1837; *Picayune,* June 4, 1837.

37 *Picayune,* June 6, 8, 1837; *Courier,* June 8, 1837.

38 *Courier,* June 8, 1837; *Bee,* June 10, 1837.

39 *Courier,* June 12, 1837.

40 *Ibid.,* June 7, 1837; *Bee,* June 7, 1837.

41 *Le Moqueur,* I (June 10, 1837), 3; *Le Moqueur,* I (June 18, 1837), 3; *Picayune,* June 13, 1837.

⁴² *Le Moqueur,* I (June 15, 1837), 3; *Le Moqueur,* I (June 18, 1837), 3.

⁴³ *Le Moqueur,* I (June 15, 1837), 2, 3; *Le Moqueur,* I (June 18, 1837), 3; *Le Moqueur,* I (July 11, 1837), 3; *Picayune,* July 7, 1837; *Bee,* July 6, 1837.

⁴⁴ *Picayune,* June 15, 1837; *Courier,* July 14, 1837.

⁴⁵ *Bee,* July 6, 1837; *Picayune,* September 28, November 1, 1838.

⁴⁶ *Bee,* May 30, 1837.

⁴⁷ *Le Moqueur,* I (September 2, 1837), 2.

⁴⁸ *Ibid.,* 3.

⁴⁹ Tasistro, *Random Shots,* I, 191.

⁵⁰ *Courier,* November 6, 22, 1837; January 2, 3, 1838; *Bee,* November 21, 22, 1837. For further comments on Julie Calve, see Kane, *Queen New Orleans,* 243–44.

⁵¹ *Picayune,* June 6, 10, 12, 16, 26, July 1, September 16, 1838; *Courier,* June 5, 1838; *Bee,* October 31, 1838.

⁵² *Bee,* October 31, 1838; Yerbury, "Concert Music in Early New Orleans," 106–107; John S. Kendall, "New Orleans Musicians of Long Ago," *Louisiana Historical Quarterly,* XXXI (January, 1948), 131.

⁵³ *True American,* December 17, 1838; *Picayune,* December 22, 1838; *Bee,* December 22, 1838.

⁵⁴ *Picayune,* November 1, 11, 1838; *Bee,* December 4, 1838.

⁵⁵ *Picayune,* January 4, 12, 18, 1839.

⁵⁶ *Picayune,* April 27, 1839; *Courier,* May 6, 1839; Kmen, "Singing and Dancing," Table III.

⁵⁷ *Courier,* May 6, 8, 1839.

⁵⁸ Dent, *Opera,* 71; *Picayune,* June 5, 1839.

⁵⁹ *Picayune,* January 29, 1840.

⁶⁰ *Bee,* February 1, 1840.

⁶¹ *Ibid.,* January 10, 1840.

⁶² *Ibid.,* April 21, December 3, 1840; *Picayune,* October 9, 1840; *Courier,* November 20, 1840.

⁶³ Tasistro, *Random Shots,* I, 191–92.

⁶⁴ *Ibid.,* I, 192; *Picayune,* March 30, 1841; Castellanos, *New Orleans as It Was,* 145.

⁶⁵ Baroncelli, *Le Theatre-Francais,* 41; Tasistro, *Random Shots,* I, 184; *Picayune,* April 13, May 13, 1841.

⁶⁶ All figures compiled from Kmen, "Singing and Dancing," Table III.

⁶⁷ Ewen, *Music Comes to America,* 48–53.

⁶⁸ See for example Riegel, *Young America,* 372–76.

CHAPTER NINE

¹ Population figures may be found in Alexander, *Transatlantic Sketches,* II, 31; Berquin-Duvallon, *Vue,* 163; Buckingham, *Slave States,* I, 343;

Norman's New Orleans, 71; Pujol, "Robin's Voyages," 20; Waring and Cable, *History and Present Condition of New Orleans*, 30, 35–36; *Courier*, June 12, 1838.

² *Argus*, May 7, June 3, 1828; *Courier*, May 18, 1829; *Moniteur*, May 13, 1807; June 20, 1812; *Le Moqueur*, I (April 23, 1837), 3; *Le Moqueur*, I (May 14, 1837), 3; *Ami*, October 10, November 8, 1817; July 25, 1820. A *quinquet* was an Argand lamp. These lamps, invented by Aime Argand about 1782, were the first to use the principle of admitting air to the interior of the flame by means of a tubular wick.

³ A. Oakey Hall, *The Manhattaner in New Orleans* (New York, 1851), 49; *Louisiana Whig*, November 27, 1834.

⁴ *Argus*, June 4, 1827; *Louisiana Advertiser*, December 4, 1830.

⁵ *Gazette*, October 30, 1819; *Ami*, May 15, 1819.

⁶ *Courier*, December 13, 1811; March 18, 20, November 25, 1812.

⁷ *Mercantile Advertiser*, January 20, 1834.

⁸ *Ami*, November 11, 1820; *Bee*, April 13, 1836; December 8, 1837; *Courier*, November 28, 1832; *Louisiana Advertiser*, April 9, 1830.

⁹ *Bee*, April 18, 19, December 29, 31, 1836. *Courier*, December 28, 29, 31, 1836. In the spring of 1838, *Gustave III*, a five-act opera by Auber, was given in both the Orleans and the St. Charles theaters during the same week—once on the same night—while yet another production of *Gustave III*, which may or may not have had music, played at the Camp. *Courier*, March 30, April 5, 1838; *Picayune*, March 30, 1838; Kmen, "Singing and Dancing," Table III.

¹⁰ *Bee*, April 2, 17, 1835; *Picayune*, April 5, 1837; *Courier*, April 18, 1835.

¹¹ *Bee*, April 17, 1835; *Courier*, April 18, 1835.

¹² *Bee*, March 5, 7, May 13, 14, 1835; *Courier*, April 1, May 14, 23, 1835.

¹³ *Louisiana Advertiser*, May 4, 1830; *Courier*, April 30, 1830.

¹⁴ *Louisiana Advertiser*, May 7, 1830; *Courier*, February 23, 1830; *Bee*, June 7, 1837; Kmen, "Singing and Dancing," Table III.

¹⁵ *Argus*, February 22, March 5, 1830; *Courier*, February 20, March 2, 3, 1830. For an account of Mme. Feron's background and ability, see George C. D. Odell, *Annals of the New York Stage* (New York, 1827–49), III, 385; and Francis Courtney Wemyss, *Twenty-Six Years of the Life of an Actor and Manager* (New York, 1847), I, 163. Wemyss called Mme. Feron "the best English singer who ever visited the United States," and he doubted that Malibran herself was any better. In view of this, it is interesting that New Orleans regarded Mme. Feron as good but no better than the soprano at the French theater, Mlle. St. Clair. Nor was this partisanship for the Orleans Theater, since Feron sang there also—in fact, Feron and St. Clair sang duets. New Orleans considered St. Clair as the best the city had ever heard, excepting possibly Mlle. Alexander, her predecessor. *Bee*, June 3, 1831; *Courier*, November 20, December 4, 1830; May 23, June 3, 1831.

¹⁶ *Argus*, March 13, 22, 1830; *Courier*, April 13, 1830.

[17] *Ami,* June 7, July 18, 26, 1823; *Courier,* July 25, 1823; February 23, 1831. See also pp. 98–99, 100, 102, 103, 106, 108 above.

[18] *Courier,* June 15, 1812; March 10, April 19, 1813; March 26, 1824; *Ami,* May 16, 1818, *Moniteur,* December 25, 1805; February 22, November 8, 1806; May 23, 1807; March 19, 1808; September 23, 1809; December 24, 1811; January 14, August 1, 1812; February 24, March 3, 5, May 12, 1814; *Telegraphe,* October 13, 1807.

[19] *Moniteur,* June 11, 25, 1808; February 4, May 29, 1813; *Ami,* June 17, 1819; *Courier,* December 26, 31, 1817.

[20] *Moniteur,* February 14, 1810; *Ami,* July 26, 1817; October 6, 1823; *Courier,* October 24, 31, 1823; June 14, 1826; May 23, 1827; *Argus,* May 22, 1827; May 23, 1828; *Bee,* April 27, 1833; *Mercantile Advertiser,* May 21, 1831.

[21] *Argus,* May 13, June 1, 1826; *Bee,* April 27, 1833. Kathryn Tierney Hanley, "The Amateur Theatre in New Orleans before 1835" (M.A. thesis Tulane University, 1940), 79–87, provides a list of musical performances and dancing in which amateurs appeared during the years from 1806 to 1835. She found no fewer than ninety such occasions.

[22] *Bee,* December 4, 1835; Kmen, "Singing and Dancing," Table III.

[23] *Argus,* January 19, February 11, 1830; *Courier,* December 5, 1829; November 20, 1830; *Louisiana Advertiser,* April 3, 1830. See pp. 118–19 above.

[24] *Courier,* May 2, 16, 1812; March 12, 1831; *Bee,* March 27, 28, 1835.

[25] *Courier,* July 5, December 9, 1811; April 29, 1812; May 28, 1821; July 26, 31, 1831; *Ami,* August 17, 1820; July 14, 1821; *Moniteur,* April 2, 1808; July 20, 1811; July 30, 1812; *Bee,* March 14, 1835.

[26] *Ami,* March 16, 1816; *Courier,* December 18, 1807; March 15, 18, 1816; June 6, August 11, 1820; March 1, 1822; December 18, 1827; *Moniteur,* February 17, July 2, October 29, 1808; June 24, 1809; March 30, 1810; January 19, June 22, 1811.

[27] *Louisiana Advertiser,* April 9, 1831.

[28] *Courier,* March 16, 1827.

[29] *Ibid.,* February 21, April 23, 30, 1827; March 25, May 7, 1831; April 28, 1832; February 18, 23, 1833; March 2, 9, 1835; *Ami,* March 8, 1817; June 4, 1818; January 24, 1822.

[30] *Argus,* April 2, 5, 1827; *Courier,* April 3, 1827.

[31] *Argus,* April 4, 1833; *Courier,* April 2, May 21, 1833.

[32] *Courier,* March 10, 15, 24, April 28, 1830; February 19, 21, 1835; *Bee,* January 26, 1831.

[33] *Courier,* January 2, March 3, 22, 1830; March 2, 1835; *Argus,* February 5, 1830. In 1833, Mrs. Knight inserted "Cupid and Me" in the same opera. *Bee,* April 13, 1833.

[34] *Ami,* September 20, 1831; April 30, 1822; March 25, 1824; *Courier,* March 25, 27, 31, April 6, May 7, 13, 1824; December 7, 8, 16, 17, 1835;

Bee, December 4, 10, 17, 18, 22, 1835; May 10, 1836; *True American,* May 18, 1836. At times this practice proved irksome. The New Orleans *Bee* protested the constant use of instrumentalists on the stage. "Their place is in the orchestra." *Bee,* December 17, 1835. On the other hand, the *Picayune* called for more solos. *Picayune,* November 10, 1837.

35 *Bee,* January 7, 1831; March 31, 1835.

36 *Moniteur,* September 30, 1807; August 24, 31, September 3, 7, 1808; December 20, 1809; *Ami,* June 1, 1818; May 31, 1822; *Courier,* March 13, 1840.

37 *Argus,* March 15, 1825.

38 *Argus,* February 10, 1830; *Courier,* April 2, 1830; Dennis Prieur, Mayor, to the City Council, February 6, 1830, in Mayor's Messages, XXXIV, January 2, 1830–December 31, 1831 (City Archives, New Orleans Public Library).

39 See pp. 8, 19–20, 36, 44–45, 95, 102 above. *Ami,* January 24, 1822; March 8, 1824; *Courier,* February 13, 15, 1822; Ripley, *Social Life,* 119.

40 *Bee,* February 18, December 1, 12, 1836; January 12, 13, 1837; *Gazette,* January 5, 16, 20, 26, 29, February 1, 1821; *Picayune,* August 11, 1841; *Courier,* June 23, 1838.

41 *Courier,* February 23, 1829; March 5, 1832; *Louisiana Advertiser,* March 2, 1831; *Moniteur,* February 26, 1811.

42 *Gazette,* January 29, 1821; Bernhard, *Travels,* II, 55–56, 72; *Bee,* October 8, 1835.

43 *Bee,* November 25, 1836; Edgar Grima, "Municipal Support of Theatres and Operas in New Orleans," in *Publications of the Louisiana Historical Society,* IX (Proceedings and Reports, 1916), 43. The advancement of $200,000 in 1836 was a striking contrast to the attitude of the council in 1830. Whether this change was simply wrought by time, reflecting the increased prestige of the opera, or whether it was due to a new form of government—the city was divided into three virtually independent municipal districts in March, 1836—is not clear. Perhaps both were contributing causes.

44 Grima, "Municipal Support," 45.

45 Letter in *Revue et Gazette des Theatres,* Paris, July 5, 1840, reprinted in *Bee,* September 16, 1830.

46 *Ami,* February 19, 1823; *Courier,* March 23, 1827; *Louisiana Advertiser,* March 31, 1832; *Moniteur,* October 8, 12, 1808; July 3, 1813.

47 Kmen, "Singing and Dancing," Table III. For examples of compositions other than operas see *Ami,* April 15, 1820; *Bee,* December 14, 1833; January 4, 1836; June 2, November 23, 1837; January 6, 1840; June 28, 1841; *Courier,* February 5, 1808; October 24, 1823; February 9, 21, March 22, 30, 1824; April 11, 1825; January 7, 1837; *Gazette,* December 20, 1824; *Louisiana Advertiser,* January 26, 1830; June 6, 1831; January 10, 1832;

Moniteur, April 5, 1806; March 14, 1807; September 21, 24, 1808; *Picayune,* January 8, July 4, 1840; May 14, 1841.

[48] *Courier,* June 9, 1823; *Picayune,* January 4, 12, March 14, May 19, 1839; *Bee,* April 29, 1840.

[49] *Ami,* February 8, 1820; April 30, 1822; October 10, 1823; *Argus,* April 30, 1828; *Bee,* October 31, 1838; *Courier,* December 18, 25, 1815; February 11, 1820; November 25, 29, 1822; December 1, 4, 6, 1826; February 28, April 14, 22, 1828; April 16, 1829; December 3, 1830; November 17, 1838; *Mercantile Advertiser,* May 5, 1831; *Moniteur,* February 4, March 19, 1806; *Telegraphe,* November 9, 1805.

[50] *Courier,* December 15, 1832.

[51] Hauk, *Memories of a Singer,* 23; Kendall, "New Orleans' Musicians," 135.

[52] *Bee,* December 3, 1836; September 16, 1840.

[53] *Courier,* November 22, 1836; *Bee,* November 24, 1836.

[54] *Argus,* February 11, 1828; *Louisiana Advertiser,* February 20, 1829; *Courier,* February 16, 1828.

[55] *Courier,* January 2, 1838.

[56] *Argus,* May 29, 1828.

[57] *Ibid.,* February 18, 1833; *Courier,* December 22, 1828.

[58] *Courier,* October 11, 14, 1822; January 13, 1823; April 14, 22, 1828; *Bee,* December 9, 1831; March 27, 1840; *Ami,* October 11, 1822.

[59] *Bee,* December 9, 1831; March 2, 1835; *Mercantile Advertiser,* May 5, 1831.

[60] *Argus,* December 16, 1826; March 25, 1828; *Courier,* February 26, 1828; *Mercantile Advertiser,* May 5, 1831; *Moniteur,* December 10, 17, 1811; *True American,* March 23, 1837.

[61] *True American,* March 23, 1837.

[62] *Courier,* February 5, 1808; January 13, 1812; July 26, 31, 1813; *Moniteur,* March 16, 20, 23, 1813; *Bee,* February 4, 1840.

[63] *Courier,* April 30, 1814; March 4, 1822; *Moniteur,* March 19, April 5, November 5, 1806; June 24, 1807; March 26, July 2, 6, 1808; May 7, 12, 1814; *Ami,* August 6, 25, 1818.

[64] *Courier,* November 20, 1822; January 13, 1823; *Ami,* March 27, 1824. The corps was imported to supply choreography for the operas and that was its primary activity. But it also presented solo dances and divertissements between pieces as well as various ballets. *Ami,* January 25, 30, February 10, May 24, 1823; *Courier,* March 10, 14, 1823. On Saturday, April 26, 1823, it staged *Le Deserteur* by Dauberval for the first time. *Courier,* April 25, 1823. *Anette et Lubin* by Dauberval received its premiere on March 16, 1824. *Courier,* March 15, 1824. *La Fille Mal Gardee* by Dauberval was danced for the first time on March 27, 1824. *Courier,* March 26, 1824. For a recent performance and contemporary view of this ballet see *Time,* LXXVI (September 26, 1960), 54.

[65] *Argus,* September 26, 1829; January 19, 1830; *Courier,* January 24, 1833; March 26, 1838; *Mercantile Advertiser,* May 5, 1831.

[66] *Courier,* January 24, 1833; March 26, 1838. Both the Guaracha Bolera and the Tarantula were eliminated. *Mercantile Advertiser,* May 5, 1831.

[67] *Picayune,* January 3, 1840.

[68] *Courier,* January 24, December 28, 1833.

[69] *Ibid.,* March 3, 1809; July 29, 1811; May 1, 1822; May 14, 1823; *Moniteur,* March 4, 1809; July 30, August 1, 1811.

[70] *Bee,* April 1, 1835

[71] *Gazette,* November 15, 1819; *Ami,* January 12, 1816; December 10, 1821; *Courier,* December 9, 1811; *Moniteur,* April 6, 1808; April 20, November 12, 21, 26, 28, 1811; March 2, 4, 1813.

[72] *Courier,* March 20, 26, 1838.

[73] *Ibid.,* December 28, 1833; January 17, 1835; January 2, February 15, 1838; *Le Moqueur,* I (May 14, 1837), 3.

[74] *Courier,* February 15, 1838.

[75] *Moniteur,* April 15, May 2, 1807; See above pp. 68–69.

[76] *Moniteur,* May 7, 1806; August 8, 1807; *Telegraphe,* October 13, 1807. Desforges, Laroque, and Valois appeared in the press frequently as arrangers, composers, soloists, and teachers. See Chapter Eleven. Also see Kmen, "Singing and Dancing," Table II.

[77] *Moniteur,* March 5, 1811; Chevalley, "Northern Tours," 37. See Chapters Six and Eleven.

[78] Ludlow, *Dramatic Life as I Found It,* 373–75; Sol Smith, *Theatrical Management in the West and South for Thirty Years* (New York, 1868), 104; *Picayune,* April 5, 1837.

[79] *Picayune,* February 5, 1837; September 28, 1838; January 8, 1841; *Bee,* November 30, 1835; *Courier,* February 7, 1837; November 8, 1839; Baroncelli, *Le Theatre-Francais,* 40.

[80] *Bee,* February 6, 1837; *Courier,* February 7, 8, 1837; *Picayune,* January 3, 1839.

[81] *Picayune,* February 16, 1838; *Courier,* February 14, 1838.

[82] Castellanos, *New Orleans as It Was,* 224–26.

[83] *Picayune,* February 16, 1838; *Courier,* April 17, 18, 1838; *True American,* April 18, 1838. The first prize went to Cioffi, trombonist in the orchestra of the St. Charles. Second prize was won by M. Guiraud of the Orleans Theater. *Courier,* April 14, 1838. Guiraud's other compositional works lead one to suspect that his was the better arrangement—but it would not have done to award first prize to a musician in the rival French theater.

[84] Fossier, *New Orleans,* 201, 238, 288–92; Bernhard, *Travels,* II, 81; *Courier,* May 5, 1831; *Louisiana Advertiser,* December 4, 1834.

[85] *Bee,* December 8, 1835; November 10, 1837; *Courier,* May 22, 1837;

Picayune, May 23, 24, 1837; January 4, 1838. See Chapters VII, VIII.

[86] *Argus,* December 7, 1829; *Ami,* March 4, 1818; November 21, 1820; *Courier,* December 14, 1818. The ordinance was passed in 1816 and again in 1823.

[87] *Argus,* December 19, 1826.

[88] Hall, *The Manhattaner,* 100.

[89] Charles Lanman, *Adventures in the Wilds of the United States* (Philadelphia, 1856), II, 204; Buckingham, *Slave States,* I, 340; Lyell, *A Second Visit to the United States of North America,* II, 114; Murray, *Letters,* 271–72; Ampere, *Promenade,* II, 133. See also Houstoun, *Hesperos,* II, 73.

[90] Wood, *Autobiography,* I, 442–43; Butler, "The Louisiana Planter," 362; Castellanos, *New Orleans,* 178–81; Coleman, *Sketch Book,* 135; *Fashion and Consequence as Now Found in High Places and Low Places. By a Minister of Many Travels* (Louisville, 1855), 76; Ripley, *Social Life,* 67; Tasistro, *Random Shots,* I, 183.

[91] *Bee,* March 19, 1836.

[92] Dent, *Opera,* 42–44, 60–67; See Kmen, "Singing and Dancing," Table III and compare with any history of opera.

[93] John A. Kouwenhoven, *Made in America* (New York, 1948), 1–117.

CHAPTER TEN

[1] Frederick Law Olmstead, *A Journey in the Back Country in the Winter of 1853–1854* (New York, 1907), I, 196; Whipple, *Whipple's Southern Diary,* 99.

[2] James R. Creecy, *Scenes in the South and Other Miscellaneous Pieces* (Washington, 1860), 34–35.

[3] *Whipple's Diary,* 100; The Reverend G. Lewis, *Impressions of America and the American Churches* (Edinburgh, 1845), 194.

[4] Buckingham, *Slave States,* I, 355; Davidson, "Journey through the South," 362; Didimus, *New Orleans as I Found It,* 34; *Picayune,* May 28, 1839.

[5] *Picayune,* February 14, 1837.

[6] Didimus, *New Orleans as I Found It,* 36; *Picayune,* August 8, 1837.

[7] Gayarre, *History of Louisiana,* III, 192; *Gazette,* December 21, 1804; Rowland, *Letter Books,* III, 353.

[8] Francois-Xavier Martin, *The History of Louisiana* (New Orleans, 1827), II, 351; Gayarre, *History of Louisiana,* IV, 414–15; Howard Corning (ed.), *Journal of John James Audubon* (Boston, 1929), 113; *True American,* December 24, 1838.

[9] Creecy, *Scenes in the South,* 44; *Whipple's Diary,* 105–106; Henry Renshaw, "Jackson Square," *Louisiana Historical Quarterly,* II (January, 1919),

43; Kendall, *History of New Orleans*, I, 191; Castellanos, *New Orleans as It Was*, 278; Bentley, "Whitman's Visit to New Orleans," 220–21; *Bee*, February 9, 1839; *Argus*, August 5, 1834; *Courier*, June 13, July 11, 1834; *Picayune*, June 25, 1837; March 5, 1841.

[10] *Bee*, March 9, 1833.

[11] *Mercantile Advertiser*, December 21, 1831; *Ami*, February 8, 1814; September 25, 1823; *Picayune*, June 25, July 6, August 8, 1837; October 2, 1838; *Bee*, November 25, 1839; *True American*, November 25, 29, 1839; Fossier, *New Orleans*, 193–203.

[12] *Picayune*, July 6, 1837; October 11, 1840; *Bee*, November 25, 1839.

[13] *Ami*, September 25, 1823; *Picayune*, June 25, 1837; February 23, 1838; *Bee*, July 6, 1837; *Courier*, July 11, 1834.

[14] *True American*, December 24, 1838; *Daily Crescent*, June 5, 1849; *Picayune*, October 20, 1860.

[15] *Picayune*, February 8, 1837; June 2, 1838; *Louisiana Advertiser*, July 6, 1832.

[16] Latrobe, *Impressions*, 60, 137–38.

[17] *Ibid.*, 60; Whittington (ed.), "The Journal of Dr. John Sibley," 479; *Moniteur*, November 16, 1808.

[18] *Courier*, January 20, 21, 1829; November 28, 1831; May 29, 1832; February 5, 1833; *Bee*, October 27, 1827; March 6, 1833; *Louisiana Advertiser*, July 28, 1834; *Picayune*, June 15, 1839. For an account of Pere Antoine's funeral see Fossier, *New Orleans*, 329–33.

[19] *Louisiana Advertiser*, July 28, 1834; Fossier, *New Orleans*, 429–35.

[20] *Bee*, October 27, 1838.

[21] *Picayune*, August 21, 31, 1853; August 31, 1858; *Daily Crescent*, August 11, 1853; August 10, September 4, 1858; *Weekly Mirror*, October 2, 1858; Robert C. Reinders, "Sound of the Mournful Dirge," *Jazz*, I (Fall, 1959), 296–98.

[22] *Moniteur*, January 28, February 4, 1807; February 5, 9, 14, 1811; March 4, 1813; *Ami*, January 27, February 8, 15, 17, 24, 1814; *Courier*, May 6, 1835; *Picayune*, February 6, 1840.

[23] *Bee*, January 23, February 8, 1834; *Picayune*, January 27, February 28, 1837; June 26, 1838; January 29, February 10, 1841; *Courier*, July 2, 1819; June 30, 1820; May 28, 1821; February 2, 1835; June 23, 1838; February 2, 1841; *Moniteur*, March 26, 1806; *Gazette*, July 8, 11, 18, 1815; *Ami*, April 21, 1817; June 30, 1820; *Argus*, August 5, 1834; *Louisiana Advertiser*, December 9, 1834; Fearon, *Sketches of America*, 275; Watson, "Notitia," 228.

[24] Levasseur, *Lafayette en Amerique*, II, 187.

[25] *Louisiana Advertiser*, September 12, 1834; *Bee*, September 18, 1835; Riegel, *Young America*, 368; Arthur Loesser, *Men, Women & Pianos* (New York, 1954), 482; *Spirit of the Times*, VI (April 2, 1836), 52.

[26] *Bee*, December 1, 4, 5, 7, 16, 1835; February 22, 24, December 6, 1836.

[27] *Ibid.*, December 4, 5, 1835; Riegel, *Young America*, 368.

[28] *Spirit of the Times,* VI (April 2, 1836), 52; *Bee,* February 24, 1836.

[29] *True American,* May 12, 1836; *Picayune,* May 24, 1839; *Spirit of the Times,* X (September 12, 1840), 336.

[30] *Louisiana Advertiser,* May 18, 1832; *Argus,* April 29, 1834.

[31] *Bee,* December 10, 1835.

[32] *Ibid.,* December 7, 8, 1835; November 23, 1837; March 2, 1838; May 2, 1839; *Courier,* June 5, 1838; March 30, May 4, 1839; April 10, December 2, 1840; *Picayune,* June 13, 1837; February 15, June 19, 1838; May 22, 1839; May 22, June 28, July 4, December 2, 1840; March 19, 1841.

[33] *Bee,* May 9, 1837; *True American,* April 21, 1837; *Picayune,* April 22, 1837; March 10, 1838.

[34] *Courier,* February 23, 1835; May 21, June 6, 1838; May 27, 1840; *Bee,* January 11, 15, December 26, 1836; June 2, 1837; April 30, May 11, 1838; May 20, 1840; April 9, 1841; *Picayune,* March 15, 28, 1837.

[35] *Courier,* December 28, 1835; May 21, June 1, 5, 6, 1838; *Picayune,* November 19, 1837; June 6, 1838; *Bee,* May 20, 1840.

[36] *Picayune,* August 2, 1838.

[37] *Courier,* August 27, 1831; January 12, 16, 17, 23, 1838; *Bee,* January 23, September 27, 1838; January 12, 1841; *Picayune,* February 6, 1840.

[38] Freund (ed. and trans.), *Dresel's Houston Journal,* 112–13; *Picayune,* May 12, 1841; *Bee,* May 13, 1841.

CHAPTER ELEVEN

[1] *Courier,* April 22, 1812.

[2] The programs were found in *Moniteur,* December 7, 1805–March 10, 1814; *Telegraphe,* October 13, 1807; *Courier,* November 18, 1807–May 27, 1840; *Ami,* January 15, 1814–February 4, 1824; *Argus,* December 8, 1824–May 30, 1827; *Louisiana Advertiser,* January 26, 1830; *Bee,* June 3, 1830–May 20, 1840; *Picayune,* June 10, 12, 1838. It is not feasible to list the numerous specific citations involved in a statistical analysis; hereafter in this chapter specific citations will be given only for material other than the analysis.

[3] *Courier,* March 18, 1814.

[4] *Moniteur,* January 14, 28, 1807; March 25, 1808; January 14, 1812; *Courier,* February 12, 1812; February 9, 1824; May 17, 1827; *Argus,* May 7, 1827; *Picayune,* September 1, 1841.

[5] *Moniteur,* January 14, 1807; *Ami,* January 2, 16, 22, 1816; *Argus,* April 26, 1827; *Courier,* January 17, 1816.

[6] *Argus,* January 5, 28, 1826; *Courier,* December 11, 1827.

[7] *Moniteur,* December 7, 14, 1805.

[8] *Ami,* January 15, 1814; *Argus,* May 30, 1827.

[9] *Courier,* February 3, 1829.

[10] *Ibid.,* July 3, 1809.

[11] *Bee,* December 24, 1838; Riegel, *Young America,* 369. See also John H. Mueller, *The American Symphony Orchestra* (Bloomington, 1951), 16–21, 31–32.

[12] *Moniteur,* March 12, 1808; December 18, 1813; *Courier,* January 5, 1814.

[13] *Ami,* January 2, 1816.

[14] *Ibid.,* January 9, 1816; *Courier,* January 10, 29, 1816.

[15] *Courier,* December 27, 30, 1816.

[16] *Ami,* February 25, 1817; April 15, 1820.

[17] *Ibid.,* January 28, February 4, 1824; *Picayune,* January 9, 1838.

CHAPTER TWELVE

[1] Marshall Stearns, "Rebop, Bebop and Bop," in Edie Condon and Richard Gehman (eds.), *Edie Condon's Treasury of Jazz* (New York, 1956), 195; Sidney Finckelstein, *Jazz: A People's Music* (New York, 1948), 35; Rudi Blesh, *Shining Trumpets* (2nd rev. ed.; New York, 1958), 155; William Russell and Stephen W. Smith, "New Orleans Music," in Frederic Ramsey, Jr., and Charles Edward Smith (eds.), *Jazzmen* (London, 1957), 9; Kane, *Queen New Orleans,* 279.

[2] Reuben Gold Thwaites (ed.), *Early Western Travels, 1748–1846* (Cleveland, 1904), IV, 363, 366; Waston, "Notitia," 232; Schultz, *Inland Voyage,* II, 197–98.

[3] Fearon, *Sketches of America,* 277–78; Thwaites, *Early Western Travels,* XIII, 317.

[4] Latrobe, *Impressions,* 49–51. For other descriptions see Creecy, *Scenes in the South,* 19–22; Ingraham, *The Southwest,* I, 162; Hall, *The Manhattaner,* 107; Flugel, "Pages from a Journal," 427, 432.

[5] Flint, *Recollections,* 140.

[6] Thwaites, *Early Western Travels,* IV, 363, 366; Creecy, *Scenes in the South,* 21; George W. Cable, "The Dance in Place Congo," *Century Magazine,* XXXI (February, 1886), 519, 527; Castellanos, *New Orleans as It Was,* 297; Ingraham, *The Southwest,* I, 162; Norman, *Norman's New Orleans,* 182; *Picayune,* June 24, 1845.

[7] Norman, *Norman's New Orleans,* 182; Hall, *The Manhattaner,* 107; Maude Cuney Hare, *Six Creole Folk-Songs* (New York, 1921), 3; Castellanos, *New Orleans as It Was,* 158–59; *Picayune,* June 24, 1845.

[8] See above Chapter Two.

[9] *Courier,* October 20, 1820; July 7, 1823; May 29, 1839; *Bee,* November 8, 1837; June 4, 1841; *Mercantile Advertiser,* August 16, 1831; *True American,* November 6, 1839; *Picayune,* November 5, 1839; January 12, July 22, 1841.

[10] *True American,* January 1, 1839; *Bee,* June 13, 1833; November 8, 1837; Tregle, "Early New Orleans Society," 33.

[11] *True Delta,* December 28, 1854; *Picayune,* August 19, 1841.

[12] *Picayune,* January 12, 1841.

[13] George W. Cable, "Creole Slave Songs," *Century Magazine,* XXXI (April, 1886), 808; Berquin-Duvallon, *Travels in Louisiana,* 26–27; Bernhard, *Travels,* II, 58; *Bee,* December 23, 1834.

[14] Captain Oldmixon, *Transatlantic Wanderings: Or, A Last Look at the United States* (London, 1855), 149; *Picayune,* August 24, 1839.

[15] Ripley, *Social Life,* 260–61; Henry C. Semple (ed.), *The Ursulines in New Orleans and Our Lady of Prompt Succor . . . 1727–1925* (New York, 1925), 96; *Picayune,* December 21, 1858.

[16] *Bee,* June 4, 1840; *Courier,* November 27, 1811; January 5, 1814; July 10, 1818; June 9, 1819; July 6, 1833. See also *Picayune,* June 5, 1839; *Courier,* July 20, 1810; June 1, 1825; August 23, 1834; *Ami,* May 21, July 9, 1818.

[17] *Moniteur,* February 1, 1806; May 9, 1807; March 5, 1808; February 14, 1811; *Ami,* February 8, 1814; January 21, 1819; *Bee,* February 19, December 10, 1833.

[18] *Ami,* October 28, 1816; January 19, 1820; October 15, 1823; *Courier,* November 19, 1819; March 11, November 20, 1822; *Moniteur,* April 15, 1807; August 24, 1808; May 28, 1811.

[19] *Telegraphe,* October 13, 1807; *Moniteur,* October 3, 1807; *Ami,* February 19, 1814; *Bee,* November 30, 1835; Pickett, *Eight Days,* 27. See Chapter Eleven above.

[20] Fossier, *New Orleans,* 193; Documents of the Cabildo, Book No. 4088, Document No. 367; Kendall, *History of New Orleans,* I, 191, 240; *Picayune,* January 8, 1854; Chapter Two above.

[21] Didimus, *New Orleans as I Found It,* 34, 36; James M. Trotter, *Music and Some Highly Musical People* (Boston, 1882), 351; Blesh, *Shining Trumpets,* 155; *Ami,* June 1, 1820; *Picayune,* May 28, 1839.

[22] Stahl, "The Free Negro," 359; Trotter, *Music,* 338–45; Kendall, "New Orleans' Musicians," 135; Everett, "Free Persons of Color," 221–22; James E. Winston, "The Free Negro in New Orleans, 1803–1860," *Louisiana Historical Quarterly,* XXI (October, 1938), 1082; Lucy Harth Smith, "Negro Musicians and Their Music," *Journal of Negro History,* XX (October, 1935), 429–30.

[23] Trotter, *Music,* 341–44, 349; Lawrence Dunbar Reddick, "The Negro in the New Orleans Press, 1850–1860," (Ph.D. dissertation, University of Chicago, 1939), 84; *Crescent,* June 26, 1860; Everett, "Free Persons of Color," 222–23.

[24] Trotter, *Music,* 351–52; *Louisiana, A Guide to the State* (American Guide Series, New York, 1941), 197; Edwin Adams Davis, *Louisiana, A Narrative History* (Baton Rouge, 1961), 227.

[25] Henri Herz, *Mes Voyages en Amerique* (Paris, 1866), 290–91.

26 *Bee,* April 3, 21, July 3, 4, 24, September 14, 1838; *Picayune,* May 22, 1838.

27 *Bee,* January 14, 18, 21, 23, 27, February 4–May 12, 1840.

28 *Ibid.,* February 10, April 6, 1840; Trotter, *Music,* 340, 347–48.

29 Ripley, *Social Life,* 162; Sarah Morgan Dawson, *A Confederate Girl's Diary* (Boston, 1913), 361.

30 Creecy, *Scenes in the South,* 21; Cable "Dance in Place Congo," 523; Hare, *Six Songs,* 3; *Picayune,* July 17, 1838; July 18, 1839.

31 Olmstead, *Back Country,* I, 216–17.

32 Castellanos, *New Orleans as It Was,* 295; *Whipple's Diary,* 112, 123; Tyrone Power, *Impressions of America During the Years 1833, 1834, and 1835* (Philadelphia, 1836), II, 117; Olmstead, *Seaboard States,* II, 258–59; *Picayune,* June 1, 1839.

33 Arthur K. Moore, "Specimens of the Folktales from Some Antebellum Newspapers of Louisiana," *Louisiana Historical Quarterly,* XXXII (October, 1949), 724; Mary Teresa Austin Carroll, *The Ursulines in Louisiana, 1727–1824* (New Orleans, 1886), 31; Cable "Dance in Place Congo," 527–28.

34 Willis Winslow Pratt (ed.), *Galveston Island: Or a Few Months off the Coast of Texas: The Journal of Francis C. Sheridan, 1839–1840* (Austin, 1954), 92.

35 Sigmund Spaeth, *A History of Popular Music in America* (New York, 1948), 81–83; Sheridan, *Galveston Island,* 90–93.

36 Pratt (ed.), *Sheridan Journal,* 93–94.

37 *Picayune,* May 12, 13, 1837; *Bee,* May 13, 1837.

38 *Picayune,* May 12, 13, 16, 1837; *Bee,* May 13, 1837; *Courier,* May 16, 1837.

39 *Picayune,* May 16, 18, 1837; *Courier,* May 16, 1837; T. Allston Brown, "Origins of Minstrelsy" in Charles H. Day, *Fun in Black, or Sketches of Minstrel Life* (New York, 1874), 6.

40 Smither, "History of the English Theatre," 223; *Courier,* May 15, 1837; *Picayune,* May 21, 1837.

41 *Picayune,* May 21, June 1, 1837.

42 *Ibid.,* September 12, 1837; July 19, 1840; July 15, 1841.

43 *Ibid.,* May 21, June 5, 1839.

44 *Ibid.,* August 25, November 14, 1839; April 28, July 18, 22, 1840.

45 *Ibid.,* February 23, March 2, *passim,* 1838; February 13, 1839.

46 *Ibid.,* June 10, 13, 1840.

47 *Ibid.,* August 4, 1838; August 28, 1839; June 13, 1840; Pratt (ed.), *Sheridan Journal,* 94.

48 Ripley, *Social Life,* 154; Pratt (ed.), *Sheridan Journal,* 91–93; *Picayune,* April 14, 1839; *Courier,* November 5, 1838.

49 Pratt (ed.), *Sheridan Journal,* 93–94.

50 *Picayune,* May 21, August 28, 1839; July 19, 1840; Brown, "Origins of Minstrelsy," 3.

51 *True American,* August 23, 1838; *Picayune,* June 19, August 21, 1839.

[52] *Picayune,* June 1, 1837; December 6, 1839; *True American,* August 23, 1838.

[53] *Picayune,* May 22, 1842; *Bee,* May 23, 1842.

[54] Brander Mathews, "The Rise and Fall of Negro Minstrelsy," *Scribner's Magazine,* LVII (June, 1915), 755; Marion Spitzer, "The Lay of the Last Minstrel," *Saturday Evening Post,* CXCVII (March 7, 1925), 118–23; Carl Wittke, *Tambo and Bones: A History of the American Minstrel Stage* (Durham, 1930), 17–18.

[55] Brown, "Origins of Minstrelsy," 5.

[56] *Louisiana Advertiser,* December 24, 1830; *Bee,* March 9, 30, May 13, 1831; *Mercantile Advertiser,* April 23, May 14, 1831.

[57] Brown, "Origins of Minstrelsy,"; *Louisiana Advertiser,* April 25, 1832; *Picayune,* June 16, 1838.

[58] *Bee,* March 23, 27, 1835; February 23, 1826; *Picayune,* March 4, 1838.

Bibliography

PRIMARY SOURCES

Newspapers and Periodicals

New Orleans *L'Abeille,* 1830–41 (alternate title, New Orleans *Bee*).
New Orleans *L'Ami des Lois,* 1813–24.
New Orleans *L'Argus,* 1824–34.
New Orleans *Commercial Bulletin,* 1836–41.
New Orleans *Courrier de la Louisiane,* 1807–41 (alternate title, New Orleans *Courier*).
New Orleans *Daily Picayune,* 1837–41.
New Orleans *Emporium,* 1832.
New Orleans *Journal de la Ville,* 1825.
New Orleans *Louisiana Advertiser,* 1826–35.
New Orleans *Louisiana Gazette,* 1804–26.
New Orleans *Louisiana Whig,* 1834–35.
New Orleans *Mercantile Advertiser,* 1831–34.
New Orleans *Merchant's Daily News,* 1834.
New Orleans *Moniteur de la Louisiane,* 1802–14.
New Orleans *Le Telegraphe,* 1804–1807.
New Orleans *True American,* 1836–39.
New Orleans *Union,* 1803–1804.

Le Moqueur, Journal des Flaneurs, I. New Orleans, 1837.
Spirit of the Times, VI–X. New York, 1836–41.

Documents and Correspondence

Acts of Pedro Pedesclaux, 1793–1811. Notarial Archives, Civil Courts Building, New Orleans.
Dispatches of the Spanish Governors of Louisiana. Photostats of the originals and typescript translation in Howard-Tilton Library, Tulane University.
Documents of the Cabildo. Louisiana State Museum Library, New Orleans.
Letter from Louis Tabary to the City Council of New Orleans, received July 13, 1805. Howard-Tilton Library.
Letters from Nathaniel Cox to Gabriel Lewis, 1802–17. Typescript in Howard-Tilton Library.
Mayor's Messages, XXXIV (January 2, 1830–December 31, 1831). City Archives, New Orleans Public Library.
Proceedings of the City Council, 1803–1807. City Archives, New Orleans Public Library.

Memoirs and Travel Accounts

"A Description of New Orleans," *Literary Magazine and American Register* (Philadelphia), IV (July, 1805), 39–42.
Alexander, James E. *Transatlantic Sketches: Comprising Visits to the Most Interesting Scenes in North and South America and the West Indies.* London, 1833.
Alliot, Paul. "Historical and Political Reflections on Louisiana," in James A. Robertson (ed.). *Louisiana under the Rule of Spain, France, and the United States.* 2 vols. Cleveland: 1911. I, 29–143.
Ampere, Jean Jacques. *Promenade en Amerique.* 2 vols. Paris, 1855.
An Account of Louisiana, being an abstract of documents in the office of the Department of State and of the Treasury. Philadelphia, 1803.
Ashe, Thomas. *Travels in America, Performed in 1806.* 3 vols. London, 1808.
Audubon, John James. *Delineations of American Scenery and Character.* New York, 1926.
Baird, Robert. *View of the Valley of the Mississippi.* Philadelphia, 1834.
Barnum, Phineas T. *Struggles and Triumphs: Or Forty Years' Recollections of P. T. Barnum.* Buffalo, 1873.
Berquin-Duvallon. *Travels in Louisiana and the Floridas in the Year 1802,* trans. John Davis. New York, 1806.

————. *Vue de la Colonie Espagnole du Mississippi ou des Provinces de Louisiane et Floride Occidentale, en l'Annee 1802.* Paris, 1803.

Bernhard, Karl. *Travels through North America during the Years 1825 and 1826.* 2 vols. Philadelphia, 1828.

Bingley, William. *Travels in North America.* London, 1821.

Brackenridge, Henry M. *Views of Louisiana together with a Journal of a Voyage up the Missouri River in 1811.* Pittsburgh, 1814.

Bremer, Fredricka. *The Homes of the New World,* trans. Mary Howitt. 2 vols. New York, 1853.

Brown, Samuel R. *The Western Gazetteer.* Auburn and New York, 1817.

Buckingham, James Silk. *The Slave States of America.* 2 vols. London, 1842.

Bullock, W. *Sketch of a Journey through the Western States of North America.* London, 1827.

Cable, George Washington (ed.). "War Diary of a Union Woman in the South," in *Famous Adventures and Prison Escapes of the Civil War.* New York, 1893.

Castellanos, Henry C. *New Orleans as It Was.* New Orleans, 1895.

Clapp, Theodore, *Autobiographical Sketches and Recollections during a Thirty-five Years Residence in New Orleans.* Boston, 1857.

Cobb, Joseph B. *Mississippi Scenes: Or Sketches of Southern and Western Life and Adventure.* Philadelphia, 1851.

Collot, Victor. *A Journey in North America.* Paris, 1826.

Corcoran, D. *Pickings from the Portfolio of the Reporter of the New Orleans Picayune.* Philadelphia, 1846.

Corning Howard (ed.). *Journal of John James Audubon, Made during His Trip to New Orleans in 1820–1821.* Boston, 1929.

Cowell, Joe. *Thirty Years Passed among the Players in England and America.* New York, 1844.

Cramer, Zadock. *The Navigator.* Pittsburgh, 1811.

Creecy, James R. *Scenes in the South and Other Miscellaneous Pieces.* Washington, 1860.

Cuming, Fortescue. *Sketches of a Tour to the Western Country.* Pittsburgh, 1810.

Cushman, Charlotte. *Her Letters and Memories of Her Life,* ed. Emma Stebbins. Boston, 1878.

Dart, Henry P. (ed.). "William Johnson's Journal." *Louisiana Historical Quarterly,* V (January, 1922), 34–50.

Davidge, William. *Footlight Flashes.* New York, 1866.

Dawson, Sarah Morgan. *A Confederate Girl's Diary.* Boston, 1913.

Didimus, Henry. *New Orleans as I Found It.* New York, 1845.

Duganne, A. J. H. *Twenty Months in the Department of the Gulf.* 3rd ed. New York, 1865.

Ellicott, Andrew. *The Journal of Andrew Ellicott.* Philadelphia, 1803.

Evans, Estwick. *A Pedestrious Tour of Four Thousand Miles through the Western States and Territories . . . 1818.* Concord, 1819.

Fashion and Consequence as Now Found in High Places and Low Places by a Minister of Many Travels. Louisville, 1855.

Fearon, Henry Bradshaw. *Sketches of America: A Narrative of a Journey of Five Thousand Miles through the Eastern and Western States of America.* 3rd ed. London, 1819.

Featherstonhaugh, George W. *Excursion through the Slave States.* New York, 1844.

Flint, Timothy. *The History and Geography of the Mississippi Valley.* 2 vols. Cincinnati, 1833.

———. *Recollections of the Last Ten Years . . . in the Valley of the Mississippi.* Boston, 1826.

Flugel, J. C. "Pages from a Journal of a Voyage down the Mississippi to New Orleans in 1817," ed. Felix Flugel. *Louisiana Historical Quarterly,* VII (July, 1924), 414–40.

Freund, Max (trans. and ed.). *Gustav Dresel's Houston Journal: Adventures in North America and Texas, 1837–1841.* Austin, 1954.

Gaisford, John. *The Drama in New Orleans.* New Orleans, 1849.

Gottschalk, Louis Moreau. *Notes of a Pianist,* ed. Clara Gottschalk, trans. Robert E. Peterson. Philadelphia, 1881.

Hall, A. Oakey. *The Manhattaner in New Orleans.* New York, 1851.

Hamilton, Thomas. *Men and Manners in America.* 2 vols. Edinburgh, 1833.

Hauk, Minnie. *Memories of a Singer.* London, 1925.

Herz, Henri. *Mes Voyages en Amerique.* Paris, 1866.

Hildreth, Samuel P. "History of a Voyage from Marietta to New Orleans in 1805." *American Pioneer* (Cincinnati), I (March, 1842), 89–105 and (April, 1842), 128–45.

Houstoun, Matilda Charlotte. *Hesperos: Or Travels in the West.* 2 vols. London, 1850.

———. *Texas and the Gulf of Mexico.* 2 vols. London, 1844.

Ingraham, Joseph Holt. *The South-west, by a Yankee.* 2 vols. New York, 1835.

Jefferson, Joseph. *The Autobiography of Joseph Jefferson.* New York, 1889.

Keller, Herbert A. (ed.). "A Journey through the South in 1836: Diary of James D. Davidson. *Journal of Southern History,* I (August, 1935), 345–77.

Kemper, Jackson. "Diary of Bishop Kemper, January 17–March 7, 1838," ed. Julie Kock. 1932. Typescript in Howard-Tilton Library, Tulane University.

Ker, Henry. *Travels through the Western Interior of the United States from the Year 1808 up to the Year 1816.* Elizabethtown, 1816.

Kingsford, William. *Impressions of the West and South.* Toronto, 1858.

Lanman, Charles. *Adventures in the Wilds of the United States.* 2 vols. Philadelphia, 1856.

Latham, Henry. *Black and White: A Journal of a Three Months' Tour in the United States.* London, 1867.

Latrobe, Benjamin Henry Boneval. *Impressions Respecting New Orleans by Benjamin Henry Boneval Latrobe: Diary and Sketches, 1818–1820,* ed. Samuel Wilson, Jr. New York, 1951.

Latrobe, Charles Joseph. *The Rambler in North America.* 2 vols. 2nd ed. London, 1836.

Laussat, Pierre-Clement de. *Memoires sur Ma Vie.* Paris, 1831.

LeGrand, Julia. *The Journal of Julia LeGrand, New Orleans, 1862–1863,* ed. Kate Mason Rowland and (Mrs.) Morris L. Croxall. Richmond, 1911.

Levasseur, A. *Lafayette en Amerique en 1824 et 1825: Ou Journal d'un Voyage aux Etats-Unis.* 2 vols. Paris, 1829.

Lewis, G. *Impressions of America and the American Churches.* Edinburgh, 1845.

Logan, James. *Notes of a Journey through Canada, the United States of America, and the West Indies.* Edinburgh, 1838.

Lowenstern, M. Isadore. *Les Etats-Unis et la Havane: Souvenirs d'un Voyageur.* Paris, 1842.

Ludlow, Noah M. *Dramatic Life as I Found It.* St. Louis, 1880.

Lyell, Sir Charles. *A Second Visit to the United States of North America.* 2 vols. London, 1849.

Mackay, Alexander. *The Western World: Or, Travels in the United States in 1846–1847.* 2 vols. Philadelphia, 1849.

Marigny, Bernard. "Reflections on the Campaign of General Andrew Jackson," trans. Grace King. *Louisiana Historical Quarterly,* I (January, 1923), 63–85.

Martineau, Harriet. *Retrospect of Western Travel.* 2 vols. London, 1838.

Memoires sur la Louisiane et la Nouvelle-Orleans. Paris, 1804.

Montlezun, Baron de. *Voyage Fait dans les Annees 1816 et 1817, de New-Yorck a la Nouvelle-Orleans.* 2 vols. Paris, 1818.

Murat, Achille. *A Moral and Political Sketch of the United States of North America.* London, 1833.

Murray, Amelia M. *Letters from the United States, Cuba and Canada.* New York, 1856.

Murray, Charles Augustus. *Travels in North America during the Years 1834, 1835, and 1836.* 2 vols. London, 1839.

Nichols, T. L. *Forty Years of American Life.* 2nd ed. London, 1874.

Nolte, Vincent. *Fifty Years in Both Hemispheres: Or, Reminiscences of a Merchant's Life.* London, 1854. Reprinted New York, 1934.

Nuttall, Thomas. *A Journal of Travels into the Arkansas Territory during the Year 1819.* Philadelphia, 1821.

Oldmixon, Captain. *Transatlantic Wanderings: Or, A Last Look at the United States.* London, 1855.

Olliffe, Charles. *Scenes Americaines: Dix-huit Mois dans le Nouveau Monde.* Paris, 1853.

Olmstead, Frederick Law. *A Journey in the Back Country in the Winter of 1853–1854.* 2 vols. New York, 1907.

——. *A Journey in the Seaboard Slave States.* 2 vols. New York, 1904.

Parker, Amos Andrew. *Trip to the West and Texas.* Concord, 1835.

Perrin du Lac, Francois M. *Voyage dans les Deux Louisianes, et chez les Nations Sauvages du Missouri, par les Etats-Unis, l'Ohio et les Provinces Qui le Bordent, en 1801, 1802, et 1803.* Paris, 1805.

Pfeiffer, Ida. *A Lady's Second Journey Round the World.* New York, 1856.

Pickett, Albert J. *Eight Days in New Orleans in February, 1847.* Montgomery, 1847.

Pope, John. *A Tour through the Southern and Western Territories of the United States of North America, the Spanish Dominions on the River Mississippi and the Floridas.* Richmond, 1792. Reprinted New York, 1888.

Power, Tyrone. *Impressions of America during the Years 1833, 1834, and 1835.* 2 vols. Philadelphia, 1836.

Pratt, Willis Winslow (ed.). *Galveston Island: Or a Few Months off the Coast of Texas: The Journal of Francis C. Sheridan, 1839–1840.* Austin, 1954.

Pulszky, Francis and Theresa. *White, Red, Black: Sketches of American Society in the United States.* 2 vols. New York, 1853.

Quaife, Milo M. (ed.). "Journal of a Quaker Merchant in New Orleans (1823)," in *Louisiana Scrapbook No. 2* (Howard-Tilton Library), 5–7.

Ripley, Eliza. *Social Life in Old New Orleans.* New York, 1912.

Robin, Claude C. *Voyages dans l'Interieur de la Louisiane, de la Floride Occidentale, et dans les Isles de la Martinique et de Saint-Domingue pendant les Annees 1802, 1803, 1804, 1805, et 1806.* 3 vols. Paris, 1807.

Robinson, William L. *The Diary of a Samaritan.* New York, 1860.

Schermerhorn, John F. and Samuel J. Mills. *A Correct View of that Part of the United States which Lies West of the Allegany Mountains with Regard to Religion and Morals.* Hartford, 1814.

Schultz, Christian. *Travels on an Inland Voyage . . . in the Years 1807 and 1808.* 2 vols. New York, 1810.

Sealsfield, Charles. *The Americans as They Are: Described in a Tour through the Valley of the Mississippi.* London, 1828.

——. *Life in the New World: Or Sketches of American Society.* New York, 1844.

Singleton, Arthur. *Letters from the South and West.* Boston, 1924.

Smith, Sol. *Theatrical Apprenticeship.* Philadelphia, 1846.

———. *Theatrical Management in the West and South for Thirty Years.* New York, 1868.

Stirling, James. *Letters from the Slave States.* London, 1857.

Stoddard, Amos. *Sketches, Historical and Descriptive of Louisiana.* Philadelphia, 1812.

Stuart, James. *Three Years in North America.* 2 vols. 3rd ed. Edinburgh, 1833.

Sullivan, Edward. *Rambles and Scrambles in North and South America.* London, 1852.

Tasistro, Louis Fitzgerald. *Random Shots and Southern Breezes.* 2 vols. New York, 1842.

Tocqueville, Alexis de. "Alexis de Tocqueville in New Orleans: January 1–3, 1832," ed. G. W. Pierson. *The Franco-American Review,* I (June, 1936), 25–42.

Thwaites, Reuben Gold (ed.). *Early Western Travels, 1748–1846.* 32 vols. Cleveland, 1904.

Trollope, Francis. *Domestic Manners of the Americans,* ed. Donald Smalley. New York, 1949.

Vandenhoff, George. *Leaves from an Actor's Notebook.* New York, 1860.

Watson, John F. "Notitia of Incidents at New Orleans in 1804 and 1805." *American Pioneer* (Cincinnati), II (May, 1843), 227–37.

Wemyss, Francis Courtney. *Twenty-six Years of the Life of an Actor and Manager.* New York, 1847.

Wharton, George M. *New Orleans Sketch Book.* Philadelphia, 1852.

Whipple, Henry B. *Bishop Whipple's Southern Diary, 1843–1844,* ed. Lester B. Shippee. Minneapolis, 1937.

Whitaker, John S. *Sketches of Life and Character in Louisiana.* New Orleans, 1847.

Whittington, G. P. (ed.). "The Journal of Dr. John Sibley." *Louisiana Historical Quarterly,* X (October, 1927), 475–97.

Wood, William. *Autobiography of William Wood.* 2 vols. New York, 1895.

Wood, William B. *Personal Recollections of the Stage.* Philadelphia, 1855.

Digests, Directories, Guides, and Contemporary Histories

Barbe-Marbois. *History of Louisiana,* trans. W. B. Laurence. Philadelphia, 1830.

Bell, A. W. *The State Register: Comprising an Historical and Statistical Account of Louisiana.* Baton Rouge, 1855.

Bunner, E. *History of Louisiana.* New York, 1842.

Collens, T. Wharton. *Analytic Digest of the Acts of the Legislature Now in Force.* New Orleans, 1846.

Darby, William. *The Emigrant's Guide to the Western and Southwestern States and Territories.* New York, 1818.

————. *The State of Louisiana.* New York, 1817.

Debouchel, Victor. *Histoire de la Louisiane.* New Orleans, 1841.

Jewell, Edwin L. *Jewell's Digest of the City Ordinances.* New Orleans, 1882.

Kimball, John F. and James. *Kimball and James' Business Directory for the Mississippi Valley: 1844.* Cincinnati, 1844.

Martin, Francois-Xavier. *The History of Louisiana.* 2 vols. New Orleans, 1837–39.

Michel, E. *New Orleans Annual and Commercial Register for 1843.* New Orleans, 1842.

Morel, Christoval, and T. Wharton Collens. *Digest of the Ordinances in Force in Municipality No. 1 on 13th May, 1846.* New Orleans, 1846.

New Orleans in 1805: A Directory and a Census, together with Resolutions Authorizing Same, Now Printed for the First Time from the Original Manuscript. New Orleans, 1936.

Norman, Benjamin M. *Norman's New Orleans and Environs.* New Orleans, 1845.

Sealsfield, Charles. *Les Emigres Francais dans la Louisiane, 1800–1804.* Paris, 1853.

SECONDARY SOURCES

Articles

Augustin, John. "The Oaks," in Thomas M'Caleb (ed.), *The Louisiana Book.* New Orleans, 1894. 71–87.

Beard, James Carter. "Composers of Music and Music Publishers in New Orleans," New Orleans *Daily Picayune,* February 18, 1912.

"Birth of Drama and of Opera in New Orleans," New Orleans *Daily Picayune,* October 24, 1909.

Bogner, Harold F. "Sir Walter Scott in New Orleans, 1818–1832," *Louisiana Historical Quarterly,* XXI (April, 1938), 420–517.

Briede, Kathryn C. "A History of the City of Lafayette," *Louisiana Historical Quarterly,* XX (October, 1937), 895–964.

Brink, Florence Roos. "Literary Travellers in Louisiana between 1803 and 1860," *Louisiana Historical Quarterly,* XXXI (April, 1948), 394–424.

Burns, Francis P. "Henry Clay Visits New Orleans," *Louisiana Historical Quarterly,* XXVII (July, 1944), 717–82.

Burns, Francis P. "Lafayette Visits New Orleans," *Louisiana Historical Quarterly*, XXIX (April, 1946), 296–340.

Butler, Louise. "West Feliciana—A Glimpse of Its History," *Louisiana Historical Quarterly*, VII (January, 1924), 90–120.

———. "The Louisiana Planter and His Home," *Louisiana Historical Quarterly*, X (July, 1927), 355–63.

Cable, George W. "Creole Slave Songs," *Century Magazine*, XXXI (April, 1886), 807–28.

———. "The Dance in Place Congo," *Century Magazine*, XXXI (February, 1886), 517–32.

———. "New Orleans before the Capture," in *Battles and Leaders of the Civil War*. 4 vols. New York: 1874.

Carpenter, H. "Theatrical Retrospection," New Orleans *Times-Democrat*, December 18, 1898.

Chevalley, Sylvie. "La Premiere Saison Theatrale Francaise de New York," *French Review*, XXIV (May, 1951), 471–79.

———. "Le Theatre d'Orleans en Tournee dans les Villes du Nord, 1827–1833," *Comptes Rendus de l'Athenee Louisianais* (1955), 27–71.

Clark, Robert T., Jr. (ed.). "A Bavarian Organist Comes to New Orleans," *Louisiana Historical Quarterly*, XXIX (January, 1946), 14–42.

Dart, Henry P. "Cabarets of New Orleans in the French Colonial Period," *Louisiana Historical Quarterly*, XIX (July, 1936), 578–83.

Davis, Jackson Beauregard. "The Life of Richard Taylor," *Louisiana Historical Quarterly*, XXIV (January, 1941), 49–126.

Dunbar-Nelson, Alice. "People of Color in Louisiana," *Journal of Negro History*, II (January, 1917), 51–78.

Durel, Lionel C. "Creole Civilization in Donaldsonville, 1850, According to 'Le Vigilant,'" *Louisiana Historical Quarterly*, XXXI (October, 1948), 981–94.

Everett, Donald E. "The New Orleans Yellow Fever Epidemic of 1853," *Louisiana Historical Quarterly*, XXXIII (October, 1950), 380–405.

Fischer, David Barrow. "The Story of New Orleans's Rise as a Music Center," *Musical America*, XIX (March 14, 1914), 3–5.

Fossier, Albert E. "Charles Aloysius Luzenberg, 1805–1848: A History of Medicine in New Orleans during the Years 1830 to 1848," *Louisiana Historical Quarterly*, XXVI (January, 1943), 49–137.

———. "The Funeral Ceremony of Napoleon in New Orleans, December 19, 1821," *Louisiana Historical Quarterly*, XIII (April, 1930), 246–52.

Grant, Georg C. "The Negro in Dramatic Art," *Journal of Negro History*, XVII (January, 1932), 19–29.

Grima, Edgar. "Municipal Support of Theatres and Operas in New Orleans," in *Publications of the Louisiana Historical Society*, IX (Proceedings and Reports, 1916), 43–45.

Hart, W. O. "New Orleans," *Louisiana Historical Quarterly*, I (October, 1918), 353–66.

Hawes, William L. "Gottschalk in New Orleans," New Orleans *Times-Democrat*, May 8, 1899.

Hogan, William R. "Amusements in the Republic of Texas," *Journal of Southern History*, III (November, 1937), 397–421.

Jaubert, Irma. "The Ghost of the Old French Opera Days," New Orleans *Item*, May 4, 1924.

Kendall, John Smith. "According to the Code," *Louisiana Historical Quarterly*, XXIII (January, 1940), 140–61.

———. "The French Quarter Sixty Years Ago," *Louisiana Historical Quarterly*, XXIV (April, 1951), 91–102.

———. "The Friend of Chopin, and Some Other New Orleans Musical Celebrities," *Louisiana Historical Quarterly*, XXXI (October, 1948), 856–76.

———. "The Humors of the Duello," *Louisiana Historical Quarterly*, XXIII (April, 1940), 445–70.

———. "Joseph Jefferson in New Orleans," *Louisiana Historical Quarterly*, XXVI (October, 1943), 1150–67.

———. "New Orleans' Negro Minstrels," *Louisiana Historical Quarterly*, XXX (January, 1947), 128–48.

———. "New Orleans' Musicians of Long Ago," *Louisiana Historical Quarterly*, XXXI (January, 1948), 130–49.

———. "New Orleans' Peculiar Institution," *Louisiana Historical Quarterly*, XXIII (July, 1940), 864–86.

———. "Old New Orleans Houses and Some of the People Who Lived in Them," *Louisiana Historical Quarterly*, XX (July, 1937), 794–820.

———. "Patti in New Orleans," *Southwest Review*, XVI (July, 1931), 460–68.

———. "The Pontalba Buildings," *Louisiana Historical Quarterly*, XIX (January, 1936), 118–49.

Lafargue, Andre. "The New Orleans French Opera House: A Retrospect," *Louisiana Historical Quarterly*, III (July, 1920), 368–72.

———. "Opera in New Orleans in Days of Yore," *Louisiana Historical Quarterly*, XXIX (July, 1946), 660–78.

———. "A Reign of Twenty Days," *Louisiana Historical Quarterly*, VIII (July, 1925), 398–410.

Laurent, Lubin F. "History of St. John the Baptist Parish," *Louisiana Historical Quarterly*, VII (April, 1924), 316–31.

Leary, Lewis, and Arlin Turner. "John Howard Payne in New Orleans," *Louisiana Historical Quarterly*, XXXI (January, 1948), 110–22.

Ledet, Wilton P. "The History of the City of Carrollton," *Louisiana Historical Quarterly*, XXI (January, 1938), 220–81.

Le Gardeur, Rene J., Jr. "En Marge d'Une Affiche de Theatre de 1799," *Comptes Rendus de l'Athenee Louisianais* (1955), 24–26.

———. "Les Premieres Annees du Theatre a la Nouvelle-Orleans," *Comptes Rendus de l'Athenee Louisianais* (1954), 33–72.

Le Jeune, Emilie. "Creole Folk Songs," *Louisiana Historical Quarterly,* XX (October, 1919), 454–62.

———. "Reminiscences of the French Opera," in *Publications of the Louisiana Historical Society,* IX (Proceedings and Reports, 1916), 41–43.

Liljegren, Ernest J. "Jacobinism in Louisiana," *Louisiana Historical Quarterly,* XXII (January, 1939), 47–97.

Lindstrom, Carl E. "The American Quality in the Music of Louis Moreau Gottschalk," *Musical Quarterly,* XXXI (July, 1945), 356–66.

Loeb, Harry Brunswick. "The Opera in New Orleans," in *Publications of the Louisiana Historical Society,* IX (Proceedings and Reports, 1916), 29–41.

Lowrey, Walter McGehee. "The Political Career of James Madison Wells," *Louisiana Historical Quarterly,* XXXI (October, 1948), 995–1123.

Matthews, Brander. "The Rise and Fall of Negro Minstrelsy," *Scribner's Magazine,* LVII (June, 1915), 754–59.

Matthews, W. S. B. "Gottschalk, the Composer," *Music,* II (June, 1892), 117–32.

McPeek, Gwynn S. "New Orleans as an Opera Center—A Vanished Era is Reviewed," *Musical Americana,* LXXIV (February 15, 1954), 25, 136, 226.

Moehlenbock, Arthur Henry. "The German Drama on the New Orleans Stage," *Louisiana Historical Quarterly,* XXVI (April, 1943), 361–627.

Moody, V. Alton. "Slavery on Louisiana Sugar Plantations," *Louisiana Historical Quarterly,* VII (April, 1924), 191–301.

Moore, Arthur K. "Specimens of the Folktales from Some Antebellum Newspapers of Louisiana," *Louisiana Historical Quarterly,* XXXII (October, 1949), 723–58.

Nathan, Hans. "The First Negro Minstrel Band and Its Origins," *Southern Folklore Quarterly,* XVI (June, 1952), 132–44.

Noble, Stuart Grayson. "Schools of New Orleans during the First Quarter of the Nineteenth Century," *Louisiana Historical Quarterly,* XIV (January, 1931), 65–78.

Overdyke, W. Darrel. "History of the American Party in Louisiana," *Louisiana Historical Quarterly,* XVI (July, 1933), 409–26.

Price, Nellie Warner. "Le Spectacle de la Rue St. Pierre," *Louisiana Historical Quarterly,* I (January, 1918), 215–23.

Reinders, Robert C. "Sound of the Mournful Dirge," *Jazz,* I (Fall, 1959), 296–98.

Renshaw, Henry. "Lafayette's Visit to New Orleans," *Louisiana Historical Quarterly,* I (September, 1917), 5–8.

———. "Jackson Square," *Louisiana Historical Quarterly,* II (January, 1919), 38–46.

Riley, Martin Luther. "The Development of Education in Louisiana prior to Statehood," *Louisiana Historical Quarterly,* XIX (July, 1936), 595–634.

Russell, William, and Stephen W. Smith. "New Orleans Music," in Frederic Ramsey, Jr., and Charles Edward Smith (eds.). *Jazzmen.* London: 1957.

Shpall, Leo. "Louis Moreau Gottschalk," *Louisiana Historical Quarterly,* XXX (January, 1947), 120–27.

Silin, Charles I. "The French Theatre in New Orleans," *American Society Legion of Honor Magazine,* XXVII (Summer, 1956), 121–36.

Smith, Lucy Harth. "Negro Musicians and Their Music," *Journal of Negro History,* XX (October, 1935), 428–32.

Smither, Nelle. "A History of the English Theatre at New Orleans, 1806–1842," *Louisiana Historical Quarterly,* XXVIII (January, 1945), 85–276.

————. Charlotte Cushman's Apprenticeship in New Orleans," *Louisiana Historical Quarterly,* XXXI (October, 1948), 973–80.

"Some New Orleans Theatre History," New Orleans *Times-Democrat,* May 13, 1910.

Spell, Lota M. "Music in Texas," *Civil War History,* IV (September, 1958), 301–306.

Spitzer, Marian. "The Lay of the Last Minstrel," *Saturday Evening Post,* CXCVII (March 7, 1925), 12–13, 123.

Stahl, Annie Lee West. "The Free Negro in Ante-Bellum Louisiana," *Louisiana Historical Quarterly,* XXV (April, 1942), 301–96.

Stearns, Marshall. "Rebop, Bebop and Bop," in Edie Condon and Richard Gehman (eds.). *Edie Condon's Treasury of Jazz.* New York, 1956.

Tregle, Joseph G., Jr. "Early New Orleans Society: A Reappraisal," *Journal of Southern History,* XVIII (February, 1952), 20–36.

Turner, Arlin. "Joaquin Miller in New Orleans," *Louisiana Historical Quarterly,* XXII (January, 1939), 216–25.

Turner, Frederick Jackson. "The Origin of Genet's Projected Attack on Louisiana and the Floridas," *American Historical Review,* III (July, 1898), 650–71.

Wellborn, Alfred Toledano. "The Relations between New Orleans and Latin America," *Louisiana Historical Quarterly,* XXII (July, 1939), 710–94.

Willink, Cecile (ed.). "An Old Lady's Gossip," *Louisiana Historical Quarterly,* VI (July, 1923), 380–87.

Winston, James E. "The Free Negro in New Orleans, 1803–1860," *Louisiana Historical Quarterly,* XXI (October, 1938), 1075–85.

Winter, Marion Hannah. "Juba and American Minstrelsy," in Paul Magriel (ed.). *Chronicles of the American Dance.* New York, 1948.

Wood, Minter. "Life in New Orleans in the Spanish Period," *Louisiana Historical Quarterly,* XXII (July, 1939), 642–709.

Yerbury, Grace H. "Concert Music in Early New Orleans," *Louisiana Historical Quarterly,* XL (April, 1957), 95–109.

Monographs and Special Studies

Allen, William Francis, and others, *Slave Songs of the United States*. New York, 1867.

Arpin, P. *Biographie de L. M. Gottschalk*. New York, 1853.

Arthur, Stanley Clisby. *Old New Orleans*. Rev. ed. New Orleans, 1944.

Arthur, Stanley Clisby, and George C. H. Kernion. *Old Families of Louisiana*. New Orleans, 1931.

Asbury, Herbert. *The French Quarter*. New York, 1936.

Audubon, Maria R. *Audubon and His Journals*. 2 vols. New York, 1897.

Augustin, George. *History of Yellow Fever*. New Orleans, 1907.

Baroncelli, Joseph G. de. *Le Theatre-Francais a la Nouvelle Orleans*. New Orleans, 1906.

————. *Opera Francais de la Nouvelle-Orleans*. New Orleans, 1913.

————. *Une Colonie Francaise en Louisiane*. New Orleans, 1909.

Barrett, Laurence. *Edwin Forrest*. Boston, 1882.

Biographical and Historical Memoirs of Louisiana. 2 vols. Chicago, 1892.

Bikle, Lucy L. Cable. *George W. Cable, His Life and Letters*. New York, 1928.

Blesh, Rudi. *Shining Trumpets*. New York, 1958.

Brown, T. Allston. *History of the American Stage*. New York, 1870.

Bumstead, Gladys. *Louisiana Composers*. New Orleans, 1935.

Burson, Caroline Maude. *The Stewardship of Don Esteban Miro, 1782–1792*. New Orleans, 1940.

Butler, Pierce. *Judah P. Benjamin*. Philadelphia, 1907.

Cable, George W. *The Creoles of Louisiana*. New York, 1889.

Carmer, Carl. *America Sings: Stories and Songs of America's Growing*. New York, 1942.

Carroll, Mary Teresa Austin, *The Ursulines in Louisiana, 1727–1824*. New Orleans, 1886.

Carson, William G. B. *Letters of Mr. and Mrs. Charles Kean Relating to Their American Tours*. St. Louis, 1945.

Caughey, J. W. *Bernardo de Galvez in Louisiana*. Berkeley, 1934.

Chambers, Henry E. *Mississippi Valley Beginnings*. New York, 1922.

Cline, Isaac M. *Art and Artists in New Orleans during the Last Century*. New Orleans, 1922.

Coleman, Will H. *Historical Sketch Book and Guide to New Orleans and Environs*. New York, 1885.

Copeland, Fayette. *Kendall of the Picayune*. Norman, 1943.

Coulter, E. Merton. *The Other Half of Old New Orleans*. Baton Rouge, 1939.

Cox, John H. *Folk Songs of the South*. Cambridge, 1925.

Curtis, Nathaniel C. *New Orleans, Its Old Houses, Shops and Public Buildings*. Philadelphia, 1933.

Dabney, Thomas Ewing. *One Hundred Great Years: The Story of the Times-Picayune from Its Founding to 1940*. Baton Rouge, 1944.

Day, Charles H. *Fun in Black, or Sketches of Minstrel Life*. New York, 1874.

Dunlap, William. *History of the American Theatre*. 2 vols. London, 1833.

Elson, Louis C. *The National Music of America and Its Sources*. Boston, 1924.

Falk, Bernard. *The Naked Lady: Or Storm over Adah*. London, 1935.

Finckelstein, Sidney. *Jazz: A People's Music*. New York, 1948.

Fisher, Miles Mark. *Negro Slave Songs in the United States*. Ithaca, 1953.

Fisher, William Ames. *One Hundred and Fifty Years of Music Publishing in the United States, 1783–1933*. Boston, 1933.

Fortier, Alcee. *Louisiana Studies: Literature, Customs and Dialects, History and Education*. New Orleans, 1894.

Fossier, Albert E. *New Orleans: The Glamour Period, 1800–1840*. New Orleans, 1957.

Gayarre, Charles E. *The Creoles of History and Romance*. New Orleans, 1885.

Hare, Maude Cuney. *Six Creole Folk-Songs*. New York, 1921.

Hensel, Octavia. *Life and Letters of Louis Moreau Gottschalk*. Boston, 1870.

Howard, John Tasker. *A Program of Early and Mid-Nineteenth Century American Songs*. New York, 1931.

Isaacs, Edith J. R. *The Negro in the American Theater*. New York, 1947.

James, Reese Davis. *Cradle of Culture: The Philadelphia Stage, 1800–1810*. Philadelphia, 1957.

Johnson, Helen Kendrick. *Our Familiar Songs and Those Who Made Them*. New York, 1887.

Jones, Howard Mumford. *America and French Culture, 1750–1848*. Chapel Hill, 1927.

Kane, Harnett T. *Queen New Orleans*. New York, 1949.

Kendall, John Smith. *The Golden Age of the New Orleans Theater*. Baton Rouge, 1952.

King, Grace. *Creole Families of New Orleans*. New York, 1921.

——. *New Orleans: The Place and the People*. New York, 1895.

Kouwenhoven, John A. *Made in America*. New York, 1948.

Krehbiel, Henry E. *Afro-American Folk Songs*. New York, 1914.

Lathrop, Elise. *Early American Inns and Taverns*. New York, 1926.

Le Gardeur, Rene J., Jr. *The First New Orleans Theatre, 1792–1803*. New Orleans, 1963.

Loesser, Arthur. *Men, Women & Pianos*. New York, 1954.

Loggins, Vernon. *Where the Word Ends: The Life of Louis Moreau Gottschalk*. Baton Rouge, 1958.

Mattfield, Julius. *A Hundred Years of Grand Opera in New York*. New York, 1927.

Monroe, Mina. *Bayou Ballads: Twelve Folk-Songs from Louisiana*. New York, 1921.

Mueller, John H. *The American Symphony Orchestra*. Bloomington, 1951.

Nolan, James Bennet. *Lafayette in America. Day by Day*. Baltimore, 1934.

Oudard, Georges. *Four Cents an Acre*, trans. Margery Bianco. New York, 1931.

Peterson, Clara Gottschalk. *Creole Songs from New Orleans*. New Orleans, 1902.

Riegal, Robert E. *Young America, 1830–1840*. Norman, 1949.

Roberts, Octavia. *With Lafayette in America*. Boston, 1919.

Roberts, W. Adolphe. *Lake Pontchartrain*. Indianapolis, 1946.

Rosengarten, Joseph G. *French Colonists and Exiles in the United States*. Philadelphia, 1907.

Saxon, Lyle, Edward Dreyer, and Robert Tallant. *Gumbo Ya-Ya*. Boston, 1945.

Semple, Henry C. (ed.). *Ursulines in New Orleans and Our Lady of Prompt Succor: A Record of Two Centuries, 1727–1925*. New York, 1925.

Sonneck, O. G. *Early Concert Life in America*. Leipzig, 1907.

———. *Early Opera in America*. New York, 1915.

———. *Miscellaneous Studies in the History of Music*. New York, 1921.

Taylor, Joe Gray. *Negro Slavery in Louisiana*. Baton Rouge, 1963.

Tinker, Edward Laroque. *Creole City: Its Past and Its People*. New York, 1953.

———. *Old New Orleans*. New York, 1931.

Trotter, James M. *Music and Some Highly Musical People*. Boston, 1882.

Wade, Richard C. *Slavery in the Cities*. New York, 1964.

Waring, George E., and George W. Cable. *History and Present Condition of New Orleans, Louisiana*. Washington, 1881.

Wittke, Carl. *Tambo and Bones: A History of the American Minstrel Stage*. Durham, 1930.

Books

Brockway, Wallace, and Herbert Weinstock. *Men of Music*. Rev. ed. New York, 1950.

———. *The Opera: A History of Its Creation and Performance, 1600–1941*. New York, 1941.

Chase, Gilbert. *America's Music.* New York, 1955.

Coad, Oral Summer, and Edwin Nims. *The American Stage.* New Haven, 1929.

Davis, Edwin Adams. *Louisiana: A Narrative History.* Baton Rouge, 1961.

Dent, Edward J. *Opera.* Rev. ed. London, 1949.

Dimitry, John B. *History of Louisiana.* New York, 1877.

Elson, Louis C. *The History of American Music.* New York, 1904.

Ewen, David. *Music Comes to America.* New York, 1947.

Fortier, Alcee. *A History of Louisiana.* 4 vols. New York, 1904.

Gayarre, Charles. *History of Louisiana.* 4 vols. 3rd ed. New Orleans, 1885.

Graf, Herbert. *The Opera and Its Future in America.* New York, 1941.

Grout, Donald Jay. *A Short History of Opera.* 2 vols. New York, 1947.

Howard, John Tasker. *Our American Music.* 3rd ed. New York, 1954.

Hubbard, W. L. (ed.). *The American History and Encyclopedia of Music.* 12 vols. New York, 1908.

Kendall, John Smith. *History of New Orleans.* 3 vols. Chicago, 1922.

Krehbiel, Henry Edward. *A Book of Operas.* New ed. New York, 1919.

Lahee, Henry C. *Grand Opera in America.* Boston, 1901.

Lavignac, Albert. *Music and Musicians.* New York, 1899.

Louisiana, A Guide to the State. New York, 1941.

Odell, George C. D. *Annals of the New York Stage.* 15 vols. New York, 1927–49.

Pahlen, Kurt. *Music of the World,* trans. James A. Galston. New York, 1949.

Rightor, Henry (ed.). *Standard History of New Orleans, Louisiana.* Chicago, 1900.

Spaeth, Sigmund. *A History of Popular Music in America.* New York, 1948.

Stringfield, Lamar. *America and Her Music.* Chapel Hill, 1931.

Taylor, Deems, and Russell Kerr (eds.). *Music Lovers' Encyclopedia.* Rev. ed. New York, 1954.

Unpublished Studies

Adams, Ben Avis. "Indexes of Assimilation of the Creole People in New Orleans." M.A. thesis, Tulane University, 1939.

Adams, Reed M. C. "New Orleans and the War of 1812." Typescript, Howard-Tilton Library.

Babin, Claude H. "Economic Expansion of New Orleans before the Civil War." Ph.D. dissertation, Tulane University, 1953.

Baudier, Roger. "The Creoles of Old New Orleans." Typescript, Howard-Tilton Library.

Bentley, Eleanor. "Walt Whitman's Visit to New Orleans." M.A. thesis, Tulane University, 1943.

Emanuel, Lena Lopez. "Education in Colonial Louisiana." M.A. thesis, Tulane University, 1931.

Everett, Donald E. "Free Persons of Color in New Orleans, 1803–1815." Ph.D. dissertation, Tulane University, 1952.

Gafford, Lucile. "A History of the St. Charles Theatre in New Orleans, 1835–1843." Ph.D. dissertation, University of Chicago, 1930. Copy in Howard-Tilton Library.

————. "Material Conditions in the Theatres of New Orleans before the Civil War." M.A. thesis, University of Chicago, 1925. Copy in Howard-Tilton Library.

Hanley, Kathryn Tierney. "The Amateur Theatre in New Orleans before 1835." M.A. thesis, Tulane University, 1940.

Hebron, Dorothy. "Sir Walter Scott in New Orleans, 1833–1850." M.A. thesis, Tulane University, 1940.

Hoffman, Beryl May. "German Education in Louisiana." M.A. thesis, Tulane University, 1939.

Laguaite, Jeannette K. "The German Element in New Orleans, 1820–1860." M.A. thesis, Tulane University, 1940.

Leigh, J. "Maunsell White, Merchant of New Orleans, 1785–1863." Typescript, Howard-Tilton Library.

"Operatic Performances in New Orleans, 1806–1915." Compiled by the Works Progress Administration in New Orleans, n.d., Louisiana State Museum Library, New Orleans.

P'Pool, E. S. "Commercialized Amusements in New Orleans." M.A. thesis, Tulane University, 1930.

Puckett, Erastus. "The Free Negro in New Orleans to 1860." M.A. thesis, Tulane University, 1907.

Pujol, Irene Blanche. "Robin's Voyages dans l'Interieure de la Louisiane, Translated and Annotated." M.A. thesis, Louisiana State University, 1935. Copy in Howard-Tilton Library.

Reddick, Lawrence Dunbar. "The Negro in the New Orleans Press, 1850–1860. A Study in Attitudes and Propaganda." Ph.D. dissertation, University of Chicago, 1939.

Roppolo, Joseph P. "A History of the English Theatre in New Orleans, 1845 to 1861." Ph.D. dissertation, Tulane University, 1950.

Index

Adam, Adolphe, 143, 144, 164; popularity of, 164
—works: *Le Brasseur de Preston,* 164; *Le Chalet,* 143, 144, 164; *Le Postillon de Longjumeau,* 164
Alexandre, Mlle., soprano, 109, 116, 118, 275
American Company, The, 76
American Theater, The New, 193, 212
Antoine, Pere, 207
Arcade Ballroom, 9
Auber, Daniel Francois, 117, 125, 142, 148, 149, 153, 163, 185, 187, 189, 191, 199, 211, 275; popularity of, 110, 113, 121, 125, 126, 144, 164, 165
—works: *L'Ambassadrice,* 164, 165, 191, 211; *Le Cheval de Bronze,* 142, 169; *Le Concert a la Cour,* 185; *Le Domino Noir,* 164, 165; *Le Dieu et La Bayadere,* 149, 153, 163, 164; *La Fiancee,* 126; *Fiorella,* 115, 144; *Fra Diavolo,* 121, 128, 144, 163, 164, 193; *Gustave III,* 163, 164, 189, 191, 275; *Le Macon,* 125, 126, 144; *Masaniello (La Muette de Portici),* 121, 125, 126, 128, 139, 144, 148, 163, 164, 189, 193, 199; *The Pages of the Duke of Vendome,* 163; *Le Philtre,* 124, 189–90
Austin, Mrs. Elizabeth, singer, 128, 129, 130

Bal de Bouquet, 12
Ballet, 67, 68, 86, 97, 116, 117, 118, 123, 132, 140, 143, 149, 153, 163–64, 171, 172, 186–89, 211, 278, 279
Ballrooms, 6–7
Balls: admittance price of, 6, 23–24; attendance at, 6, 13, 16; bachelors, 24; *Bal de Bouquet,* 12; carnival, 7–8; Catholic attitude toward, 10–11; character balls, 24; charity, 8,